Tom —
FROM ONE BLUE SUITER
to ANOTHER
Bernie
Hale

TOM
14

Jungle Fighter Pilots

A Vietnam Memoir

Bernie Hale

Published by PC Publishing
931-B South Main Street #307
Kernersville, NC 27284

LIBRARY OF CONGRESS CATALOGING-IN-PUBLICATION DATA

Printed in the United States of America
by Kieger Graphic Communications
Winston-Salem, NC

This Story is Dedicated to My Children

Shannon, Shevaun, Sheila and Shane

Thank you, Shane,
for planting the seed.

Lieutenant Bernie Hale

ACKNOWLEDGEMENTS

Mentor:	Ray Russell
Editors:	Ryan Gay Michael Hale
Design & Layout:	Jasmin Orlando
Contributors:	Tums: Ted Bama, Bob Butler, Dohrm Crawford, Pat Dowling, Steve Drummond, Ted Gamlin, Larry Howerton, Gary Lohr, Bill Lutz, Ken Montague, Jake Morrison, John Murphy, Ted Olsen, Dave Rogers, Bill Schoder, Bob Snyder, Ron Tribo, Frank Wisenski Others: Frank Cheshire, Craig Duehring, Joe Finley, Pat Hale, Jim King, Bud Leithiser, Jim Myers Barry Ream, Raymond Ried, Chris Rogers, Joe Tamowski, Paul Urschalitz
Photos:	Dohrm Crawford David Jauquet (OV-10 Bronco) E.J. van Koningsveld (SR-71) Dave Rogers
Maps:	Phillip Schwartzberg
Special Thanks:	Thank you, Janis, for reading hundreds of pages of gibberish and always telling me it was brilliant.

CONTENTS

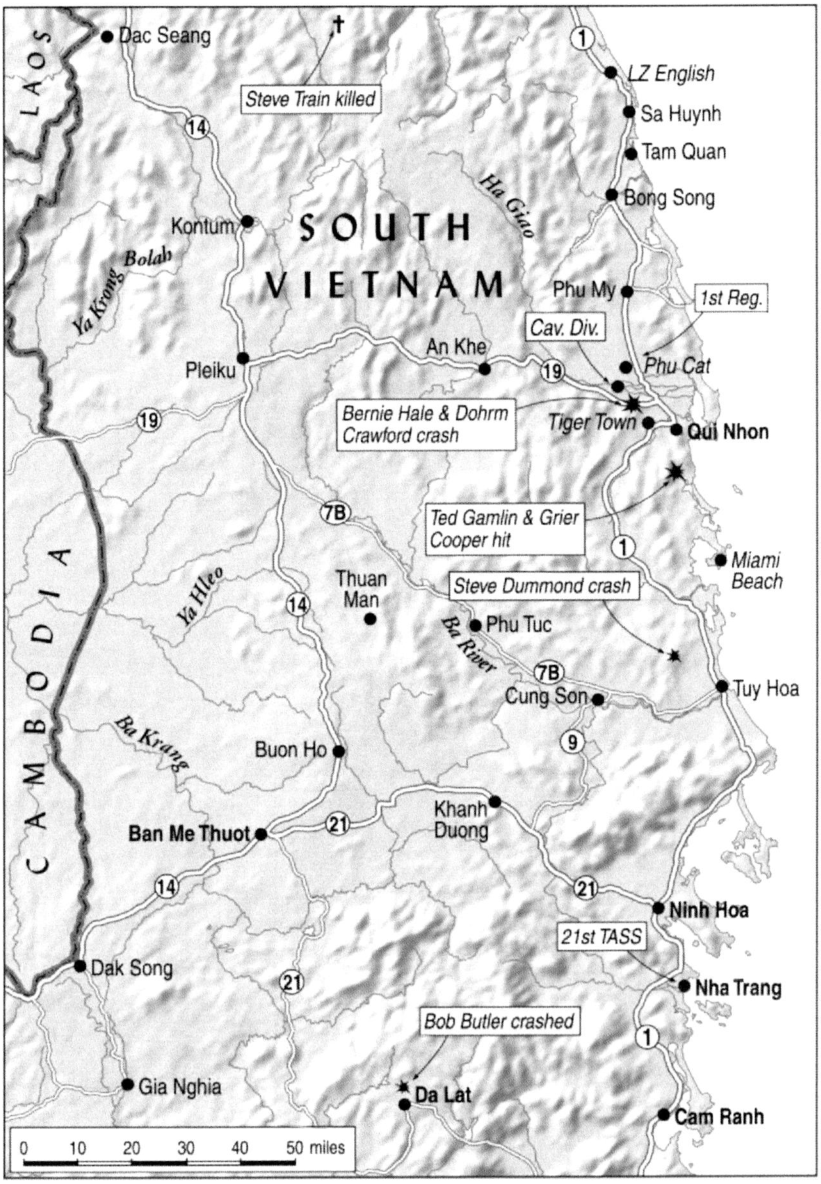
LAOS
Dac Seang
Steve Train killed
14
1
LZ English
Sa Huynh
Tam Quan
Bong Song
Ha Giao
Kontum
SOUTH
VIETNAM
Ya Krong Bolah
Phu My
1st Reg.
Cav. Div.
An Khe
Pleiku
19
Phu Cat
Bernie Hale & Dohrm
Crawford crash
Tiger Town
Qui Nhon
19
CAMBODIA
7B
Ted Gamlin & Grier
Cooper hit
1
Miami
Beach
Ya Hleo
Thuan
Man
14
Steve Dummond crash
Phu Tuc
Ba River
7B
Tuy Hoa
Cung Son
9
Ba Krang
Buon Ho
Khanh
Duong
Ban Me Thuot
21
14
21
Ninh Hoa
21st TASS
Dak Song
Nha Trang
21
Bob Butler crashed
1
Gia Nghia
Da Lat
Cam Ranh
0 10 20 30 40 50 miles

CHINA
Jim Cross
NORTH VIETNAM
Nanning
Hanoi
Haiphong
Gulf of Tonkin
Hainan (CHINA)
Cease Fire Line
Hue
Danang
Chuck Engle
THAILAND
LAOS
Bangkok
SOUTH VIETNAM
CAMBODIA
Da Lat
Phan Rang
Phnom Penh
Saigon
Gulf of Thailand
0 100 200 miles
DMZ
Quang Tri
Khe Sanh
Hue
Da Nang
South China Sea
Kham Duc
Tam Ky
Tien Phouc
Chu Lai
Dak Pec
Quang Ngai
Steve Train crashed
LZ English
1st Reg
Kontum
Phu Cat
Pleiku
An Khe
Tiger Town
Qui Nhon
SOUTH
Miami Beach
Tuy Hoa
CAMBODIA
Ban Me Thuot
VIETNAM
Nha Trang
Mekong
Da Lat
21st TASS
Ba Ra
Cam Ranh
Phnom Penh
Phan Rang
FAC U
Tay Ninh
Bob Butler crashed
Bien Hoa
Saigon
Long Xuyen
My Tho
Vung Tau
Rach Gia
Can Tho
Mekong Delta
Gulf of Thailand
Ca Mau
International boundary
Corps boundary
0 50 100 miles

"Never have so few, been unrecognized by so many, for so long."

~Pat Dowling, Tum 12

PROLOGUE

0-1 Bird Dog

Binh Dinh Province, South Vietnam

20 December, 1969

It was my turn to fly the daily Dawn Patrol, a boring, three hour visual reconnaissance (VR) mission around our Area of Responsibility (AO). We Forward Air Controllers (FACs) were tasked with directing tactical air strikes in support of the Korean Tiger Division, one of three stationed in Vietnam.

My unit consisted of twenty pilots, radio call sign Tum. Our mission was to provide the Korean Army close air support whenever they engaged the enemy. We marked targets with white phosphorous rockets fired from pods beneath our wings, and directed fighter bombers in the deployment of their ordnance. We were responsible for the safety of the Korean soldiers and took every precaution to ensure safe separation while directing weapons close to the friendly troops.
We rolled out of bed much too early, strapped into our planes before first light and flew over our AO looking for signs of enemy activity: black pajama-clad folks; smoke from breakfast campfires rising through the jungle canopy; tire tracks or vehicles; the twinkle of muzzle flashes from enemy weapons. Nothing caught my attention or surprised me during the flight, and I headed back to our base.

We hated the Dawn Patrol but somebody had to do it.

I yawned as I approached Phu Cat Air Base, anxious for breakfast and a morning nap.

I called the tower for landing clearance, "Phu Cat tower, Tum One Four one mile south for landing."

"Tum One Four, Phu Cat. You're cleared to land runway three-three. "

Before I could acknowledge, my radio came to life.

"Tum One Four, Tum One Zero. Are you still airborne?"

"Roger that, One Zero. I'm on final approach at Phu Cat."

"Get your ass up here, Hale! We've got troops in contact and a flight of F-100s en route with an ETA of three-zero minutes." I slammed the O-1's throttle forward and told the tower operator I would continue north. Sensing the urgency in my voice, he replied,

"Roger, Tum One Four. Good luck."

Captain Dave Rogers had been embedded with the Korean 1st ROK Infantry Regiment for three days, there to support them should they need close air support. I made a mail and cigar drop the previous day and knew exactly where he was located. I soon arrived at his location which overlooked a wide valley with steep, rocky slopes to the north. I called Dave to get a briefing. "Tum One Zero, One Four's on station. What's going on?"

Dave replied, "Our guys are engaged with enemy troops at the base of the mountain across the valley."

He gave me the target coordinates, which I wrote on the plexiglass window with a black grease pencil. I marked them on my topographic map, compared the chart to the landscape and pinpointed the target.

"One Zero, I've got the target in sight. Have the friendlies pop a smoke and I'll be ready to go to work when the fighters arrive."

I had to know the exact location of the Korean soldiers before I could authorize a strike. Our Republic of Korea (ROK) soldiers carried red, yellow and green smoke canisters.

"Roger, One Four. Standby for friendly smoke."

Seconds later the fighters checked in. "Tum One Four, Bobcat Lead. How do you read? Over."

"Bobcat Lead, Tum One Four. You're loud and clear. What's your lineup and ETA?"

"We're a flight of two Huns (F-100 jet fighters) carrying snake (Mark 82 high drag bombs), nape (napalm) and guns (20 millimeter cannon). We'll be ready to go to work in ten minutes."

"Roger that, Bobcat. I'm an O-1 in a left hand orbit two zero miles north of the runway at Phu Cat. Your target is located at the base of a steep mountain at the north end of an east to west valley. Our target is hot, we have troops in contact. If you take ground fire and can't make it to Phu Cat, bail out south, over the friendlies. Make your runs east to west in a left hand pattern. I'll mark the target when we're ready."

"Roger that, Tum. Bobcat has you and the target area in sight. We're standing by for a mark."

Yellow smoke rose from the valley floor and I called Dave. "If the ROKs popped a yellow smoke, they're too close to the target. You've got to move them fifty meters south." I didn't ask for a specific color because the enemy monitored our radios and they also had smoke canisters they could ignite, confusing the issue of troop identification.

The jungle foliage was so thick I couldn't see the troops on the ground and had to rely on the colored smoke.

"Standby, One Four. We'll move them back and give you another smoke."

I imagined the scene on the valley floor: Korean soldiers, fierce warriors, engaged with the enemy. They could hear Air Force jets overhead, and knew they carried weapons they desperately needed, and some officer in the relative safety of the regiment commander's tent was ordering them to move back, retreat like cowards. They wanted the ordnance right on top of them, something I couldn't let happen.

Several minutes later I saw red smoke and called Dave. "I've got red smoke, One Zero. Acknowledge it's the good guys and we'll go to work."

"Roger the red smoke, One Four. We're ready for the fighters. Give us hard bombs first".

"Bobcat Lead, Tum One Four. I'm rolling in with a mark."

"Roger, Tum. Bobcat Flight's ready."

I pulled the throttle to idle, dove into the valley, fired a rocket and watched it explode in a brilliant white cloud. As I pulled off the target, Dave, communicating with the Korean radio operator at the battle site, called me, "Tum One Four, your mark's good.

Then he said, "Bring it on."

"Bobcat Lead, Tum One Four, you're cleared in hot, hard bombs in pairs. I'm in a right hand turn. Hit my smoke!"

"Roger that, Tum. Lead's in hot from the east. I've got you in sight."

I blinked away sweat dripping in my eyes and focused on the lead F-100. From an altitude of 5,000 feet, he entered a steep dive, a four hundred knots-per-hour falcon, sun reflecting from his wings, prey in sight, anxious for the kill. At eight hundred feet above the valley floor he released a pair of bombs that disappeared in the center of my mark and exploded in a roar of thunder claps, filling the sky with foliage, rocks and dust. I banked hard left, looking for the second jet, ready to clear him to follow his leader down the chute.

My heart stopped when I heard Dave's voice. "Tum One Four, we've hit the friendlies!"

How could this happen? I did everything I could to protect the ROKs. My hand shook as I engaged the radio. "Bobcat Two, go through dry! Don't release your weapons! Acknowledge!"

The fighter jock replied, "Roger that, Tum. Two's going through dry and will hold at altitude."

I watched the deadly cloud dissipate with the help of a gentle, peaceful breeze and had one thought. *Please, God, don't let there be any Korean casualties.*

One

The Adventure Begins

I began to understand the meaning of patriotism as a youngster in the mid-fifties. Persistent news coverage of the arms race and Cold War we waged with the Russians impressed upon me how fragile our freedom was. Preparing for nuclear fallout from Russian missiles, millions of American families, mine included, stocked their basements with jugs of water, canned goods stacked high, medical supplies, transistor radios and plenty of batteries. On cue from our school principal, we practiced the "duck and cover" exercise, diving under our desks to safety.

In February 1962, my junior year in high school, our principal broadcast current updates of the Cuban missile crisis throughout our classrooms. Any minute I expected to hear an announcement telling us to go home and seek shelter with our families. World War II images of the carnage in Japan and the thought that a nuclear attack could take place on American soil petrified me. When the standoff was over, I thanked God for giving our leaders in Washington the courage to stand up to the Communist threat. I believed we were on the brink of nuclear war.

I discovered flying three years later when I was a sophomore at the University of Montana. My first flight was in a Cessna 172, a four-passenger plane flown by Larry Wilkinson, one of my father's friends. Dad and I followed the tall, gray-haired pilot as he walked around the aircraft and performed the preflight inspection. He looked for freedom of movement on the control surfaces, noted the tire pressure and made sure there were no hydraulic leaks around the brakes. When a ramp attendant filled the gas tanks and checked the oil level, we were ready to go. I jumped in the back seat, choosing the right seat so I could see

Larry and watch his every move. The instrument panel with its dials, lights and switches fascinated me. Butterflies swarmed in my stomach when the propeller sprang to life and the tower operator cleared us to taxi. Larry stopped short of the runway where he pulled, pushed and turned the control yoke. It was imperative, he said, that the flight controls were free of obstruction and worked properly. He revved the engine and checked the RPM and oil pressure, tapping each gauge as he did so with his right index finger. Larry looked over his shoulder and gave me a thumbs up. Raised eyebrows asked, 'You ready?'

I nodded and we taxied onto the runway. As the plane accelerated slowly, my heart pounded. The anxiety I felt vanished the moment we rose into the brisk, fall sky.

The scenery captivated me as we climbed. From above, the winding rivers seemed much smaller. Dense red maples, golden aspens and oaks tried their best to conceal the University Of Montana Campus. Rocky mountain peaks reflected the morning sun. Puffy white clouds drifted by, close enough to touch.

The university was a land grant institution and required male students to enroll in either the Army or Air Force Reserve Officer Training Corps (ROTC). I was in the Army class and thought I would serve our country as an Army officer. However, my brief introduced to aviation in Larry's Cessna convinced me I wanted to be an Air Force pilot.

At the beginning of my junior year I joined the Air Force program, intent on qualifying for flight school.

A month after my maiden flight, a national tragedy occurred. President Kennedy was assassinated November 22, 1963. At the time of his death, there were 16,000 American military advisors stationed in South Vietnam.

Many Americans saw a direct parallel in Vietnam and the Korean War a decade earlier, when our ally asked for military assistance to fend off a Communist invasion. President Johnson and a majority of Americans felt our involvement in the conflict was justified, and our long involvement in Vietnam began. By early 1966, there were 235,000 soldiers in South Vietnam. This dramatic escalation began to elicit antiwar protests in parts of the country. Rallies took place on many colleges throughout the country, including the sleepy campus of the University of Montana.

Charlie Brown Artman, a rotund, wandering hippie from California, discovered

Missoula and proclaimed himself leader of the few malcontents among our enrollment of three thousand. Around thirty, Artman wore a full-length brown leather trench coat. Long, gnarly black hair dangled below his shoulders and a round, pudgy face peered through a bird nest beard. Charlie loitered outside the student union building urging small groups, never more than a dozen, to use marijuana, LSD and protest the military presence on our campus.

He railed at the top of his voice, "The government is corrupt, evil! All soldiers are baby killers! Drive the ROTC scum from your campus! We are all cells in a large green plant, and must unite against those who seek our destruction!"

Lieutenant Colonel Means, the ROTC commander, told us to avoid Artman. "I know you guys want to kick his ass, but I won't tolerate any violence. Ignore him and he'll go away."

He was right, Charlie didn't last more than a month. The morning after two members of the Rodeo Club hog tied him and shaved half his head and beard, he disappeared. However, his message lingered. Our presence in Vietnam, like an open wound, continued to fester and erode civilian-military relations.

When my junior year ended I joined a hundred ROTC Cadets at Fairchild Air Force Base near Spokane, Washington. We came from universities throughout the northwest to attend summer camp, a four-week program designed to prepare us for active duty. We didn't have the stereotypical drill sergeant leading us through "boot camp," but an ROTC instructor. Captain Jerry Cover, a former F-100 fighter pilot, had that All-American look--Johnny Unitas in a flight suit. He did his best to act like a badass Marine drill sergeant, but he was a pussycat.

Late one afternoon he told us he was going to take us to the Officer's Club for dinner.

He said, "Gentlemen, it's time you guys got acquainted with the O'club."

Captain Cover felt it was important to expose us to the revelry and camaraderie exhibited by the B-52 Bomber and KC-135 tanker crews stationed on the base. The bar was full of pilots and navigators dressed in flight suits adorned with shoulder patches identifying their squadrons and the aircraft they flew. They were a boisterous lot that exuded confidence. Oh, how I wanted to be a pilot! On a trip to the Base Exchange (BX), a huge shopping center, I bought a silver tie tack adorned with Air Force wings. I had no idea when, if ever, I would be able to wear it, but carried it as a good luck charm.

Our curriculum included early morning physical training, hours of marching and lessons in military protocol.

We polished our brass belt buckles, shoes, the wooden floors in the barracks, the chrome fixtures in the latrine and the tile in the showers. Individual lockers held our toiletries and clothing, all neatly organized. Captain Cover inspected us and our quarters each morning, handing out demerits for failure to conform to standards. Marching laps around the parade ground Friday afternoon erased the black marks accumulated during the week.

On the final day of our training we marched to the flight line for a ride in a T-33 jet trainer, a modified F-80 Shooting Star, a Korean War vintage fighter. The T-33 had tandem seating, the copilot's seat located directly behind the pilot's. I climbed a bright yellow ladder to the rear cockpit where a crew chief sat perched on the side of the aircraft, ready to help me into the seat. He fastened the shoulder harness and connected the radio to the speaker in my helmet. Wearing a sly grin he winked and handed me a barf bag as he descended the ladder. Getting air sick had never entered my mind. I thought, *If I puke in this thing, I won't ever live it down.*

After engine start, the crew chief directed us out of the parking spot and saluted our pilot as we taxied toward the runway. The fighter pilot engaged the intercom.

"My name's Captain Walsh, who are you?"

"Bernie Hale, sir."

"Welcome to the T-33, Bernie. I'm going to give you a flying lesson and introduce you to her performance, but with all those cadets lined up, it'll be a short flight. If you have a problem, engage the mic and talk to me. Understand?"

"Yes, sir," I replied.

I studied the console in front of me. Round, black dials with yellow numbers displayed the pilot's altitude, airspeed and heading. A vertical velocity indicator let him know at what rate he was climbing or descending. The artificial horizon, a gyro operated sphere, grey on the top half, black on the bottom, occupied the center of the panel. It illustrated to the pilot how his aircraft was oriented relative to the horizon. Levers for raising and lowering the landing gear and flaps protruded from the panel. Circuit breakers and switches that controlled the lights, radios and navigation equipment littered the cockpit. The accelerometer, a silver dollar-sized instrument that displayed the G-forces on the plane, occupied a space on the lower right side of the instrument panel.

We stopped short of the runway and the speaker in my helmet came to life.

Captain Walsh called the tower and said, "Fairchild Tower, T-Bird One Zero is ready for takeoff."

"T-Bird One Zero, Fairchild Tower, you're cleared for takeoff."

"Roger, tower. One Zero is rolling."

We taxied onto the runway and the captain held the brakes, and slowly advanced the throttle. The jet howled and quivered, anxious for the pilot to set her free. When the pilot released the brakes, the plane leapt forward and soon became airborne. When we leveled off, Captain Walsh said, "Hold the stick with your right hand, the throttle with your left, and put your feet on the rudder pedals. I want you to feel the pressure I exert on the controls."

"Roger," I said, hoping that was the proper response.

We made several level turns, and I felt the stick and rudders move. The throttle eased forward, the stick moved back and to the side, and we started a climbing turn. The captain retarded the throttle and we descended. He leveled off and said, "Okay, I want you to shake the stick left to right and say, 'I've got the airplane.' That's how we acknowledge the transfer of control from one pilot to another."

With a few quick lateral movements of the stick and the words, "I've got the airplane, sir," I relegated Captain Walsh to the role of copilot. Giddy with excitement, I thought, *Holy smokes! I'm flying a jet fighter! If Dad and Larry could see me now!*

The captain talked me through a series of maneuvers. "Using the horizon as your reference, enter a level left hand turn with pressure on the stick and left rudder pedal. The nose is dropping below the horizon, ease the stick back. That's it, gentle pressure on the controls. Now reverse the direction of turn. Keep your eyes moving. Always scan the horizon looking for planes and birds. A midair collision would ruin our day. Retard the throttle and descend five hundred feet."

For five minutes I gently maneuvered the jet through the blue Washington sky. I could have stayed aloft all day.

"Good job, Cadet," the captain said as he shook the stick. "I've got the airplane. Let's ring her out, see what she'll do."

The throttle shot forward and the plane rolled inverted, which gave me a look at the earth through the top of the canopy. We made several steep, high-speed turns, a few barrel rolls and headed back to the base. When we turned off the runway I noticed our crew chief, arms extended above his head, motioning for Captain Walsh to follow his directions to a parking spot. The aircraft came to a stop, the crew chief put the ladder in place and scampered up to the open cockpit. He reached in, unplugged the radio connection, released the shoulder harness and extended a helping hand as I climbed out of the cockpit. With the same wink and smile I received from him twenty minutes ago, I handed him the barf bag and hustled down the ladder. As I stepped on the tarmac, another cadet, eager to get in the silver bird, jumped on the ladder and scampered up to the waiting crew chief. I turned and smiled up at the cockpit.

Captain Walsh, oxygen mask dangling from the side of his helmet, gave me a thumbs up. A grin and a nod seemed to say, *I know, Cadet, it is pretty cool stuff.*

Summer camp flew by like a jet breaking the sound barrier. I returned home full of enthusiasm, anxious for my senior year to begin. In a few months I'd know if my first assignment would be flight school.

Two

Silver Wings

When my senior year began, I started to check off the requirements for acceptance to flight school: basic math skills; manual and mental dexterity tests; and the physical exam given annually to all Air Force pilots. Our administrative clerk, Sergeant Basil Fogge, drove four of us two hundred miles to Malmstrom Air Force Base where we spent all afternoon getting weighed, measured, poked with blood sucking needles, prodded, x-rayed and questioned about our families' medical and psychological history.

A week later, Lieutenant Colonel Means told me I had passed the physical and would begin flight training at our local airport. If I earned a private pilot's license I'd receive orders to Undergraduate Pilot Training (UPT) upon graduation. If I failed to meet the FAA private pilot requirements, the Air Force would assign me elsewhere: navigator training, aircraft maintenance, administration, intelligence, weather school, missiles or a number of other career fields, none of which interested me.

I drove to the airport early in October of 1966, where I met my flight instructor, Dick Komberec. Four years older than I, Dick was a "ramp rat," a guy who washed and waxed airplanes, gave lessons and flew charter flights, shuffling customers and freight from point A to B. He longed to be an airline pilot.

On our eighth flight, while practicing touch and go landings, Dick told me to pull off the runway and let him out. "You're on your own, Bernie. Make three landings and I'll see you on the ramp."

My heart jumped in my throat. Dick hopped out of the plane, reached in the cockpit, patted me on the shoulder and shouted over the roar of the engine,

"Relax, Bernie. You're ready for this or I wouldn't turn you loose. Enjoy it, you only solo once!"

In shock, I could only nod an acknowledgement. I did, however, manage to speak to the tower operator, and after one trip around the traffic pattern, was ecstatic. After my third landing, I taxied to the ramp where Dick greeted me with a broad grin, a firm handshake and a pair of scissors. He cut off my shirttail, and with a black marker noted the date of my solo flight. I understood how much I had to learn, but at that moment felt like a real pilot.

I flew as often as the fall and winter weather permitted, and studied for the written exam, which I passed. Six months later, I flew with a Federal Aviation Agency check pilot and qualified as a private pilot. That December I graduated with eleven ROTC Cadets and received my commission as a second lieutenant. I didn't have to wait long before a letter from the Air Force arrived.

Like a kid opening his first present on Christmas morning, I ripped open the envelope and flipped through an atlas looking for Lubbock, Texas, home of Reese Air Force Base. One of my classmates, Dave Peterson, a tall, handsome blond, also received orders to report to the base in west Texas. We studied together while taking flying lessons and shared the cost of renting a plane when we became licensed pilots. Now we were on our way to Texas and class 69-05, the fifth class to graduate in 1969.

Dad, never one to be emotional, told me he was proud of me and eager to hear all about Texas and the airplanes. Having to say goodbye to my mother broke my heart. I lived at home while going to college and except for one month at summer camp, was never away from her for more than a few days at a time. My brothers, Mike and Pat, six and nine years my junior, left the house and headed for their respective schools, no doubt thinking how great it would be to finally have their own bedroom.

Mom, however, was a wreck. Sobbing uncontrollably, she walked to my room and collapsed face down on the bed. I patted her on the back and told her I loved her. With tears streaming down my face, I left my home of twenty-three years.

Dave and I had 1,500 miles ahead of us, plenty of time to ponder the future. The closer we got to Lubbock, the more I questioned my qualifications. The academics were going to be complex. Was I smart enough? Probably not. The flying was certain to be demanding, the competition fierce. Was I a good enough pilot? Not likely. I'd logged a measly seventy hours of flying time. Until now, the thought of washing out of the program hadn't been a concern. The closer we got to Texas, however, the more it became a certainty. I wondered if every member of our class felt the same apprehension I did. Three days after leaving Missoula, we presented our orders to the guard at the entrance to Reese AFB,

drove to the Headquarters building and reported for duty.

We were two of seventy-seven wannabe pilots in our class. Most of us came from ROTC programs, but we had a few guys who attended Officer's Training School (OTS) upon graduating from college. The class included two Norwegian officers, an Air Force navigator, a former corporate pilot who had been accepted to OTS, an Air Force Academy graduate, a NASA scientist who joined us during the advanced stage of our training and two haughty Marines, Captain Jim Hare and Lieutenant Mike Ryan. They came to us by way of the inter-service transfer program. We were divided into two sections and Captain Dave Sanford, the navigator, was my and Dave's Section Commander.

On January 31st, 1969, the first day of the Vietnamese lunar calendar and the most important Vietnamese holiday, the two-day celebration of Tet began. Both North and South Vietnamese forces had agreed on a cease fire during the holiday period, however, the early morning calm was shattered by synchronized attacks from the North Vietnamese Army (NVA), and the Viet Cong (VC) forces. Their targets ranged from the Marine firebase in Khe Sanh, just south of the Demilitarized Zone (DMZ), to the southern part of the country. U.S. forces were taken completely off guard, but recovered quickly.

Militarily, the Tet Offensive was a failure for the NVA and VC forces who lost 45,000 and 14,000 soldiers respectively. Our losses were high, 1,500 soldiers lost their lives, but the enemy failed to capture any real estate in South Vietnam. What they did earn, however, was increased support from antiwar supporters and select members of the press. When Walter Cronkite told his audience "The war is lost," antiwar sentiment increased. The enemy touted the Tet Offensive as a huge success and Ho Chi Minh, the leader of North Vietnam, said, "We don't need to win military victories, we only need to hit them until they give up and get out." Tet was designed to influence public opinion and it accomplished just that. Antiwar sentiment continued to escalate and President Johnson announced he would not accept the nomination of his party to seek another term.

Class 69-05 faced twelve months of flight training followed by, it appeared, a tour of duty in Vietnam. We had a few free days before classes and flying began, which gave us time to pick up our flying gear, academic material, get settled in the Bachelor Officer Quarters (BOQ) and learn our way around the base. Dave and I looked up two friends from Montana who were in the class ahead of us. At the whim of some clerk in the Military Personnel Center, Mike and Marsh Reese, twins from Missoula, had been assigned to Reese AFB. We got together for a beer at the Officer's Club and met a classmate of theirs, Bubba Williams, a Georgian who grew up in Atlanta. He grinned at us beneath unkempt red hair and drawled, "I just love the way ya'll Montana boys talk. I've never heard anything like it!" Dave and I felt the same about him. For some unknown reason, Bubba nicknamed me "Lizard" and it stuck.

Barry Ream and Murry Green, two of our classmates, became our good friends. Barry grew up in Pennsylvania, loved the Pittsburgh Steelers, had an incredibly dry sense of humor and played a mean game of golf. Murry, a tall, lanky, slowtalker from Mississippi, lived close to me and Dave and we all studied together. I loved hanging out with guys from other parts of the country who grew up in different cultures. Bubba and Murry spoke of racial strife in their southern communities. They dealt with conflicts in their schools and on their athletic teams, something we Montanans couldn't imagine.

Captain Sanford summoned our section to the stag bar, a saloon adjoining the Officer's Club, for a get-acquainted session. Upon entering, the first thing one noticed was a sandhill crane mounted above the bar. With its long wings fully extended, it appeared to be in a steep left bank. Prominent in west Texas, this large bird had a wingspan up to seven feet and weighed fifteen pounds or more. It posed a serious threat to pilots. Striking a bird of this size always damaged the aircraft and sometimes proved fatal.

A few years before my arrival, a student and his instructor struck a sandhill crane while on a training flight. The impact shattered the canopy in a catastrophic explosion of plexiglass, blood, guts and feathers. The instructor died instantly. The student, who had not yet soloed, maintained control of the damaged twin engine jet trainer, returned to the base and landed safely.

The crane displayed in the bar had one feature that distinguished it from the rest of its species--a pitot tube, a pointed pressure measuring device installed on the nose or leading edge of a wing on all aircraft--protruded from its ass.

Close to the crane hung a brass bell, its purpose to announce a less-than-alert officer had entered the bar without removing his flight cap. The culprit singled out by the clanging bell had to buy a round of drinks for everyone, a head count that could total fifty or more on a Friday afternoon. Every club in the Air Force maintained this protocol, a bell ready to summon any offender, regardless of rank, to the bar to ante up.

Several small tables were crowded together next to the long, dark mahogany bar. Pool balls clicked in the background. A neon-colored juke box belted out tunes from the Beach Boys, Elvis, The Beatles and an occasional number from Old Blue Eyes, Frank Sinatra. A popcorn machine worked nonstop, as did the enlisted men who moonlighted as bartenders. We mingled for several hours, not enough time to get to know everyone, but putting a face with a name wouldn't take long as we were going to spend long hours together, beginning early the next morning.

Our work day consisted of flying and academics. One week, our section flew in the morning and spent the afternoon in the classroom while the other half of our class did the opposite. The following week the schedules flipped. At the flight line we flew, critiqued our flights and studied emergency procedures. Our academics consisted of aircraft systems, navigation, weather, aerodynamics and instrument procedures. None of us knew why, but we also studied Morse Code.

We spent time in an altitude chamber, exposed to the dangers of high altitude flight. At 25,000 feet our instructor, a sergeant, told us to remove our oxygen masks. In seconds we began to experience hypoxia, lack of oxygen to the brain. The symptoms included a feeling of euphoria, slurred speech, blue fingernails and dizziness. The sergeant told us to write numbers from one to ten on a scratch pad. Initially, they were legible but soon became scribbles. We learned to recognize our own individual symptoms and a valuable lesson: with a sudden loss of cabin pressurization, descend rapidly or die.

From a platform four feet from a sawdust pit, we learned how to execute the parachute landing fall (PLF). For hours, we jumped and rotated upon contact in such a manner that the shock upon landing was distributed from our feet to our calves, thighs, buttocks and shoulders.

A parasailing exercise taught us how to make a safe landing when floating to earth in a parachute. Strapped into an inflated chute, we ran a few steps behind an accelerating pickup and became airborne. At an altitude of four hundred feet we were cut loose, floated to earth and executed a PLF.

We flew three different planes while at Reese. The first was the T-41, a small Cessna, ideal for basic instruction. We travelled by bus from the base to the Lubbock airport for initial training. Several of us had some flying experience, which meant nothing to the Air Force. As my instructor, James Adam Needham, and I approached a T-41 for my first flight, he looked at me and said, "Lieutenant Hale, this is an airplane."

"Yes, sir," I replied.

The rules were understood, the game on. Mr. Needham, like all the T-41 instructors, was a civilian, contracted by the Air Force. A large man, he struggled cramming his linebacker-sized frame into the small cockpit.

Major McQueen, assisted by Major Finch and Captain Landor, managed the T-41 program, which lasted six weeks. They flew periodic check rides with us and monitored our flying and academic progress.

It was important to Major McQueen and his staff that every student recommended for advanced training was capable of meeting the challenge. Sending a less-than-qualified student to the next level would have been a failure on their part. Consequently, they subjected us to intense scrutiny. Nineteen members of our class, twenty-five percent, failed to complete the T-41 program. One guy suffered from air sickness, a few were afraid of flying, and the remainder washed out due to a lack of coordination. They were known as "ham-fists."

The three Air Force officers were a surly lot. They barked at us the moment we got off the bus and treated us as raw recruits, and we understood why. Their peers were on the other side of town, flying high performance jets with advanced students while they spent every day boring holes in the sky with rookies in a small Cessna, wondering what they had done to deserve such a miserable assignment.

We referred to the operations building as Happy Ops, a satiric reference to the attitudes of the three officers in charge. There we met with our civilian instructors to study emergency procedures, brief each day's flight and critique our performance upon landing. Four of us flew with Mr. Needham. My table mates were Bob Crane, a stocky farm boy from Ohio; John McKenzie, a short feisty red head; and Lyndon Johnson, a lanky Texan who was quick to point out he wished the other Lyndon Johnson would have remained a little-known Senator from the hill country. Ever since he was a young boy, Lyndon dealt with the same incredulous look when meeting someone for the first time and we were no exception. When he introduced himself to us we all had the same "you've-got-to-be-shitting-me" expression on our faces.

We flew the T-41 for one month and logged thirty hours. Those of us who thought we were accomplished pilots quickly understood we had been fooling ourselves. The manner in which the Air Force approached flight training was much more intense than we experienced as civilians.

Putting the airplane through a maneuver with a less-than-precise technique was not acceptable. Headings were to be maintained to the exact degree. Flying level at 5,000 feet meant just that.

Our class members with no experience had the opportunity to learn the basics of flying, and when we completed our T-41 training, the playing field was level. With the blessing of Major McQueen and his henchmen, we were deemed ready to enter the second phase of training, a transition to a twin engine, jet powered aircraft.

The Cessna T-37, known as the "Tweet" or "3,000 pound dog whistle," due to the high-pitched whine of its twin jet engines, introduced us to jet-powered flight. It topped out at three-hundred-and ninety miles per hour and could reach a height of 25,000 feet. We flew the Tweet for five months and practiced aerobatics, instrument flying and navigation. The latter phase of our T-37 training included an introduction to formation flying.

I flew my first overnight cross country flight with Captain McClellan, our assistant flight commander. We landed at Del Rio Air Force Base on the Mexican border. These flights tested our navigation skills, and believing the adage that there are two kinds of pilots--those who have been lost and those that one day would be--we paid attention. Flying an airplane from point A to B without getting lost was not difficult if the pilot could read navigational charts and follow landmarks and terrain features, something hard to do in the flat lands of west Texas. If low visibility deprived the pilot of visual references, he had to transition to instrument flying and interpret radio signals from navigational aids located at all military and most civilian airports.

To prepare for the inevitable day we would become disoriented, a rescue procedure was in place, one we practiced often. We called the FAA traffic control center, the facility tasked with radar monitoring of every airborne flight in a given region, and requested a practice direction finding (DF) steer. If the center had time to perform the exercise they were happy to do so. The controller directed us to execute a series of ninety degree turns, which we repeated until the air traffic controller could identify our position on radar. He then gave us a heading that would take us to the base. If too busy to accommodate us, they would tell us to call back later.

One afternoon, a classmate of mine flew a solo mission, working on aerobatic maneuvers in the local practice area, a pie-shaped piece of airspace 30,000 feet thick. He became disoriented and made a call to Fort Worth Center. Everyone flying at the time heard him speak to the controller.

"Fort Worth Center, Golf Three Two, a Reese T-37 west of the base, requesting a practice DF steer."

The center replied, "Golf Three Two, be advised we are unable to work a practice exercise for you at this time."

Forced to admit he was lost, the student said to the controller, "Uh, Center, would you have time to do a real one?"

Word of the embarrassing conversation spread throughout the squadron. When the lost pilot entered the stag bar that afternoon, we greeted him with a standing ovation. He bought a round of drinks.

After countless landings, loops and spins, we passed our final check rides and were deemed qualified to strap on the advanced trainer, the supersonic T-38 Talon, known as "The White Rocket."

Our class was six months into the program when we were given a week off, a short break to relax and reflect on what we'd accomplished to date and prepare for the final lap of our year-long marathon. Some of the guys went to Dallas to escape the mundane environment of Lubbock for a few days, but most stayed at the base to play golf and study the T-38 operating manual.

I flew to Montana and got married.

Kay deMers and I were ten years old when we met. A cross-town move took me to the south side of town and a home one block from hers. The neighborhood teemed with healthy, active kids. A softball field, located across the street from my house, served as a skating rink during the winter months. Mount Sentinel stood guard over the valley and we sped down her slopes on our Flexible Flyers, cheating death with each daring run. The *thump, thump, thump* of bouncing basketballs on the school playground echoed for blocks. The blue-eyed girl with auburn hair and just the right number of freckles became one of my best friends.

One of the most popular kids in our high school, Kay excelled athletically and in the classroom. Everyone, teachers and students alike, admired her. She and I were never high school sweethearts, but always close friends. She went to the University of New Mexico to play on the women's tennis team but returned to Montana after her freshman year. We dated occasionally while in college and she visited me in Lubbock in the spring of 1968, not long after I began the T-37 program. It was then we decided to get married.

The time in Missoula was fantastic. Being reunited with Kay, family and friends from high school and college made for an exciting, fun-filled week. Kay and I settled into an apartment in the complex where I lived with Dave and Bubba and began our transition from single to married life. It was a challenge for both of us considering my military experience consisted of a mere six months. Kay had no idea what to expect of the Air Force environment, and I faced deployment to Vietnam within the next six or seven months. Then there was the demanding White Rocket waiting for me on the flight line. I had a spouse and a mistress.

The T-38 could attain a speed of 1.4 mach, nearly one-and-a-half times the speed of sound, and reach an altitude of 50,000 feet. Capable of climbing at a rate of 33,600 feet per minute, the White Rocket set four climb records in 1962. In a second it could roll at the rate of seven-hundred-and-twenty-degrees, two revolutions around its longitudinal axis. The aircraft seated a student and instructor in tandem and had engine air intakes located at the wing roots, aft of the cockpits. With anxious anticipation, we reported to the T-38 squadron briefing room for the introductory "dollar ride," a flight in which we sat quietly in the back seat, kept our hands away from the controls and marveled at the T-38's performance. Major Sheldon Brown, a veteran instructor who had flown the T-38 for several years, commanded my group, E Flight.

We enjoyed Major Brown's pleasant demeanor. Having advanced to the T-38 program, we were treated more like fellow pilots than students. Major Chuck

Thomas, a grizzled F-100 fighter pilot, commanded our sister section, A Flight. He had thinning red hair, a furrowed brow and bright green eyes that seldom revealed a hint of levity. His face displayed the impression made by a tight-fitting oxygen mask, no matter how long it had been since his last flight. He appeared to be tattooed, permanently marked as a fighter pilot.

I was assigned to Captain Bill Cathey's training table but flew my dollar ride with Major Thomas. Giddy with excitement, I walked with the major to the equipment room, where we picked up our parachutes and G-suits, tight fitting garments worn over the lower body and pressurized through a G-sensitive valve, which inflated during periods of high acceleration, restricting the flow of blood from the head to the lower extremities.

Major Thomas, like several of the T-38 instructors, had recent combat experience in Vietnam. Consequently, he and the other fighter jocks were held in higher esteem by the students than the instructors who had been assigned to UPT right out of flight school. Experience, more important than rank, determined one's position in the pecking order of respect.

A van took us to our assigned aircraft. I followed close behind the major as he walked around the jet performing the exterior preflight check list. He spoke to me as he noted the critical items. "Air intake ducts clear, gear safety pin removed, pitot tube clear, no damage to control surfaces, tailpipes free of debris and cracks." With the exterior checklist complete, he said, "Let's saddle up, Lieutenant."

"Yes, sir," I replied as I slipped into the straps of my parachute.

Once I had the bulky thing strapped on tight, I climbed the ladder to the rear cockpit. The crew chief made sure my radio connection, oxygen mask, and G-suit were properly hooked up. He scampered down the ladder and started the auxiliary power unit, a device that provided airflow to the turbines, facilitating engine start. Major Thomas obtained clearance to taxi and our crew chief guided us out of our parking area. We taxied to the runway and stopped short of the hold line, a white stripe on the taxiway, not to be crossed without clearance from the control tower. I wondered how long my heart could pound at its current rate before exploding. Often I watched the T-38s in the traffic pattern as I practiced landings in the Tweet. Couldn't wait to strap one on.

There I sat, poised at the end of runway one seven right, my dream about to become a reality. The tower cleared us for takeoff.

"Echo One Two, you are cleared for a max performance takeoff. Climb to, and maintain ten thousand feet and contact Fort Worth Center."

"Roger, Tower," the fighter pilot acknowledged, "Echo One Two is rolling"

Major Thomas taxied into takeoff position, applied and held the brakes. Slowly, he advanced the throttles to the Military Power (MIL) setting. With the engines screaming at one hundred percent power, he checked the engine instruments for proper values and said, "Hang on, Hale. Here we go."

The White Rocket leapt forward. I watched the throttles move slowly through a friction stop to the MAX setting, which ignited the afterburners and injected additional fuel into the engines, increasing the thrust. Slammed into my seat, I focused on the airspeed indicator, which moved rapidly to one hundred-and-fifty-five knots. Major Thomas gently pulled the control stick back, and the jet leapt from the runway. He retracted the gear, then the flaps, and leveled off a few feet above the ground. We accelerated to five hundred knots as the end of the 8,000 foot runway flashed beneath us. He jerked the stick into his lap and put us into a forty-five degree climb, which we maintained until he leveled the jet at an altitude of 10,000 feet.

We had been airborne forty-seconds. *Holy smokes! What just happened?* I was shocked by how quickly we became airborne and reached altitude. There was no way I could keep up with such a fast airplane. An airspeed restriction was in place to reduce stress on the landing gear. Once airborne, the gear had to be retracted before the T-38 reached one-hundred-and-seventy-five knots. The flaps, too, had an airspeed limit. It was two-hundred-and-ten knots and was upon the pilot seconds following gear retraction.

I heard the words, "Oxygen check," a reminder we were going higher and needed to ensure our system worked properly. Major Thomas reported, "I've got a hundred pounds of pressure, five-and-half liters and a blinker." I replied that I, too, had adequate pressure, volume and my eye-shaped indicator winked at me with each breath.

The air traffic control center cleared us to climb and enter our assigned practice area. Major Thomas advanced the throttles and we began a twenty-five degree climb. Our airspeed settled at four hundred knots, which we maintained until we leveled off at 40,000 feet.

Following several dizzying max-rate rolls, we rolled inverted and changed our heading one-hundred-and-eighty degrees by descending in a high-speed, high-G maneuver called a split S. My G-suit inflated, a python attacking my skinny legs. The accelerometer indicated two, three, four Gs. My blood flowed toward my feet despite the inflated G-suit and my vision began to fade...five, six Gs. My field of vision was sucked into a dark tunnel and I blacked out. When we leveled off and the G-forces subsided, I quickly recovered. Knowing I had "taken a nap," Major Thomas keyed the mic and said, "it will be easier for you to withstand high Gs when you are flying the plane, not just along for the ride. Check the mach indicator, Hale, you're about to go supersonic. Shake the stick, you've got the airplane. Ease the throttles forward and gently light the burners."

We were flying at .98 mach. I gently eased the throttles forward, lighting the afterburners, and we flew faster than the speed of sound. I felt no turbulence or buffeting, just a slight bump and a momentary decrease in indicated airspeed as the air struggled to get out of our way. For a few moments we rocketed through the atmosphere at eight hundred miles per hour.

I had joined an exclusive club.

Major Thomas took control of the plane and did more aerobatics. We landed an hour after takeoff. I was soaking wet and hadn't even touched the stick except for my brief super sonic moment. When we got out of the plane, Major Thomas smiled and exclaimed, "I love these dollar rides!"

After we dropped off our G-suits and chutes in the equipment room, we walked toward the squadron briefing room and Major Thomas said, "It's your turn tomorrow, Hale. Captain Cathey expects you to be prepared. You'll be responsible for completing the check lists and handling the communications. You'll perform the engine start, taxi, takeoff and execute the flight plan. I suggest you sit your ass down, replay the details of the mission we just completed and start studying."

"I'll be ready, sir. I really enjoyed our flight, Major."

With a wink and a pat on my shoulder, he said, "I know you did, Lieutenant, but not as much as I. Now hit the books."

I spent the rest of the day with Captain Cathey, a 1966 graduate of the Air Force Academy, discussing the curriculum we would follow the next six months. He had been an instructor since graduating from flight school and was ready to move on to another assignment, preferably a fighter. He respected us and considered us fellow pilots who needed tweaking before moving on to our next assignments.

Two other students, Mike Ryan and Larry Farmer, joined me at Captain Cathey's training table. Mike could have appeared on a Marine recruiting poster. Six-feet tall, handsomely square-jawed and sporting a blond flattop, he epitomized the Corps. Mike enjoyed our company and the flying, but longed to return to the Marine Corps.

Larry was an avid runner and led the pack when it came to long distance work. Even Mike Ryan couldn't keep up with him. He also excelled in academics and was an excellent pilot, a "good stick." Larry wanted desperately to fly the North American F-100 Super Saber jet fighter. He was an artist, and his sketch book contained dozens of drawings of the "Hun." He designed the class patch we wore on our flight suits. It featured a wide-eyed, sexy, miniskirted blonde struggling to keep a gust of wind from exposing her derrière. The caption read, 69-05 *Up Up and Away.*

Captain Cathey took the three of us under his wing and helped us become excellent pilots. I flew twenty-five hours with him before I soloed in the White Rocket. I didn't have to be taught how to make a takeoff, landing, execute a loop or any other aerobatic maneuver. I simply needed to understand how the T-38 demanded to be flown. Much feistier than the T-37, she required a more gentle caress and total concentration.

Making my first takeoff, I struggled to react to each critical action promptly. Holding the brakes with all the strength I could muster, I advanced the power to one hundred percent. With strained legs quivering, I checked the engine instruments. The plane lunged forward when my boots came off the brakes. I lit the afterburners and maintained directional control with gentle pressure on the rudder pedals, eyes darting between the runway and airspeed indicator. With heart pounding, lungs sucking oxygen from my mask, I coaxed the jet into the air when we reached a hundred-and-fifty-five knots.

Okay, Bernie, lots to keep up with. Relax. Stay focused. Keep the wings level and maintain a hundred-and-seventy-degree heading and a fifteen degree climb angle. Check the engine instruments. Scan the horizon for birds and other aircraft. Monitor the air speed indicator...oops.

"Hale, you just passed a hundred-and-ninety knots!" Captain Cathey barked. "Retract the gear!" A second later, "The flaps are going to blow off the jet! Raise the flaps!" Then a dagger to my heart, "Lieutenant, you are so far behind the airplane, if it crashed you wouldn't even get hurt!"

Too busy flying the airplane to feel sorry for myself, I brushed off his scathing tirade. Obviously, I needed some prodding. It took a few flights for me to catch up to the jet and I wondered why I struggled so, taking care of business.

We spent hours in the practice area working on aerobatics learned in the T-37. The performance of the Tweet compared to that of the White Rocket was like the difference between a sparkler and a Roman candle. Several hours were devoted to instrument flying. Tucked in the back seat on each of these flights, I covered the canopy with a canvas curtain and flew the sortie "under the hood." For the entire flight I focused only on the instrument panel. This included the takeoff, performed using the heading indicator for directional reference.

With Captain Cathey in the front cockpit, I departed Reese airspace and flew several navigation legs over west Texas. The traffic control center directed me to different civilian airports where, guided by the instruments, I executed approaches to the runway. I didn't land, but at an altitude of two hundred feet, advanced the throttles and initiated a go around. I raised the gear and flaps and flew to another airport to repeat the exercise. After an intense hour, I returned to Reese soaked with sweat and exhausted, thinking, *one more approach, Bernie. Nail this baby and you'll be at the club in an hour.* A few feet above the ground, Captain Cathey took control of the airplane and made the landing. What a relief to feel the stick shake and hear him say, "I've got the airplane, take the hood down and relax."

After twenty-nine hours under the hood, I began the pre-solo phase of training. The dual sorties focused on stick and rudder work in the practice area honing aerobatic skills, pushing the White Rocket to her limits in high-G maneuvers. We also spent hours in the traffic pattern where we practiced landings. Cleared by the tower to land, we flew a three-hundred-and-sixty degree overhead pattern. We entered our initial leg at two-hundred-and-eighty knots, 1,500 feet above the ground, flying parallel to the runway in the direction we would land. Approaching the midpoint of the runway, we executed a snappy sixty degree banked turn to the left. We maintained this turn for one-hundred-and-eighty degrees, and rolled out on the downwind leg, parallel to the runway, opposite the direction of our landing.

Extending the speed brakes created drag and reduced our speed. We lowered the flaps, checked the gear down and locked and maintained heading and altitude until the touchdown point was forty-five degrees behind our shoulder. We then reduced our speed to one-hundred-and-seventy-five knots and began a descending turn toward the runway, rolling out on final approach at one-hundred-fifty-five knots, plus one knot for every hundred pounds of fuel onboard. Our speed at touchdown was one-hundred-thirty knots plus the fuel consideration. Safely on the runway, we raised the nose to induce aerodynamic braking. This maneuver created drag on the airplane and extended brake life. As the speed dissipated below one hundred knots, the nose settled on the runway, at which time we tested the brakes and completed the landing roll.

We practiced single-engine and no-flap approaches, preparing for the day we might experience an emergency.

After six weeks of flying under the watchful eyes of our instructors we soloed and began formation work, for me, the most difficult phase of our training. We learned how to fly formation in the Tweet, but doing so in the White Rocket proved more difficult due to the higher speeds and G-forces. Maintaining proper spacing depended on our ability to maneuver so that the lead aircraft's wingtip covered the star painted on its air intake duct. If we made smooth changes in attitude and airspeed, and maintained proper position by keeping the wingtip on the star, we could safely follow the lead aircraft wherever he went. We pulled up to five Gs and executed climbs, descents, and aerobatic maneuvers. After several dual rides we soloed in formation, but our two and four-ship flights always contained at least one instructor in the formation to keep a close eye on us. After thirty-five hours of practice, we could maintain close formation with our wingtips three feet apart while flying at speeds of up to five hundred knots. Ham fists need not apply.

We flew two cross country flights, one dual and the other solo. One of our instructors, Captain Lewis, and I flew to Las Vegas, home of Nellis Air Force Base and the Air Force Thunderbirds. I planned a route to Holloman Air Force Base in New Mexico where we refueled. We then continued on to Phoenix for two practice instrument approaches at Luke Air Force Base followed by a high speed, low-level visit to the Grand Canyon. The magnitude and beauty of the canyon took my breath away. Brilliant shades of red, orange, yellow and purple blended in a kaleidoscopic blur.

From a higher altitude, we flew over Hoover Dam, my second awe-inspiring sight in a matter of seconds, then descended into Las Vegas airspace for a landing at Nellis. I taxied past the Thunderbird's F-4 Phantom jets, and with goose bumps tingling, parked the T-38 and shut down the engines. I took a moment to reflect on the previous thirty minutes and thought, *Hale, you are one lucky guy.*

My solo cross country flight, a month later, was as exciting as the one with Captain Lewis but for different reasons. I planned an out-and-back flight that would take me back to Holloman Air Force Base where I refueled on the way to Las Vegas. I planned to fly three navigation legs and figured it would take me an hour and thirty minutes to get to Holloman. I flew the route dozens of times in my mind and was well prepared when I taxied to the runway to start my journey.

"Reese tower, Echo One Two is ready for takeoff."

"Echo One Two, standby, we have an emergency in progress."

"Roger, tower," I replied, hoping the delay would be short.

With hundreds of sorties flown each day, occasionally a plane would have a problem and declare an emergency. I looked to my left expecting to see a distressed T-38 on a long final approach, but saw nothing. Fire trucks and emergency vehicles, sirens wailing and lights flashing, arrived and lined the runway. Ten, fifteen, thirty minutes passed. Thinking of my fuel requirements, I began to wonder how long the delay would be. I had plenty of gas, but wanted to get on my way. The tower dispatched the planes in the traffic pattern to the practice areas to await the conclusion of the emergency. Parked at the hold line fifteen yards from the runway, I had a front row seat. The pilot would land right in front of me.

Billowing black smoke on the horizon announced the arrival of the crippled aircraft. I couldn't identify it but assumed it was a T-38.

As the plane rapidly approached the runway, I realized I had never seen anything like it. The large, black aircraft had a fuselage shaped like the body of an elongated stingray. Swept wings well aft of the cockpit each supported a huge engine, the one on the right spewed smoke and flames. The pilot flying this thing had a handful of airplane. It yawed left and right, the pilot struggling to stabilize on the center of the runway. I estimated its speed at over two hundred knots. When the plane touched down, a huge orange parachute billowed from the rear of the aircraft. The jet came to a stop at the far end of the runway, fire trucks and ambulances in tow.

With the mystery plane safely off the runway, I received a call from the tower.

"Echo One Two, Reese tower. You are cleared as filed. Contact Fort Worth Center when airborne."

"Roger, tower. Echo One Two. What was that thing that landed in front of me?"

"Uh, Echo One Two, tower. You are cleared for takeoff."

"Roger that," I replied. *Hmm, he doesn't know what it is either, or he's not saying.*

As I flew over the end of the runway, I banked to get a look at the sight below. The jet appeared to be over one hundred feet long with a wingspan half that distance. It looked like something out of a science fiction movie, a craft capable of escaping earth's gravity. Several onlookers surrounded the plane, sharing the surreal experience with me. I amended my flight plan with the air traffic control folks to make up for my late departure and couldn't wait to get back to Reese and tell the guys what I'd seen. When I landed in New Mexico, I asked the crew chief for a quick turnaround. I wanted to get refueled soon and head home without delay.

I walked to the Base Operations building, got a sandwich and filed a flight plan for my return flight. The place was full of F-4 jocks. A few of them spoke to me, asking where I was stationed. One guy told me he had been a student at Reese and wondered if I knew his T-38 instructor. I did not, but our conversation continued. We talked about the F-4 and T-38 and how lucky we were to fly such aircraft. I didn't feel like a student but a real jet jockey, shooting the breeze with a peer.

Strapped into my White Rocket and ready to go, I called for clearance to taxi and requested a max performance, unrestricted takeoff, one not restricted by airspeed or altitude. I certainly didn't think I would impress any F-4 pilots, but like my classmates, wanted to emulate the excitement we experienced on our dollar rides. We never got the opportunity to execute this exciting climb at Reese due to the heavy traffic, but we all requested one when we flew our one and only solo cross-country sortie. The tower operators didn't always grant this request as it depended on the amount of traffic in the area, but it was my lucky day.

Approaching the runway, I received a call from the tower.

"Echo One Two, Holloman tower. You are cleared for a max performance takeoff. Climb to and maintain flight level two five zero (25,000 feet) and contact center."

Shit hot! I thought, grinning behind my oxygen mask. That expression described any person, place or moment considered to be outstanding.

Roger, tower. Echo One Two is rolling".

I centered the plane on the runway, held the brakes (I hated this part), advanced the throttles and urged the jets to quickly spool up to one hundred percent. The engine instruments indicated we could safely execute the takeoff and I released the brakes and lit the burners.

My White Rocket and I leaped forward and raced down the runway, working together as one. She responded to my every command, and aware of her limitations, I didn't ask too much. In the length of two football fields, the jet exceeded a hundred knots.

Seconds later we leveled off twenty-feet above the runway, airspeed increasing rapidly. I retracted the gear and flaps, streamlining the aircraft. My heart pounded as I watched the airspeed indicator exceed two hundred, three hundred, four hundred knots.

The end of the runway flashed beneath the nose, I yanked the stick into my lap and maintained a forty-five degree climb angle. Passing through 10,000 feet I checked the oxygen system and slammed the stick all the way to the left, inducing high-speed rolls. An aggressive thrust of the stick reversed the direction of roll and seconds later I leveled off at my assigned altitude. I leveled the wings, slowly retarded the throttles and the additional thrust provided by the afterburners subsided. The White Rocket slowed as though brakes had been applied. Like a jockey patting his mount after a winning effort, I gently rocked our wings back and forth. *Well done, my friend. Let's go home.*

Upon landing, I asked my crew chief if he knew anything about the mystery plane and he told me everyone was talking about it but no one knew what it was. When I entered the briefing room, Captain Cathey said, "Welcome home, Bernie.

You missed some excitement while you were gone."

"No, sir, I didn't. I was stuck at the hold line and the black jet landed right in front of me."

That afternoon I learned a bit about the SR-71 Blackbird, now a not-so-secret-spy plane stationed at Beale Air Force Base in California. The replacement for the U-2 spy plane that the Russians shot down in 1960 with Gary Powers aboard, could cruise at 85,000 feet and fly at a speed of more than three times the speed of sound. Some of the guys said they'd heard of a secret plane on the west coast but no one knew its name or had seen it until now. By the time I returned from my flight, an Air Force transport plane had landed at Reese carrying a maintenance crew, a new engine, and several armed Air Police (AP). The Blackbird had been towed to one of our maintenance hangars and was well guarded. The next day, we students were allowed to walk through the hangar and view the plane from a distance of thirty feet.

Cameras and Larry Farmer's sketch book were not permitted.

A month later, my time in the T-38 was over. When I touched down on my final flight, a year after driving through the front gate of Reese AFB, I knew I could fly any airplane in the Air Force inventory, even the SR-71.

Colonel Clyde Morganti, the Wing Commander, presided over our graduation ceremony in March of 1969. As he spoke to our class, I recalled a flight I had with him two weeks before.

We flew a four-ship formation flight, and he was in my back seat. It wasn't a check ride, but I had a serious case of "checkitis," a nervous condition experienced by all students being scrutinized in flight by a check pilot or in this instance, the Wing Commander. Once airborne, I relaxed and performed well. As our formation entered the traffic pattern, Colonel Morganti engaged the intercom. "Lieutenant, what would you think of a rusty old fighter pilot making the landing?"

That's a great idea, Colonel," I replied. "You have the airplane." He shook the stick as the tower cleared us to land. The Boss, as we referred to him, flew frequently with each class and always got all the landings and stick time he wanted.

During the last week in March of 1969, pinning silver wings on my chest, The

Boss shook the hand of a proud Air Force pilot.

The day we received our wings, the number of American troops in Vietnam was 495,000, a figure more than double the number of three years before.

President Nixon threatened to resume bombing in North Vietnam and authorized B-52 strikes in Cambodia, targeting NVA supply and troop sanctuaries located along the Vietnamese border. The NVA and VC were being supplied with weapons, ammunition, missiles, heavy equipment, and aircraft from Russia and China. Support for our war effort continued to deteriorate.

Reese Air Force Base Class 69-05

Forty-Three Years Later

Barry Ream, Andy Gambardella, Bernie Hale, Wayne Schnell, Bill Baker, Neil Stringer, Fred Smith, Charlie Hulse, Mike Ryan, Dave Peterson, Dave Sanford, John Quinn, Ralph Femrite, Wes Westenrieder.

Three

Preparing for Combat

We were given our choice of four categories of aircraft, which we ranked in order of preference: fighters, cargo, UPT, and Forward Air Control (FAC). Assignments were based on academic and flying performance.

Our selection of aircraft included twenty fighter slots, my first choice. They were taken when my name appeared on the class roster. I was assigned an O-1 Bird Dog, a small, single engine Cessna flown by FACs, pilots who directed tactical air strikes in support of ground forces.

Nineteen percent of our class were going to be FACs. My ticket was punched to Vietnam.

Barry Ream, John Murphy, Bob Crane, Ted Barna, John McKenzie, Fred Clark, Dick Ross and Bud Leithiser were going to fly the twin engine O-2 Skymaster, the Cessna designed to replace my 1940s vintage aircraft. Bob Heft and David Jauquet were assigned the armor-plated OV-10 Bronco, a North American Rockwell twin engine turboprop considered to be the ultimate FAC aircraft--fast, maneuverable, outstanding visibility and capable of expending rockets and machine gun fire.

I envied the guys who were going to fly the newer aircraft, but once I began training, I fell in love with the Bird Dog and wouldn't have traded places with any of them.

Dave got an F-4 fighter, Larry received his F-100, Mike Ryan went on to fly Marine A-4 fighters, and Murry drew a C-123, a cargo plane modified to spread Agent Orange over the Vietnamese landscape.

The day after graduation, our class flew to Fairchild Air Force Base, the site of my ROTC summer camp. We went there to attend the Air Force Survival School, a requirement for all pilots. The two week program consisted of two phases: a field exercise where we were taught basic survival and evasion techniques, and exposure to life as a prisoner of war in a realistic prison compound.

March signaled the end of the long northwest winter and the feeling of spring filled the air. My group of six boarded an Air Force bus and headed to the Pend Oreille forest located in the Idaho panhandle. Sergeant Jim Griffith, our instructor, briefed us on what to expect.

"Gentlemen, you're going to do navigation exercises, learn how to protect yourselves from the elements, trap game, and communicate with search and rescue personnel. Yours is the first class to go through the exercise without snow shoes, but two weeks ago the snow wasn't too deep so there shouldn't be a problem."

Ted Barna nudged me and whispered, "What the Sergeant means is, we're screwed." Ted enjoyed the outdoors and looked forward to plodding through the forest. When we got off the bus and unloaded our gear, I noticed Sergeant Griffith strapping a pair of snow shoes to his backpack. Not a good sign. Ted grinned and shook his head.

For three days, we hiked through the woods, sometimes in thigh-high snow while our instructor skipped merrily along on top of the stuff. We cut pine boughs on which we slept, lit fires with survival kit matches, navigated with a small compass, and lived on rabbit soup and a few candy bars, contraband smuggled in our clothing. The guys thought that I, being a native Montanan, would revel in the woods, no matter how cold and wet. They were wrong. I couldn't wait to get back to the warm barracks.

The prisoner of war exercise began at midnight the day after our return from the boondocks. The plan was for us to maneuver through an obstacle course in an attempt to escape enemy soldiers, but the field was closed due to the recent heavy snowfalls. We marched a mile from the barracks to the Prisoner of War (POW) camp, accompanied by armed enemy soldiers, watching our every move and threatening to kill us if we tried to escape.

The prison, previously a bomb storage revetment, was a dank subterranean structure. It contained several bare, one-man cells, five feet square with cinder block walls. Low ceilings prohibited standing and we sat on the cold cement floor.

In total darkness, we spent countless hours in solitary confinement, deprived of sleep. A guard roamed the floor, banging a wooden stick on the door of each cell. Occasionally, the guard passed tins of broth and water through a small sliding door. We relieved ourselves in a plastic bucket that was kicked over if we were caught sleeping.

I have no idea how long we were locked up, but each of us hallucinated due to lack of sleep. Several times I saw a bunk in my cell and leaped into it, only to crack my head against the cold, black wall.

Periodically, a guard took us to a small room for interrogation. A single, bright light hung from above, dangling over a small table. I faced a lone, hostile officer. *Name, rank and serial number, tell him no more.* Following several minutes of verbal abuse and threats of physical violence, we were returned to our cells.

Stuffed into a wooden box not much larger than a suitcase, I played mind games. Having a panic attack or passing out weren't options. *I've got to relax. Deep, slow breaths. Think about open spaces: football fields, airports, seaside beaches. Play an imaginary round of golf. Wiggle your toes, it takes concentration. You're breathing too fast, slow down.*

Wiggling my toes was a superstition my mother told me about when I was a boy. She said, "Bernie if you're in a pickle and need to relax, just wiggle your toes. It takes concentration and you'll be at ease." Not being in a position with many alternatives, and following the old adage that mother always knows best, I wiggled my toes like crazy.

We were instructed to knock on the door if we were beginning to panic and the exercise would be halted. They also rapped on each box every few minutes and we were instructed to answer by rapping back with our knuckles to let the instructor know we were okay. They didn't want an Air Force pilot losing consciousness. When one of the guys several boxes down the row failed to respond to a knock, the instructor flung open the door to find him grinning broadly. When asked why he failed to rap he replied, "I didn't hear you, sir. I was in the back room." Laughter echoed throughout our cages. The guards were pissed and quickly whisked us back to solitary.

Following two or three sleep-deprived days and nights, a reunion with my buddies took place in a compound reminiscent of the POW camps seen in World War II movies. A few hours later we were released. Relieved to be out of jail, we silently trudged back to the barracks, pondering our fate should we be shot down and captured. We didn't undergo physical abuse, but it was a realistic, dramatic exercise designed to get our attention.

The thought of checking into the Hanoi Hilton POW camp was frightening.

Upon our return to Lubbock, we processed out of Reese Air Force Base, bade our classmates farewell and headed for our next duty stations. I was given a week to report to Hurlburt Field, home of Air Force Special Operations Command located in the Florida panhandle. Kay and I lived in nearby Fort Walton Beach from late April until early June of 1969.

Five days a week I drove twenty miles to Holly Field, a small naval airstrip where I learned how to fly the Bird Dog and direct airborne fighters in the deployment of their weapons. Air Force, Army and Naval aviators shared the crowded airspace and trained in short takeoff and landing (STOL) aircraft. A lone Naval Shore Patrolman guarded the entry gate. "Welcome to Holly Field, Lieutenant, have a safe flight."

His routine never wavered.

I might have walked into World War II. We studied in two Quonset huts identical to the ones in which Gregory Peck briefed his haggard air crews in the movie, Twelve O'clock High. I could smell the aroma of well-worn, sweat-stained leather flight jackets and Lucky Strikes as my instructors and I prepared for and evaluated each flight. A control tower directed traffic on two cement runways and one short dirt strip. A sailor managed a fuel storage area and topped off the tanks of the various aircraft that shared the crowded airspace.

The O-1, a tandem-seat Cessna, weighed 2,400 pounds and was powered by a two-hundred-and-thirteen horsepower engine. Maximum speed was advertised at one hundred knots, but ninety was more like it. Outstanding visibility and slow-flight capability made it the perfect platform for the mission of directing fighters in their role of close air support.

The Bird Dog was unique in that the third landing gear was located under the tail rather than the nose, she was a "tail dragger." This configuration made the aircraft unstable while taxiing, taking off, or landing since the center of gravity was aft of the main landing gear. If a preoccupied pilot allowed the tail wheel to swing either left or right of the intended direction, centrifugal force would result in a tight turn and perhaps a ground loop. Should that occur at a high rate of speed, a wing would contact the ground resulting in severe damage to the aircraft as well as the pilot's ego.

I flew ten hours my first week at Holly, most of them spent in the traffic pattern. I logged seventy landings and fell in love with the airplane. The Bird Dog was certainly no White Rocket, but the seat-of-the-pants feeling I felt while putting her through her paces at less than one hundred knots was somehow exhilarating. We were going to make a great couple.

After two sessions on the cement runways, Captain Pat Rooney, my instructor, told me to move to the dirt strip, a short, narrow runway. I noticed a captain standing on the side of the runway, obviously watching one of his students. When I made my first approach and touchdown, he extended both hands, ten fingers in front of his face,. The captain repeated the gesture on my next pass and I said to my instructor, "What's that guy doing?"

"He's grading your landings. You numbah ten, G.I."

Obviously, being "numbah ten" sucked, as my landings were less than smooth. My theory proved correct, when, following a perfect touchdown the critic smiled and saluted me with the middle finger of his right hand.

Captain Rooney clicked the intercom and said in a cheesy, oriental voice, "You numbah one, G.I."

Proficient in flying the airplane, we focused on navigation. Using a topographic map, I learned to identify terrain features and plot longitude and latitude coordinates, which was difficult while flying over the flat, nondescript, Florida landscape. It would have been easier in Montana with its plentiful lakes, rivers and mountainous terrain. In one of the Quonset huts before a flight, Captain Rooney gave me a list of coordinates and told me to find them and report what I found. Using a map, I identified highway intersections, small ponds, notable hills, etc.

We flew most days, but spent some time in a classroom where we studied the weapon systems and techniques we would use in controlling airstrikes in Vietnam. Our mission was to identify enemy locations and direct tactical fighters to a position where they could deploy their ordnance without risk to friendly troops. The fighters we would control would be armed with bombs, napalm, rockets and twenty millimeter canon. We had to understand their limits and know exactly how close to friendly forces they could be deployed.

Field exercises were held on a Naval artillery range. We new FACs identified a specific target and worked with student fighter pilots deploying weapons on an imaginary enemy. I flew in one tactical fighter, an A-1 Skyraider, to observe the performance of a FAC from the fighter pilot's perspective. The A-1 was a single engine WWII dive bomber. In Vietnam it performed as a close air support aircraft, and aided air rescue missions by suppressing enemy fire while downed pilots or injured ground troops were hoisted to the safety of a helicopter.

I flew with several instructors, all Vietnam FACs. It was beneficial to fly with different teachers, as each had his own technique. Besides instruction in the intricacies of flying the aircraft, they provided information on the environment I would soon encounter. I spent hours listening to war stories about missions they'd flown, descriptions of the places they lived, and the importance of the work that lay ahead.

The last flight I had at Holly was with Bob Crane, a classmate at Reese and O-2 pilot. Bob's mission was psychological warfare operations. He would not pound the enemy with bombs and napalm, rather propaganda-laced leaflets and recorded messages broadcast from loud speakers, urging the bad guys to give up the fight. His Cessna Skymaster was known as the "Bullshit Bomber."

I had just finished the critique of my final check ride and was leaving the airstrip when I saw Bob walking across the flight line. He waved and said, "Hey, Lizard, I've got a solo flight, come along and I'll let you fly a real airplane."

"I'd love to, but don't we need clearance from someone?"

I wasn't trained in the O-2 and Bob wasn't supposed to take passengers on his training flights.

"What'll they do? Send us to Vietnam?"

"Yeah, you're right. Let's go."

I enjoyed getting a little stick time in the O-2, but would not have traded assignments with any Skymaster driver. I loved flying the O-1. Lighter than the O-2, with a quicker response to control pressures and a superior field of vision, the Bird Dog was perfect for our mission.

The day before Kay and I were scheduled to leave for Montana where I would await orders to my next duty station, a tragedy occurred. One of my classmates at Reese, John McKenzie, was killed when his O-2 crashed during a dual training flight. His instructor, a veteran pilot, also died. I never learned the cause of the accident.

Dying in an airplane never occurred to me. I was more worried of making a mistake: missing an item on a check list; getting lost; failing a check ride or disappointing an instructor. Losing a friend and fellow pilot was devastating, a grim reminder that the sky, while exciting, peaceful and beautiful, was an unforgiving environment. Shortly after arriving home, I received my orders. Before reporting for duty at the 21st Tactical Air Support Squadron (TASS), Nha Trang Air Base, Republic of Vietnam, I was scheduled to attend Jungle Survival School at Clark Air Base in the Philippines. All pilots were required to attend the eighteen day course known as "Snake School."

The days before my departure grew short and the magnitude of what was taking place overwhelmed me. For the past nine years I believed that by the time I finished whatever phase of my life I happened to be currently living--high school, college or flight school--the war would be over and my life as a pilot would take place in a peacetime environment. Going to war was now inevitable and I was well trained and ready to go.

Kay and I had been married a mere nine months and were facing a separation longer than that. The often repeated adage, "If the Air Force wanted you to have a wife, they would have issued you one," was true. The UPT curriculum was demanding and there were no days off except a short Christmas break. The only extended breaks we had were our leisurely drive from Lubbock to Fort Walton Beach and the few weeks in Montana before my deployment.

Kay was going to live with her mother in Missoula and busy herself with tennis. She planned to play regional tournaments, give lesson and work with kid's programs. We looked forward to Rest and Relaxation (R&R) in Hawaii, midway through my tour in Vietnam.

The morning I left, my mother said, "Bernie, is it too late for you to tell the Air Force you made A's in typing class? They must need clerks as well as pilots." Her quivering lower lip belied her clever attempt at humor. As a young girl, she sent her brother, Buzz, off to the Navy and World War II. The anguish and fear she felt then gripped her now as we parted. I held her close and vowed to return unscathed as Buzz did twenty-four years earlier.

My father was exempt from military service. He told me a back problem kept him from joining the Army. As he hugged me and said to take care of myself, I wondered if he regretted not serving his country.

Four

Beware The Snake

Getting from Missoula, Montana to the Philippines wasn't easy. The adventure began with Kay driving me two hundred miles west to Spokane, Washington, where I boarded a flight to San Francisco. After a lengthy layover, I hopped on an Air Force bus and rode a short distance to Travis Air Force Base, "The Gateway to the Pacific." It was there I boarded a flight bound for Clark Air Base. Our flight plan took us to Anchorage for refueling, then on to Guam where we changed flights at Anderson Air Force Base. Five hours later, my flight arrived at Clark. Two jet-lagged days later, I began to understand life in the jungle.

For five days, we received classroom instruction on jungle survival, escape and evasion techniques and rescue operations. Charlie, an eight-foot boa constrictor, greeted us each morning from his two-story cage as we entered the auditorium. Well-fed on a diet of rats the size of cocker spaniels and chickens, he led a good life.

Instructors taught us how to find water and edible vegetation. They discussed evasion techniques and the importance of concealing ourselves from pursuers. Downed pilots were a valuable commodity in Vietnam and the prisoner of war exercise at Fairchild instilled in us a fear of being captured. We were an attentive audience.

A four hour bus ride took six of us, four lieutenants and two captains, to a training area where we practiced the lessons learned in the classroom. We were met by our instructor, Sergeant Unger, and his assistant, Felix, a native of the Philippine Islands. They made a great team. The sergeant could communicate with Felix, was familiar with the area we would travel and understood the importance of us learning our lessons. Felix, a twenty-five year old, thrived in the jungle. On his tip toes, he may have topped five feet. He had dark skin, piercing black eyes, kinky hair and the build of a middleweight boxer. Despite his sinister appearance, Felix was a jovial guy. He always had a grin on his face that seemed to say *don't worry, guys, I'll take care of you.*

A blazing sun played peek-a-boo with the dense triple canopy jungle. We began a single file trek at noon, and at times, it seemed we were in twilight. Countless birds flitted among the branches. Lizards adorned tree trunks. Bees the size of badminton birdies buzzed us. The anxiety, exertion and stifling humidity drenched us.

Felix was not always with us, but he was never far away. Sergeant Unger made sure we understood Felix's role. "When one of you sees a snake, stand still and yell for Felix."

I noticed he didn't say *if* we see a snake.

When he heard his name echoing through the hardwoods, Felix magically appeared, just like Tinker Bell. With the tip of his bolo knife he flipped the reptile high in the air. While the snake was airborne, Felix identified it as friend or foe.

"FEEELIIIIIX!" came the cry from a pilot ahead of me. I froze and dared not look down to see what might be preparing to coil around my boot.

Poof, there was Felix.

"OOH, OOH, good snake," he exclaimed. "We like!" Those creatures hit the ground unscathed and slithered away, much to my chagrin.

A few minutes later...

"FEEELIIIIIX!" screamed the last man in our troop.

Poof

"OOH, OOH bad snake! He kill you ass!"

The killer landed in two pieces. Felix enjoyed this exercise, but it scared the hell out of me and most of the other guys. Jim Williams, a helicopter pilot from Florida, was the exception. He volunteered to take the point on our single-file treks.

What a stud.

Sergeant Unger stopped mid-afternoon so we would have plenty of time to set up camp and eat before darkness engulfed us. There was a stream nearby and he told us to take a dip and cool off. We peeled our soaked flight suits off our steaming bodies and got in the cool water. Thousands of small, black snails floated in the lazy creek. They enhanced our supper of rice and tubers.

Felix cooked every meal. It concerned me that he used his snake-killing knife to prepare our vegetables, but was not about to object. With his razor-sharp weapon he tapered one end of a short bamboo stalk to a sharp point and thrust it into a vine clinging to the trunk of a huge hardwood tree. Water flowed from the vine, filling our canteens. In cooking chambers fashioned from pieces of bamboo, water, snails and rice boiled over a fire created by rubbing two pieces of wood together. Fine bamboo shavings served as kindling.

We slept suspended in hammocks made from parachute canopy and covered with mosquito netting. Sleeping on the jungle floor would not have been wise as the rats were fearless, the insects omnipresent. Sergeant Unger told us to put our boots in our hammocks or the rats would carry them off. He also warned us to keep our arms tucked inside our cocoons.

"If you eat a chocolate bar and your Hershey-scented fingers extend outside your hammock, there's a good chance a rat will smell it and believe he's stumbled upon a hundred-and-eighty pound candy bar."

Darkness fell with the speed of a Broadway curtain. When I hear people use the cliche "It was so dark I couldn't see my hand in front of my face," I snicker.

A multitude of creatures serenaded us with an endless cacophony. Our banter didn't last long and we settled down with our own thoughts, hoping for a few moments of sleep. I imagined myself in this setting alone, pursued by the enemy. No jungle expert like Sergeant Unger or fearless guide like Felix to take me by the hand and lead me to the rescue chopper. *This is serious stuff, Hale, serious.*

When morning light filtered through the jungle, we packed our gear and continued our lessons. We watched Felix burrow into dense bush, disappear and remain motionless for several minutes. I didn't see a single movement from the bushes where he hid.

"You've got to dig deep into the foliage, gentlemen," said Sergeant Unger. "It's imperative you relax and keep your breathing under control, like Felix is, or you won't hide from the bad guys."

We scattered in a game of hide and seek. Felix was "it." We did this several times and not once did any of our guys elude him. We were certain he could smell us.

When it was time for us to be the hunter, we couldn't find him even though we knew his general location. Giving up on our last attempt to capture him, Jim Williams said to Sergeant Unger, "We give up. He's beaten us again."

Hearing that, Felix, twenty-five yards from where we stood, leaped straight up out of the weeds as if bounced from a trampoline.

"OOOWEEE! G.I.s no can find Felix!"

He floated to earth and graciously accepted our applause, bowing from his narrow waist, triumphant grin beaming.

For the next two days, we humped through the boonies navigating with a small compass, trying to find and hide from Felix, filling our canteens with vine water, starting fires and trying to sleep while sharing the night with who-knew-what lurking in the darkness: lizards, snakes, rats, tigers or discus-sized tarantulas.

Our final exercise was the act of being rescued. We used items found in the survival vests issued to all flight crews. We had a map, a hand-held radio, a pen gun the size of a fountain pen that fired red flares and a mirror we could use to signal a helicopter.

When we heard the *"whop, whop, whop"* of an approaching chopper, we radioed the pilot. He asked us to estimate our location and describe the terrain where we were hiding. Jim Williams, listening to the sound of the approaching rotor blades, vectored the aircraft to our location. When the rescue bird appeared overhead, we took turns reflecting light from our mirror onto the cockpit window. We each fired a flare from our pen gun. The pilot hovered above and lowered a jungle penetrator, a sleek apparatus designed to slither through dense foliage. When it was on the ground, three steel legs sprang open, creating a seat on which the downed pilot rode to the safety of the chopper. We didn't make the ride up, but had we been in Vietnam, would have clung to it with all our strength.

We marched a few miles to our pickup location and boarded a bus for the trip back to Clark Air Base. Sergeant Unger and Felix wished us good luck and sent us on our way. We left Snake School with a tremendous respect for the jungle environment and the training we received. I understood what a dreadful, life-threatening situation I would face if forced to survive alone in the jungles of Vietnam.

Five

In-Country

The Boeing 737 taxied to the runway at Clark Air Force Base, Republic of the Philippines, as the sun rose July 3rd, 1969. Our destination was Saigon's International Airport in war-torn South Vietnam.

A petite, blue-eyed blonde flight attendant, with dimpled cheeks and Doris Day hair welcomed us aboard. She strolled, no--flirted--her way down the aisle looking for unfastened seat belts and letting us know she would return soon with coffee and snacks. Fawningly, the audience followed her every step. A few moments later, the jet sped down the runway, lifted off and I was on my way to join nearly a half million American servicemen and women. Eight-and-a-half years had passed since we joined the fight on behalf of the South Vietnamese. In that time 35,551 U.S. troops had lost their lives and 435 were missing in action (MIA).

Doris' melodic words echoed in my mind, que sera sera...

I nodded off and woke when I felt the pilot retard the throttles and begin the descent. I saw narrow, sandy beaches that gave way to lush vegetation. Tall green and brown grass, nudged by the wind, offered a greeting: *Welcome, Bernie. Enjoy your stay.*

Inland, we flew over jungle-covered hills. A gentle, descending turn to the south took us over a flat area, the center of which was home to a sparkling blue lake with rocky shores. West of the lake were six bomb craters, each the size of a single car garage and filled with reddish brown water.

A surreal setting, serenity and devastation side by side.

Due to its high volume of military traffic, Saigon Airport was one of, if not the busiest airports in the world. The plane leveled off and the pilot announced we were entering a holding pattern. A gentle three-hundred-and-sixty degree turn afforded me a view of the countryside. Huge mountains to the west, perhaps 10,000 feet high, defined the Cambodian border. Rocky peaks protruded from dense jungle. To the south, several rivers zigzagged their way eastward to the South China Sea. Our captain retarded the throttles. The joy ride was over, it was time to land. We began a steep descent. The threat of gunfire at the end of runways in Vietnam forced pilots to make such approaches, sacrificing customer comfort for safety.

We deplaned amid dozens of chartered airliners and waited on the tarmac for our luggage. No baggage claim here. Thirty minutes passed before a canvas bag bearing my name appeared on the ramp: LT. B. HALE, USAF. The fetid, humid air was stifling. Sweat streamed down my back as I lugged my gear fifty yards to the terminal. The bag grew heavier with each step.

In the center of the terminal the size of a basketball floor, stood an elevated platform occupied by two heavily armed Military Police (MPs). Both were large men, one black, one white. They shuffled in slow circles; bouncers in a rowdy bar, expecting trouble any minute.

I noticed the information desk and told an Army sergeant I was scheduled to report to Bien Hoa Air Force Base, twenty miles northeast of Saigon. He directed me to an area where I could board a military bus leaving in thirty minutes. At a currency exchange booth, I joined the "Arrival" line and traded my cash for Military Pay Currency (MPC). Brightly colored artwork depicted Vietnamese people, jungles and seascapes adorned each denomination.

I stopped in the men's room before leaving the terminal. While doing my business, an elderly Vietnamese woman sauntered up to me and began cleaning the adjoining urinal. A major wearing pilot wings approached, noticed my surprise, smiled and said, "Welcome to Nam, Lieutenant." At the exit, he turned toward me and said, "Good luck. Keep your head out of your ass."

"Thanks, I will," I replied, wishing he could take the time to share a beer with me. I assumed he was on his way home, his quick pace that of one not wanting to miss a flight.

The blue bus was typical of those on bases in the states with one exception. Heavy-gauge steel wire covered the windows--protection from dangerous projectiles. Our driver, a short, skinny airman first class, packed a .38 revolver on his hip. He wore a uniform one size too large and had a sparse mustache that didn't have a chance to succeed. The only armed guy on the bus looked like I did when I was fifteen, something I found unsettling

"Gentlemen, I'm Airman Smith. The trip to Bien Hoa will take approximately one hour. Our route is secure, but let me know if you see anything that would indicate an unsafe condition. We are in radio contact with the dispatcher here and at Base Operations in Bien Hoa."

What the hell does that mean? If the Viet Cong attack the bus, will a company of Green Berets magically appear like Felix?

Airmen and officers filled the bus. There were no weapons, flak jackets, steel helmets, survival radios, first aid kits or even drinking water. A cumbersome, defenseless, luscious target; our bus lacked only a bull's-eye. It was going to be a long hour on the road.

Our driver departed the congested airport on a northerly heading, away from Saigon. A Saint Christopher's medal, suspended from the rearview mirror, swayed to and fro. We passengers were quiet, restless.

The driver took us through several small villages. Thatched roofs covered wooden structures, homes and storefronts. Small, shoeless children, several naked from the waist down, scurried through the streets. Bicycles and scooters clogged the roads.

Rice paddies lined both sides of the road. Workers wearing conical hats, bent at the waist, tended to business in ankle-deep water. Saddle-bagged water buffaloes meandered among them. Surely, their cargo was drinking water. The heat was suffocating.

Smith's head swiveled from side to side, eyeing the laborers. Small motor scooters, most carrying two riders, occasionally approached from the front. Identifying a potential threat, he always sped up.

I was relieved when he announced we were nearing Bien Hoa. We were met at the gate by an AP who boarded the bus, checked each passenger's orders and cleared us to enter the base. We drove to Base Headquarters where I checked in and was assigned a room in the Visiting Officer's Quarters (VOQ). I confirmed my flight the next morning to Phan Rang where I would receive my in-country ı the Bird Dog.

gave me directions and I lugged my bag to my room, a single story buuu. The door in the hallway opened to a small room containing two single beds separated by a night stand. Two of the walls, screened two-thirds of the way to the ceiling, opened to a grassy field. Across the open area sat a cinder block structure, identified as the latrine.

My cigarette-pack-sized transistor radio picked up an Armed Forces Network transmission of a baseball game, the Giants versus the Pirates. I stripped to my shorts, turned on the fan, stretched out on my bunk and listened to the game. When Juan Marichal struck out Willie Stargell in the top of the ninth inning to end the game, I grabbed some clean clothes and went for a shower.

In the locker room I noticed a pile of filthy clothes on one of several wooden benches: Army fatigues adorned with embroidered captain's bars; an olive drab tee shirt; socks and boots soiled with grime and covered with red dust.

The only guy in the shower room was lathered from head to toe. Dark eyes peered at me through thick soap. I avoided his stare and turned on the water. I stood there a few moments waving my hand to and fro in the stream of cold water, anxious for it to warm up. It was then I engaged my mouth before my brain.

"How do you get the hot water on?" I asked my shower-mate.

"Hot water?" he exclaimed, soap bubbles spewing from his mouth. "Where the hell do you think you are, New York City?"

I hopped in the shower and stood there for several minutes, giving the surly captain plenty of time to get dressed and on his way.

Sporting a clean flight suit, I walked to the Officer's Club for an early dinner. I tucked my flight cap in a pocket on my flight suit, entered the club and stopped at the bar to order a beer. Four pilots, all captains, played a dice game. Their shoulder patches indicated they were F-100 jocks. A leather cup, shaken in a gentle manner, stirred the dice. The cup was then slammed on the bar and lifted up, revealing the score. Groans and cheers followed each toss as the dice were passed to the next shooter.

I must have looked like I had Fucking New Guy (FNG) tattooed on my forehead. One of the fighter jocks asked where I was stationed, and when I told him I was an O-1 pilot on my way to the 21st TASS, one of the other Hun drivers turned and smiled at me.

He told the bartender to put however many beers I drank on his tab and said, "Good luck, FAC. Maybe we'll work with you one day. Keep your head out of your ass."

They were obviously more interested in shooting dice than shooting the breeze with a rookie, so I thanked them for the beer and moved to a nearby table. I ordered a cheeseburger with fries and thought, *In the last five hours, two combat pilots have told me to keep my head out of my ass. I'm going to give myself that briefing every morning.*

I had a couple more beers and got back to my room as the sun was setting. I set my alarm, read Michener's *The Drifters* for a few minutes and fell asleep listening to the sound of jets perhaps a half mile away, taxiing, taking off and landing. My first day in Vietnam was over. Only three-hundred-and-sixty-four days to go before I boarded a flight bound for home.

I woke before my alarm sounded and followed the aroma of bacon to the mess hall. A rectangular sign suspended from the ceiling admonished the diners: Take All You Want, Eat All You Take. The servers wore white coveralls and hats and worked at a fast pace; heads down, eager to get the troops on their way. I asked for scrambled eggs, bacon, hash browns, mixed fruit and pancakes. It was outstanding and I ate it all.

I hustled back to my room, picked up my bag and headed for Base Operations. It wasn't a cool morning, but I managed to get to the flight line without breaking a sweat. A clerk told me the plane would leave as scheduled. I had a few minutes to stroll the flight line.

The ramp buzzed with activity. Crew chiefs teamed up to service several O-1s. I hadn't flown in a month and itched to strap one on. Cargo planes landed and off-loaded troops and large wooden pallets containing equipment wrapped in black plastic. F-100s, with bombs and napalm canisters hanging under their wings, taxied in flights of two. Army choppers swarmed the base perimeter.

A C-47 transport plane landed and parked in front of the operations building. I assumed it was my ride and headed to the boarding area. The twin engine tail-dragger, known as the Gooney Bird, made its military debut in the early 1930s. She rested on her tail wheel, dolphin-shaped nose proudly raised high.

Ten passengers entered through a door aft of the left wing. A plywood floor rose steeply toward the cockpit. Six rows of brown vinyl-clad seats, four per row, filled the cabin. I chose a window seat, assuring a scenic flight to Phan Rang, a trip that would take less than an hour.

A captain entered the plane and led a lieutenant to the cockpit. He settled into the left seat and the copilot faced the cabin. He told us to strap in as we would be taxiing shortly. Before all the seat belts clicked shut, the left propeller began to turn. The 1,200 horsepower engine sputtered, belched a puff of dark smoke and roared to life. I could see the shoulders of the pilots, separated by a console that housed the throttles. As the pilot cranked the right engine, the copilot put on a headset and turned a radio knob on the console. A moment later, we began to taxi.

I was eager to get to Phan Rang and begin the in-country checkout process. I wanted to get it behind me and report to the 21st TASS in Nha Trang. It was the parent unit for all FACs in the Central Highlands area of Vietnam, where I would be assign to an operational unit. I wanted to get settled and meet the guys with whom I would fly.

The C-47 taxied on the runway. Our captain eased the throttles forward and after a short takeoff roll, the Gooney Bird rose from the runway and banked gently to the east. We leveled off as we approached the ocean at an altitude that appeared to be 4,000 feet. The terrain became more mountainous as we flew north--steep rocky peaks, narrow valleys, thick jungle vegetation and narrow white-capped rivers that sped toward the South China Sea.

The roar of the engines filled the cabin, making conversation difficult; but, it didn't appear the passengers were interested in anything except watching the ominous environment disappear beneath our wings. There was no announcement from the cockpit thanking us for flying Air Force Airlines or promising an on time arrival. No peanuts, sodas, or permission to unfasten our seat belts and move about the cabin.

The plane slowed, descended and turned east over the water. I saw our destination located in a broad, arid valley, its rocky floor covered with red dirt. The runway was three or four miles from the coastline. Without a warning, the pilot yanked the throttles back and began a steep, descending left bank aligning the aircraft with the valley. Several Army helicopters approached an open area left of the runway. Soldiers wearing flak jackets and carrying bulky backpacks stood in a red, rotor-induced dust storm. A flight of two F-100s sat at the hold line waiting for us to land and get out of their way.

When we touched down, the pilot made a sharp right turn onto a taxiway. We stopped in front of Base Operations, and while I waited for the baggage to be dropped on the ramp, watched the hectic scene on the airfield. Two F-100s taxied rapidly from their revetments, eager to get airborne. Maintenance and munitions vehicles sped along the tarmac. Dozens of pilots, parachutes slung over their shoulders, hurried toward waiting jets, others walked slowly away from the flight line, their missions completed. I expected to see an accident any minute. *Holy smokes! This place is out of control!*

I grabbed my bag and headed toward Base Operations to check in and get directions. I stopped after a few steps. I didn't need any guidance because off to my right sat a Quonset hut like the ones at Holly Field. A large white sign hung on the front of the building:

Welcome to FAC U

Seeing the bold letters on the sign, I knew I was about to join a very old and honored fraternity. Supporting ground troops from the air was nothing new. Two hundred years ago, the French army used aerial reconnaissance to help defeat an Austrian force in the battle of Fleurus. Tethered balloons floated aloft for several hours, each carrying an observer who dropped written messages in leather, rock-filled pouches advising infantry commanders of movements made by their enemy. Unlike today's brightly colored balloons, theirs were blue-gray to blend with the sky and clouds.

The Union Army created the Balloon Corps to spy on Confederate forces in the Civil War. During the First World War, both sides gathered information with aircraft. Before our involvement in WWII, the War Department directed the Air Corps to find a way to control aerial bombing in ground battles. They created the Forward Observer. It was necessary for a controller to be on the ground at the front lines to direct aircraft as they attacked enemy forces in proximity to friendly troops, and assess bomb damage for intelligence purposes. This was not the glorious mission the fly boys envisioned when they joined the Army Air Corps, but essential to the success of the mission.

The first airborne FACs worked above the beaches of Normandy. Light, radio-equipped aircraft directed naval artillery in support of the D-day invasion. As U.S. forces moved inland and established gun sites, the FACs went with them and provided assistance in pinpointing targets identified by the ground commanders.

Having a pilot positioned to gather real-time intelligence was a tremendous advantage. Well-versed in the capabilities of air power and able to deliver its wrath upon the enemy, the FAC became a valuable asset for the ground troops he supported.

My pulse quickened as I approached FAC U. The hectic activity on the flight line left no doubt that I was up to my ass in a war.

Two metal desks were located at the entrance. Each had a manual typewriter, in and out boxes, and a ceramic coffee cup bearing the image of Snoopy on top of his dog house, goggles firmly in place, scarf trailing behind his leather helmet. Floating above his head in a bubble, were the words, "FAC U, Charlie!" The VC were also referred to as Mr. Charles.

Airman First Class Bailey, busy typing, rose and said, "Good morning, Lieutenant. What can I do for you?"

I handed him my orders and said I was reporting for Theater Indoctrination School. He looked at my documents and with his right index finger pointing the way, scanned a list of names, and noted mine on the roster.

A dozen small metal tables filled the room. Pilots, working in sets of two, hunkered over maps beneath a white and orange parachute canopy hung from the ceiling. Two captains sat at a table close to the front sipping coffee. One of them rose and ambled toward me.

"You must be Hale. I'm Ace Hutzler."

"Yes, sir. I'm Bernie," I said as we shook hands.

He motioned for me to follow him to a briefing table. Captain Hutzler looked like a football player; stocky build, square jaw, a handsome no nonsense guy. We sat down and he said, "We're going to fly two sorties today. It's going to take me ten minutes to know if you can fly the airplane. If you can't, you've got a problem. I won't send you to the field and you can't stay here. I'm going to call you Bernie and you're going to call me Ace. If I refer to you as 'Lieutenant Hale,' you'll know things aren't going well. We're going to fly ten to fifteen hours together. Most of the time will be spent working on navigation. If you can't find the target, you can't do your job. We won't work hot targets with fighters because you don't have a survival vest or weapons. You'll get those things at the TASS. We'll simulate air strikes and fire plenty of white phosphorous rockets (Willie Petes) we use to mark targets. This morning we're just going to fly the airplane and after lunch we'll work with a map and start navigating. Get your helmet and we'll get started."

I liked this guy. I'm sure he was pulling my chain a bit, giving me a test, but I was confident we would get along fine.

Ace watched as I walked around the airplane and performed the preflight checklist, making sure the fuel and oil levels were okay, the aircraft had no dings, and there were no hydraulic leaks on the brakes. As we taxied to the runway amid dense ground traffic, Ace spoke on the intercom. "Relax, Bernie. Just fly the airplane. Put her through a good workout: stalls, spins, steep turns, slow flight; you know what I want. Have some fun. Show me whatcha got."

"Roger that," I replied, feeling relaxed and ready to go.

When we were airborne, Ace directed me to a coastal area he used for practice and I performed several sets of the maneuvers Ace mentioned. The traffic around the airport was heavy and I constantly scanned the sky, looking for other aircraft. Ace liked that.

After thirty minutes, he said, "If you can land this thing as well as you fly it, and read a map, you've got it licked. Let's go back to the base and shoot some landings."

I made three landings on Runway 22, using the numbers as my touchdown point. Ace wanted to see me land and stop in as short a distance as I could. We did short field takeoffs with me holding the brakes while advancing the power to full power, which was a lot easier in the Bird Dog than the T-38. My knees didn't shake once. While on the downwind leg of our last landing he pulled the throttle to idle, simulating an engine loss, a dead-stick landing. I nailed it.

My first flight in Vietnam lasted two hours and ten minutes. I couldn't wait to do it again.

It was lunch time and Ace told me to get my bag and we would drop it off in my room, then get something to eat.

"All the rooms in the VOQ are occupied so you've got to bunk in Ho Jo's," he said. "It's a cheesy motel but you won't be here long."

Speeding on a dirt, pot hole-littered road, our Jeep spewed red dust in the air. We passed the mess hall that reeked of sauerkraut, base headquarters and a sign that advertised The Happy Valley Theater. The screen, a white plywood panel the size of a highway billboard, sat in front of a dozen or so benches that rose from ground level to an elevated structure that was obviously the projectionist's stand. The amphitheater looked like it could hold fifty viewers.

As we passed the theater I saw my quarters on the left. A sign read Howard Johnson's. A tin roof covered a single story cinderblock building protected by a four-foot high cement wall. We skidded to a stop and a red cloud engulfed our Jeep. I grabbed my bag and Ace gave me a tour.

There were twelve rooms, each door painted bright red. Inside there was one set of bunk beds, a wooden chair, one three-drawer chest and an air conditioning unit mounted in the wall. A latrine with three shower heads was located at the far end of the building, which sat no more than a hundred yards from the western boundary of the base. Beyond the perimeter, two steep mountains formed a serene background.

There was an underground bunker, four or five feet deep, ten wide and twenty long, a few yards from the latrine. Piles of dirt, two or three feet high, covered with tin and sandbags, formed the aboveground protection. Heavy, wooden beams supported the structure. Ace tapped me on the shoulder and said, "When the alert siren goes off and the shit hits the fan, don't screw around. Get your ass in the bunker. Most of the incoming attacks are directed at the flight line, but this area gets hit occasionally."

With my duffle bag stored in my room and the tour complete, we headed for the Jeep. Passing my room, Ace stopped at the cement wall in front of my room and pointed to several silver-dollar sized holes and said, "Shrapnel. Do not stay in your room! Got it?"

"Yes, sir," I replied."

"Good. Let's get something to eat."

Eating a plate of smothered hot dogs, I thought about Ho Jo's, the dark, dank bunker and the pockmarked cement wall. I didn't have a clue where the TASS was going to send me, but I was ready to get out of this place.

Following a quick lunch, Ace and I spent an hour studying topographic maps of the local area. They provided a detailed representation of cultural and natural features: villages, rivers, roads, airports and lakes. Contour lines, representing areas of equal elevation above sea level, gave the pilot a picture of the terrain below. The space between each line depicted an elevation change of five hundred feet, making it easy to identify steep terrain. The closer the lines, the steeper the mountain.

Ace said, "It's going to be a piece of cake to navigate here compared to Holly Field where the flat land all looked the same. After a few hours practice, terrain features will jump off your map. However, you might get disoriented and if you do, just fly east until you hit the coast. It's lined from the Delta region in the south to the DMZ with Air Force bases."

He went on to illustrate his point.

"I flew with a guy a month ago who had no idea where we were. We both knew he was lost but he wouldn't ask me for help. I let him bore holes in the sky for several minutes then asked him where we were." 'I don't know, sir,' was his reply. I asked if there was anything on the ground he could identify. He still didn't have a clue where we were so I shot back, 'How about the fucking ocean, Lieutenant? The big blue thing. Can you find that?' "He didn't say a word but turned east and located Nha Trang when we hit the coast."

I told Ace I understood, folded my map and we headed for the ramp and our waiting Bird Dog. We planned to fly an hour with Ace giving me navigation exercises. We were airborne and clear of the congested airspace surrounding Phan Rang when Ace said, "I'm going to give you the coordinates of your target. Find them and tell me what you see."

I pulled a black grease pencil from one of two slots sewn on the left shoulder of my flight suit and wrote the longitude and latitude numbers on the left window. I learned to use the window as a clip board, noting radio frequencies, fighter call signs, ordnance available and anything else of importance.

A mark of the grease pencil also served as our unsophisticated sighting mechanism for firing our rockets. Flying straight and level, we noted the horizon and marked it on the windscreen (cockpit window) with an X. In a steep dive we put our sight on the target and fired the smoke rocket. It wasn't high-tech, but effective.

Like finding a city using an atlas, I plotted the coordinates on my map where the vertical and horizontal lines intersected. Then I compared the terrain below to the features on the map. "I've got the target, Ace. It's a small village located in the valley below us. There's a river running through it that makes a ninety degree turn to the east."

"Good job. Now imagine you have a flight of F-100s on the way. Direct them to the target. I'll play the part of flight lead. My call sign is Tiger. You're Bird Dog."

"Roger that, Tiger," I replied.

"Bird Dog, Tiger Lead. How do you read? Over."

"You're loud and clear, Tiger Lead," I replied.

"Tiger is a flight of two F-100s over Nha Trang, headed south. Over."

Roger Tiger. Our target is three-zero miles south and ten inland from your current position. I'm an O-1 at two thousand feet, ten miles due west of Cam Ranh Bay. When you turn inland you will see an east-west river. We'll rendezvous where it makes a ninety degree turn to the south."

So it went for the next hour. Ace gave me coordinates to locate and imaginary fighters to direct to the targets. As we headed back to the base he said, "Tomorrow we'll shoot rockets and simulate air strikes, which will be our program for the next few days."

Back at FAC U, with the map spread out on a long table, we studied each set of coordinates I'd located. He pointed out certain terrain features I overlooked that might have been more prominent and easier for the fighter pilot to identify. It was a short critique, which he ended by saying, "Okay, let's get out of here. It's time for you to buy your instructor a drink."

The Officer's Club sat on a hill overlooking the south end of the runway. A short flight of steps led to the entrance. The smoke-filled bar was standing room only, and we waited several minutes for our scotch. Phan Rang hosted a few flying squadrons and their insignias adorned the walls. F-100 fighters, C-123 airlift and defoliation (Agent Orange) birds, AC-47 "Spooky" gunships, Australian twin engine Canberra bombers, C-119 "Shadow" gunships and the FACs all proudly displayed their plaques in the club.

A flight of stairs led to an open deck. We grabbed a table on the patio as the sun began its descent behind the mountains a short distance from the runway. Pilots gathered around a barbecue grill fashioned from a fifty-five gallon drum. It sat on a steel plank, a safety feature designed to keep flying pieces of charcoal from igniting the wooden floor. The crowd took turns cooking steaks, chicken and burgers. Ace ordered a couple of steaks and more scotch from our Vietnamese waiter.

The white runway lights became more prominent when twilight turned to darkness and we had a clear view of the departure end. F-100s roared down the runway, afterburners spewing blue-tipped flames. Ace noticed the activity and said, "The Hun drivers are busy tonight. The hills on the far side of the valley are full of bad guys. There must be something going on."

We chatted about the day's flights. Ace told me I did a good job and wouldn't have a problem getting through the program.

"Our job is to send qualified FACs to the field. We take major flak when the brass at the TASS tell us we've sent them a ham fist."

We talked about how we would spend hours firing Willie Petes, simulating air strikes and effective communication with fighter pilots. I listened and nodded as Ace spoke, but it was hard to focus due to the activity on the flight line and in the hills to the west.

An AC-47 gunship, radio call sign "Spooky," lumbered down the runway and rose slowly into the night. The aircraft carried six gatling guns, each holding 15,000 rounds of 7.62 mm ammunition. The gunners could put one bullet in every square foot of a football field in one minute. I flew in one of those planes that morning, but it carried passengers, not bullets.

Watching the bird turn north, Ace grinned and said, "He'll be on station soon. Fasten your chin strap."

What the hell does that mean?

A few minutes later bright flares, dropped from Spooky, lit up the hillside no more than three miles away. I couldn't see him, but somewhere close to the battle site a FAC communicated with the gunship and any fighters that might be circling above. He would brief the pilots on the location of the bad guys as well as any friendly forces in the area. A puff of white smoke marked a target in the illuminated area. The battle was about to begin.

The moment was surreal. On a balmy, starlit evening, I sat on an outdoor patio swilling scotch and eating a steak while a Hollywood scene played out before me. The audience on the balcony whooped and hollered with every *whomp, whomp* of exploding bombs or brilliant red tracers streaming toward the enemy. We were a raucous crowd watching a sporting event. The Montana Grizzlies and their despised cross-state rival, the Bobcats, spilling their guts on the gridiron, the losers paying the ultimate price.

The drama lasted thirty minutes and as the excitement settled down I realized how tired I was. In the process of traveling from Bien Hoa to Phan Rang, flying two missions with Ace and the time spent at the club, I'd been awake for over twenty hours. I told Ace I was whipped and we headed down the hill to Ho Jo's.

I showered and donned a pair of shorts, a tee shirt and tennis shoes tied tight. If I had to race to the bunker I would be prepared. Trying to relax and listening to the sounds of jets departing, I relived the action I'd observed from the deck at the Officer's Club. Having seen the local work environment up close, I prayed our flight crews would return to the base unscathed.

It was the Fourth of July, and I fell asleep reliving the most incredible fireworks display I'd ever seen.

Six

"Hit My Smoke"

The night passed without incident and I woke rested and refreshed, ready to get to the flight line. I had a leisurely breakfast in the mess hall and met Ace at FAC U. He told me the munitions crew were loading rockets on our plane and we would launch shortly. I grabbed my helmet and headed for the flight line, maps tucked in a zippered pocket on my flight suit.

Four Willie Petes, each five feet long and slightly larger in diameter than a beer can, hung under each wing. Each rocket was secured to its launching rail with a steel pin tagged with a red streamer, a reminder for the pilot to pull the pins before takeoff. It would be embarrassing to show up at a target and not be able to fire the rockets. "Uh, Fighter Lead, this is your FAC. I'm having a system malfunction and am unable to launch my rockets. We'll have to abort the mission."

That would not be good.

Ace arrived as I completed the walk-around inspection and said, "Let's launch."

As we taxied to the runway Ace said, "When we're airborne go feet wet (over the ocean) and head south. I'm going to give you some coordinates to locate, we'll have a little target practice and work on strike procedures. We'll be in the air a couple of hours and tomorrow we'll fly the same profile twice."

The tower cleared me for takeoff and as we flew over the coast, I made a right turn and leveled off at two thousand feet. Ace gave me a pep talk. "At Holly Field you flew with an instructor in your back seat while you controlled A-1 Sky Raiders flown by rookie fighter jocks who were also flying with an instructor.

They carried dummy bombs, which you dropped on well-defined, easy to locate undefended targets. It's different here. There won't be anyone in your back seat telling you what to do, and each flight of fighters you control will be led by seasoned, hard-nosed fighter jocks expecting you to be on top of your game every second. Friendlies on the ground will trust you to drop the ordnance where they want it. The only thing you were afraid of at Holly was failing a chicken-shit check ride. Here you're going to be scared, not necessarily of getting shot down or killed, but of screwing up and looking bad in the eyes of the fighter pilots and grunts needing your support. You'll always be one bad decision away from humiliation, or worse--casualties among your troops."

Ace wasn't trying to scare or intimidate me, but prepare me for what lay ahead. He wanted me to understand how serious the mission was and the magnitude of the responsibility we FACs carried. He told me wherever I was assigned I'd fly the same types of missions: Troops In Contact (TIC); Known Enemy Location (KEL); Suspected Enemy Location (SEL); Landing Zone Prep (LZP), which involved knocking down trees and foliage, clearing the way for helicopters delivering troops and supplies; forest defoliation missions; C-123 aircraft spraying Agent Orange; and Visual Reconnaissance (VR) flights, sorties in the AO looking for signs of enemy activity--smoke rising from the jungle canopy in areas where no friendlies were supposed to be, tire tracks, camouflaged trucks or barges on the rivers.

Ace told me to turn inland and keep an eye out for pedestrian traffic. He gave me a set of coordinates to locate and we went to work. A small stream that zigzagged through tree-covered hills led to the spot I'd marked on my map.

"Ace, it looks like our target is the remains of a wooden structure just west of the stream below us."

"Good job. Put a rocket in the middle of it."

Eight toggle switches that armed the rockets were located on the lower right side of the instrument panel. A safety pin locked the trigger, which was mounted on the control stick. When released, the pin dangled a short distance from the trigger so it wouldn't fall through the cabin floor, potentially jamming the flight controls.

I made a steep three-hundred-and-sixty degree turn, looked for air traffic, pulled the safety pin, armed an outboard rocket with the flip of a toggle switch, retarded the throttle to idle, and in a steep dive, centered my grease-pencil sight on the center of the target and fired my first Willie Pete. *WHOOSH!* The rocket ignited and streaked earthward, trailing fire like a jet's afterburner. In three or four-seconds, the rocket hit the ground and exploded, lighting up the jungle with a bright plume of smoke. It hit fifteen meters short and left of my target. As I rammed the throttle forward and began a climb, I pressed the mic button.

"That sucked," I said to Ace.

"No shit," he replied. "Try it again. This time make sure you're not putting any pressure on the stick or rudder pedals. You want to release the rocket when the aircraft is not subjected to any G forces, positive or negative."

I launched two rockets with much better results and Ace said, "Okay, let's simulate an air strike. You've got two F-4s circling overhead, each carrying snake-eyes, nape and guns. They're waiting for you to tell them what to do. Friendlies are to the north. I'm Gunfighter lead, your call sign is Rookie. Talk to me."

"Gunfighter Lead, Rookie. I'm an O-1 in a right hand orbit fifty meters north of our target. Make your passes east to west, with a right hand pattern. We have friendlies one hundred meters north. Bail out north, I want hard bombs first, then nape and guns. When you're ready, I'll put in a mark and circle north of the target."

Ace responded, "Roger that, Rookie. Give us a mark." I replied, "Rookie's in with a mark, Gunfighter. Stand by."

I wanted to fire an accurate rocket and make all the correct radio calls. Ace expected me to be in control of the simulation and I didn't want him to have to say a word. I pulled the throttle to idle, pointed the nose at the target and gently squeezed the trigger. The Willie Pete was a direct hit, a "shack."

"Gunfighter Lead, Rookie. You're cleared in hot. Hit my smoke!"

For two hours I plotted coordinates, fired Willie Petes, dropped smoke grenades out the window and played war. We returned to the base and had a quick sandwich at Base Operations while the crew chief replenished our plane with gas and rockets. Then we did it again.

I made four more flights with Ace and they were all the same with one exception. We flew a night mission with the support of an AC-47 gunship. We didn't fly the O-1 at night or in the weather, but with flares, clear weather and being close to the brightly lit base, it was safe. The crew dropped flares and I simulated a strike under their bright lights. I pictured myself in the place of the FAC who worked the mission my first night at Phan Rang. Flares floating to the ground, tracers filling the sky, fighters streaking toward the target, bombs exploding and people dying. I recalled what Ace said that night on the patio, "Fasten your chin strap."

I flew thirteen hours with Ace, landed the airplane forty times and fired dozens of rockets. It was important for him that his students went into combat well prepared. He was an outstanding instructor. I left Phan Rang confident, eager to get to the TASS and get my assignment. Not once did I have to sprint to the bunker at Ho Jo's.

Seven

The Tum FACs

The morning after my last flight with Ace, I signed out of FAC U and boarded a C-47 for the thirty minute flight to Nha Trang. We landed on a runway that was less than the distance of a football field from the South China Sea. The brilliant white sand was beautiful. I could have been arriving at a Hawaiian resort.

Captain Frank Cheshire met me at the flight line and we drove a short distance to the TASS where I presented my orders and signed in. While the clerk processed my paperwork, Captain Cheshire briefed me on what would be a short stay at Nha Trang. He told me I was going to fly twice today, once with him and a second flight with Captain Sellers.

"If Ace Hutzler sent you to us, we know you're prepared, but we've got to check you out. We'll fly around the local area for an hour or so and shoot some landings. Tomorrow morning we'll go over the Rules of Engagement (ROE), give you weapons and survival gear and send you on your way."

I nodded an acknowledgement and asked, "Do you know where I'm going, captain?"

"Yes, I do. You're going to be a Tum (radio call sign), stationed in Qui Nhon, an hour and a half flight up the coast. One of your guys is going to pick you up tomorrow afternoon. You'll be assigned to one of three regiments of the Korean Capitol "Tiger" Division, headquartered a short distance west of Qui Nhon at a place called Tiger Town. Lieutenant Colonel Frank Wisneski, call sign Tum Zero One, is the Division Air Liaison Officer (ALO), the head Tum. Each regiment has an ALO who is the highest ranking guy. The ROKs are extremely rank-conscious and the ALO is the FAC who spends the most time working with them. They don't want a lieutenant giving them advice if a captain or major is available. I can tell you one thing about the ROKs. They are tough sons-a-bitches. They have one Marine and two Army Divisions here in Vietnam. They are warriors. You'll enjoy working with them and we're glad to have them close by. Five years ago, before the ROKs joined the fight, the Central Highlands were controlled by the VC and NVA. The area is still dangerous, but not like it used to be."

I didn't know there were Korean troops in Vietnam, but the tone of Captain Cheshire's voice led me to believe I had drawn a good assignment. I was a category "B" FAC, one with no tactical experience, and consequently, not deemed qualified to work with U.S. ground troops. The "A" FACs were experienced pilots with tactical experience and were assigned to American fighting units.

We walked to the flight line and I pre-flighted an O-1. Captain Cheshire got in the back seat, and we flew down the coast a few miles. We circled around Cam Ranh Bay, a sprawling Air Force Base, home to an F-4 fighter wing, several transportation squadrons and an Air Force hospital. The airspace was crowded with military aircraft as well as chartered airliners offloading fresh troops from the States and returning home, those veterans who had completed their tours of duty.

Our destination was a dirt runway close to the beach and Highway 1A, the north and south road that ran from the southernmost part of South Vietnam to the Chinese border. Captain Cheshire wanted to see me do short field takeoffs and landings, and this type of runway was more like those I might come across in the field, rather than the 10,000 foot runway at Nha Trang. I made five trips around the short, narrow strip and we headed back to the base.

After lunch I met Captain Sellers. He handed me a map of the local area and said, "Frank told me you could fly the airplane and I'm going to see if you can read a map. We'll go up to Tuy Hoa, shoot a few landings, then do some navigation work. It'll be a short flight."

We launched and headed north, hugging the beautiful coastline. Tuy Hoa was the third seaside base I'd seen and the smallest. Dozens of F-100 fighters were parked in revetments close by the single runway. I wondered if my classmate, Larry Farmer, would be stationed there. I made two landings and we flew inland where I found several coordinates for the captain. I was thankful for the time spent with Ace and hoped I would be as good at directing fighters as I was reading a map.

After we landed, Captain Sellers told me I passed my check ride and wished me luck with the ROKs. Captain Cheshire and I went to the club for an early dinner and a few beers. The place could have been Fort Walton Beach or Destin on the Florida panhandle. There was white sand, gentle breezes and a beautiful, blue ocean. If you had to be in a war zone, this place wasn't too bad.

Before coming to Vietnam, Captain Cheshire flew the F-106 fighter interceptor in the Air Defense Command, assigned to the Hat in the Ring squadron, Eddie Rickenbaker's WWI outfit. He was a Tonto FAC before being assigned to the 21st TASS, and lived north of where I was destined. I pressed him for details on the area where I would live and I looked at my map as we talked.

South Vietnam was divided into four Major Military Regions, I CORPS pronounced (eye-core) was the northernmost region and extended a hundred-and-eighty miles south of the DMZ. Laos comprised the western border. II CORPS spanned two hundred miles and included an area known as the Central Highlands, where I would be stationed. III CORPS took in the area surrounding Saigon, the capital city, and IV CORPS was the Mekong Delta region, the southern tip of South Vietnam. Cambodia bordered III and IV CORPS.

When the sun started to fade, the captain said he would take me to my room. "It's crusty, but it's all we've got," he said. I told him I didn't care as long as I could get a shower and hit the rack. We jumped in a Jeep, and drove a short distance to a two-story barracks, reminiscent of the one in which I bunked at Fairchild AFB while in ROTC summer camp. I climbed the stairs and tossed my duffel bag on a lower bunk. On the way to the shower room, I noticed a small wooden box nailed to one of the vertical beams. It contained small paper pouches with the words "Crab Powder" printed on the bags.

I hoped the bunk I chose had clean sheets.

After a cold shower, I donned a flight suit and walked a block or two to the outdoor theater just in time to watch John Wayne save the day for *The Sons of Katie Elder.* While the projectionist changed the reel, there was a brief intermission. A dozen enlisted men in the front row stood as one and executed a snappy "about face" maneuver and serenaded the officers sitting on the upper benches: "Let's all go to the lobby, let's all go to the lobby, let's all go to the lobby and get ourselves a treat."

When the flick was over, I walked back to the barracks, shook the linens on my bed and nodded off, recalling the good old days at the Roxy Theater in downtown Missoula, Montana.

You're a long way from home, Tum FAC.

When I arrived at the TASS the next morning, Captain Cheshire told me my ride to Qui Nhon was scheduled and I needed to be on the ramp at two o'clock. That gave me plenty of time to get my gear and complete the administrative process. He gave me manual on the ROE and told me to study it. "You've got to pass a test before we can turn you loose."

While wading through volumes of bureaucratic blather, I realized the extent to which we were waging a political war.

"Let me get this straight. If I come upon a group of bad guys who begin firing at me, I have to contact the Province Chief and ask permission before I call the Direct Air Support Center (DASC) to request a set of fighters?"

"That's right."

"How long does it take to get a clearance?"

"It depends."

That wasn't a good answer, but the best one he could give me. I studied the ROE manual for a few hours and passed a test which qualified me to engage the enemy with the full force of the United States Air Force. Woe be to me if I infringed upon the Province Chief's authority.

After lunch I went to the armory where I signed for a .38 caliber revolver, an AR-15 automatic rifle and several clips of ammunition. At the supply center I got a survival vest which contained a radio, spare batteries, medicine kit, ration packet, waterproof matches, small compass, flare gun, strobe light and mirror. I was also given a steel helmet, a flak jacket, three sets of camouflaged fatigues and two pairs of sun glasses.

Captain Cheshire dropped me off on the ramp in front of Base Operations, shook my hand, and wished me well. "I enjoyed flying with you, Bernie. You're going to get along great with the ROKs. Work hard for them and fly safe."

He sped away leaving me on the tarmac, searching the northern sky for the sight of an O-1. I didn't have to wait more than a few minutes. A Bird Dog touched down and taxied to the ramp. The pilot returned my wave and followed a crew chief's directions to a parking spot. A short, thin captain hopped out of the plane and greeted me with a broad grin and firm handshake.

"Welcome to the Tums, Lieutenant. I'm Bob Moore."

"Thanks, Captain. I'm Bernie Hale."

"Call me Bob. Let's load your stuff and go get a soda."

He asked the crew chief to top off the tanks, we crammed my bag and weapons into the small storage area behind the rear seat and walked to Base Ops to cool off. The guy never stopped grinning. *He's sure glad to see me. I must be his replacement.*

We were airborne fifteen minutes later. I'd flown fifty hours in the Bird Dog, all in the front seat, and I enjoyed sitting in the back, taking in the landscape and listening to Bob talk about the Tums.

"We've got three regiments and you're going to work for the 1st ROK Infantry Regiment. Dave Rogers is the ALO. He's Tum One Zero, the numbah ten Tum." I grinned, thinking about the guy grading my landings at Holly Field.

"I'm Tum Two Three, stationed at the ROK Cav Regiment, about thirty miles west of Qui Nhon. Major Chuck Hadley is our ALO. We're going to fly over the 26th ROK Infantry Regiment in a few minutes. Everyone refers to this coastal regiment as Miami Beach and Captain Grier Cooper is the ALO. We'll call their hooch (wooden structure) when we pass Tuy Hoa."

When we flew over the Air Force Base, Bob called Miami Beach.

"Miami Beach Ops, Tum Two Three. Over."

Ted Gamlin, one of their radio operators, answered Bob's call. "Tum Two Three, Miami Beach Ops, go ahead."

"I'm en route to Qui Nhon with a new Tum in the back seat. We'll say hello to you guys in a few minutes."

"Roger that, Two Three. We'll be looking for you."

Bob pulled the throttle back and we dove toward the sea and leveled off twenty feet above the water. "Check out the sharks," he said.

Hundreds of small sharks flitted about. Obviously, it was dinner time at a favorite feeding area. We skimmed the South China Sea for a few minutes, then turned inland and flew above the sandy beach. I saw two hooches ahead of us and three Jeeps parked in the sand. A handful of shirtless guys wearing fatigue pants, some with cameras hiding their faces, watched us approach. Bob pulled the stick back and we zoomed over their heads, wings wagging as we made a climbing turn. Qui Nhon was on our nose, no more than twenty minutes away.

When we approached our destination, a crescent shaped bay with anchored ships waiting to unload their cargo, appeared on the horizon. The tip of the bay was close to a long, narrow, rocky peninsula with scattered patches of green foliage. It extended a mile up the coast.

Bob keyed the mic and announced our arrival. "Tum Ops, Tum Two Three. How do you read? Over."

"Loud and clear, Two Three. What's your ETA?"

"Three minutes."

"Roger that. We'll be standing tall."

I wonder what that means?

Bob continued his description of my new home. "We've got rooms in a MACV (Military Assistance Command Vietnam) compound located on the beach. We're renting space from the U.S. Army's 1st Cavalry Division. It's just to the left of the cargo ships, the spot surrounded by foliage. I'll give you a closer look."

Bob made a lazy turn and pointed out the complex, a three story building surrounded with concertina wire. Fifty yards of palm trees on the beach marked its location.

Bob said, "Our rooms are on the top floor. There's a balcony overlooking the beach. Let's see if we have a welcoming committee."

He pulled the throttle back and descended as we continued our approach. He leveled off a few feet above the water, headed straight for the compound and wagged the wings. Bob opened the window and waved to four guys wearing flight suits, and leaning over the edge of the balcony, thumbs extended.

Giddy with excitement, I pushed the mic button and shouted, "Shit hot!"

Bob said, "Welcome to Qui Nhon, Bernie."

The airport was a U.S. Army facility located in the northern part of Qui Nhon, no more than a mile from our compound. The south end of the 6,000 foot runway was fifty yards from the South China Sea. The ramp was congested with Army helicopters, Air Force cargo planes and O-1s.

Bob landed to the north and taxied to our parking area where a crew chief, an airman first class, directed us to a parking spot in a revetment lined with sand-filled fifty-five gallon drums stacked two high. He chocked the wheels, opened the door and greeted us. "Welcome home, Captain Moore." The crew chief looked at me in the back seat, and said, "Howdy, Lieutenant, they call me Buddha. Welcome to the Nam." I shook his hand when I got out of the plane and thanked him as he reached in the back to grab my bags. Buddha was railroad-spike thin and about six feet tall. A .38 caliber shell casing dangled from a leather necklace.

Bob and I walked across a dirt road to a pair of conexes, large steel-reinforced containers used for shipping and storing military equipment. When Bob spun the combination lock and opened a conex, we were greeted with a blast of hot air. It was well over a hundred degrees inside the steel box. We weren't allowed to take our weapons off the post, and we hung them along with our helmets, flak jackets and survival vests on hooks spaced along the walls of the storage facility.

We hurried out of the stifling heat and I tossed my duffle bag in a Jeep adorned with Korean lettering. From the revetment, Buddha shouted to Bob, "I'll fill her up and check the oil, Captain."

"Thanks, Buddha. See ya tomorrow."

When we drove off, I said, "Buddha seems like an interesting character."

"That's an understatement. He lives in our compound in the enlisted barracks and hangs with the Army guys. He's always got a case of the clap. Qui Nhon is dangerous after dark, and is off limits when the sun goes down. Buddha has a knack of sneaking off the compound in the van used to shuttle the mama-Sans (housemaids) home at the end of the day. Somehow he makes it to the flight line every morning."

The five minute drive to our quarters took us around the bay. Dozens of small fishing boats lined the coast.

An MP guarded the entrance to the compound. He saluted Bob and waved us in. It appeared the only identification we needed was the Korean lettering on our

Jeep. As we drove through the gate I looked up at the vacant balcony Bob buzzed a few minutes ago.

We parked at the back of the building and got my stuff out of the Jeep. The mess hall occupied the ground level and two flights of stairs took us to our rooms. A hallway extended from the stairwell to the balcony. The Tums occupied eight of the ten rooms on the top floor.

We walked to the far end and entered the lounge, the last room on the left. Four pilots stood and introduced themselves; Captains Chuck Quisenberry, Rod McClellan, Jake Morrison and Major Chuck Hadley each shook my hand. Captain Quisenberry, who told me to call him Quiz, was assigned to the ROK Cav Regiment; Rod worked at the 26th ROK Infantry Regiment at Miami Beach; Jake was an instructor, the check pilot for new guys.

He spent time at Tiger Town, the division headquarters, and in Qui Nhon. Major Hadley was Bob's boss, the ALO at the ROK Cav Regiment. Jake said, "In a few minutes you're going to meet your ALO, Dave Rogers. He just called to let us know he'll be landing soon."

Jake handed me a beer and said I could toss my bag in the room next to the lounge. He told me I'd bunk with Dave and the next day the three of us were going to end up in Tiger Town, where we'd spend a couple of days with Lieutenant Colonel Wisneskie and his staff.

There were two single beds, one strewn with clothes. A bathroom and shower accommodated ours and an adjacent bedroom. The furniture consisted of one chest of drawers, a night stand and a couple of chairs. The room was crowded but clean.

In the lounge there was one black vinyl sofa, four frayed leather chairs, three wooden chairs, a refrigerator, an end table that held a radio and a coffee table that was so cluttered I couldn't see its surface. It was covered with cans of peanuts, whiskey bottles, empty beer cans, magazines and newspapers stacked two feet high. Gaudy, gold drapes hung above the sofa. A map of the local area was taped to one wall and a felt painting of a tiger adorned another. A portion of a parachute canopy hung from the ceiling.

I joined the guys on the balcony and admired the view of the bay while we got acquainted. Jake, a husky blond, was an Air Force Academy graduate who flew C-141 cargo planes before getting the O-1 assignment. Chuck Hadley had been a

C-141 pilot, too. Bob Moore's experience was in a smaller cargo plane, the C-130. Rod was a UPT instructor.

When I saw the captain enter the far end of the hallway, I knew it was Dave. He walked with a purpose, map case draped over his shoulder. His eyes never left mine. A mischievous grin appeared when he was halfway down the hall and it never left his face. Dave entered the balcony, eyes still trained on mine. He extended his hand, and as he crushed my fingers, said, "Hale, I'm Rog. Welcome aboard."

He then asked Jake, "Have you given him a Him yet?"

What's a Him? I wondered.

Jake replied, "No, we wanted to wait for you."

"All right, guys, his call sign is One Four." With a forceful voice, as though introducing someone important, he barked, "Gentlemen, let's say hello to Tum One Four!"

In unison the Tums bellowed, "Helloooo, ass hole!"

Dave shouted, "Let's say hello to the ass hole!"

The group replied, "Helloooo, Tum One Four! Himmm, himmm, fuuuck himmm!"

The Tums applauded, laughed, pounded me on the back and another beer appeared. I was speechless. Four captains and a major made a second lieutenant's day.

Dave nodded toward our room and said, "Let's go unpack your stuff and we'll talk about what we're going to do the next couple of days." I told him the first thing I needed to do was figure out how to get my laundry done. He told me to pile my dirty clothes on the bed and mama-San would take care of it. "The woman loves us," he said, "and works hard to keep the place tidy, which is a chore. Of course, we take good care of her, too. Every time one of us goes to the Post Exchange (PX) we pick up candy and sodas for her kids and cigarettes, detergent and sundries for her. She sneaks the booty on the shuttle bus that takes them downtown each afternoon." *Yeah, along with Buddha.*

Dave tossed a map of our AO on the bed and pointed out the location of the 1st

ROK Infantry Regiment, a complex located twenty miles north of Qui Nhon, on the perimeter of Phu Cat Air Base. "I'll get you over there after you spend a few days at Tiger Town."

Dave explained the organization and training I would receive before I'd be cleared to direct air strikes.

"Each regiment has an ALO and ideally, three or four Tums. Along with our pilots, each regiment has a Senior NCO and three ROMADs (radio operator, maintenance and a driver).

"The ROKs are aggressive, and one of the three regiments seems to always be out in the boonies executing an offensive operation. One of our FACs and a ROMAD go into the field with them. We load our radio Jeep in an Army CH-47 Chinook helicopter and set up camp next to the regiment commander's tent. The Jeep has four radios: a high frequency, single side band radio that has a range of hundreds of miles; a UHF radio for communicating with the fighters; an FM radio used to communicate with ground troops; and a VHF for talking with our Tums who are airborne."

Dave told me we would fly around the local area for a couple of hours in the morning and fly to Tiger Town after lunch. Jake was scheduled to meet us there and begin my check out process. I would fly with him a few times then observe a couple of air strikes from the back seat.

He said, "You'll hang out with Colonel Wis and his staff for three or four days. I've got to get back to the regiment and relieve Pat Dowling. One of us has to always be there and we're short handed. More guys are due to arrive any day, so you won't be the only FNG for long."

We walked down to the first floor and found the mess hall full of Army officers, none of whom acknowledged our presence. I had the feeling we were intruding on sacred ground, outsiders invading hallowed space. Perhaps it was Dave's Korean shoulder patch, or simply the fact we were Air Force guys. We ate quickly and retired to the friendly confines of our lounge.

We grabbed a couple of beers and went out on the balcony. I asked Dave about the attitude of our Army hosts and he said they never attempted to hang out with us, not even share a few beers at the Officer's Club located next door or our quarters on the third floor.

He motioned for me to follow him to the south side of our balcony and we leaned over the edge. He pointed to a bungalow below and said, "Their boss is a two-star general and that's his house. We Tums work hard, play hard and like hanging out with each other. I'm sure they resent us for the camaraderie we enjoy as well as the fact we have air conditioners and our own Jeeps, which they don't. That's not our fault. Air Force regulations require us to have air conditioned quarters. It's a sleep issue thing, and we've got to have transportation to the flight line. We come and go as we please, fly the missions we are assigned and bust our ass to support the ROKs who keep this entire province secure. We don't need a two-star general looking after us, and the surly guys we see in the mess hall and O'Club don't either, but like it or not they have one, and they always seem pissed off about something."

The general's abode looked like a Hollywood set from the movie, *"South Pacific."* A narrow, gated entrance led to the front of the house and was flanked by foliage and palm trees. An octagonal patio table sat on a strip of plush grass directly below our balcony. A sandy beach across the street, with spot lights nestled in the palm trees, was the icing on the general's cake.

I wonder if the two-star likes the Tums any better than his troops do.

Eight

Tiger Town

Early morning light brought a low ceiling and drizzling rain, weather not conducive to flight in the O-1. The aircraft contained basic instruments: airspeed; vertical velocity and turn and-bank indicators; altimeter and artificial horizon. We didn't have the high-tech navigational equipment we had in the T-38 that allowed us to fly safely in bad weather. There was, however, one piece of navigation equipment that could lead a pilot to safety. An Automatic Direction Finder (ADF) was a receiver that could be tuned to the local radio beacon, and a needle pointed the way to the station. The Bird Dog was a Visual Flight Rules (VFR) airplane, one flown by the seat of the pants, not instruments.

Dave and I had breakfast in the mess hall and watched the weather, looking for signs of improvement. In mid morning, the solid overcast began to break up and we drove to the flight line, hoping the weather would continue to improve. With me in the front seat, we took off at noon and headed north toward Phu Cat Air Base. Dave wanted to begin our tour of the AO by giving me a look at the 1st ROK Infantry Regiment headquarters, where I would eventually spend a week at a time working with the Koreans. We flew over the east side of the base, which gave us a good look at the Korean compound. There were several barracks, a dozen single story offices, an artillery site located close by a structure that was the Tum hooch and a helicopter landing pad. Dave called the regiment and Airmen First Class, Harold Schaffer, Charlie Amonett and Mike Halderman, rushed out and saluted us, as did a tall, lanky staff sergeant named Swen, the Noncommissioned Officer In Charge (NCOIC).

Our AO was rectangular shaped and extended along the coast a hundred and twenty miles from the Phu Cat Mountains to a short distance south of Tuy Hoa, the F-100 base not far south from Miami Beach. Our territory extended thirty to forty miles inland.

Dave told me to head north and we flew a short distance following Highway 1A. We turned inland and headed toward the ROK Cav Regiment. We 1st ROK Infantry Regiment guys could fly from Qui Nhon to Phu Cat when it was our turn to spend a week at the regiment, but the FACs assigned to the ROK Cav Regiment and 26th ROK Infantry Regiment at Miami Beach had to travel by Jeep. The ROK Cav Regiment was located in the An Khe Pass region on Highway 19, a major route from the port at Qui Nhon to Pleiku, the defensive post for the entire Central Highland region. The Cav Regiment's presence in this area was instrumental in securing the flow of war materials from Qui Nhon to Pleiku. The North Vietnamese Army lurked just over the Cambodian border, a mere twenty miles from Pleiku.

The roads were easy to follow and the steep, mountainous terrain provided many unique landmarks which made navigating throughout our AO easy. An example were the Mansfield Peaks, twin rocky spires, as big around as school buses, which extended a thousand feet above the valley floor. They were so close together, an O-1 couldn't fly between them.

We flew south from the Cav Regiment, passed over the sprawling compound at Tiger Town, and continued toward the southern boundary of our AO. We were thirty or forty miles inland, and the farther south we went, I noticed a paucity of prominent landmarks, no small streams, roads or villages. Whenever I flew, going back to my pre-solo days with Dick Komberec, I always tried to have a place picked out where I could land in case of an engine failure, but this place was covered with dense jungle. The trees were so thick, I figured I could gently touch down in the tree tops, and hopefully come to rest without tumbling to the ground, a wounded bird perched high upon a nest. The place gave me the willies. I mentioned it to Dave and he said, "We're in bad guy territory, Bern."

I turned the Bird Dog east and soon saw the South China Sea and an air base with F-100s parked on the tarmac. It was Tuy Hoa and we headed up the coast to Qui Nhon. When we were a few miles from Qui Nhon, the weather went south. The ceiling dropped and it began to rain. Dave told me to dial in the frequency for the Qui Nhon radio beacon and said, "Let's treat it like an instrument check ride. Pretend you're under the hood."

I turned on the ADF and adjusted our heading until the needle pointed to twelve o'clock. Qui Nhon was on our nose. I was able to maintain visual contact with the ground, and after two and a half hours we touched down, drove to the hooch, packed a Remain Over Night (RON) kit with clean clothes, got a sandwich at the mess hall and headed back to the flight line for our short ride to Tiger Town.

Fifteen minutes after leaving Qui Nhon, I touched down on the narrow, one thousand foot long Pierced Steel Planking (PSP) runway at Tiger Town. There was a steep drop off on the side of the runway, perhaps ten feet from the landing surface. Concertina wire, a hundred yards from the runway, defined the southern border of the ROK compound. Dave told me mines were planted between the landing strip and the wire.

Airman First Class Ken Montague, a radio operator, greeted us.. We tossed our gear in his Jeep and sped off in a cloud of red dust, our destination a mile away. The Tum hooch was U-shaped, and we were met by two mangy dogs who recognized Ken, but gave me and Dave a cursory checkout. Their names were Buddha and Nam. Ken helped us unload the Jeep and said, "Lieutenant Hale, when you want a tour of the underground command post, let me know."

Sergeant Landry and Lieutenant Col.Wis

As Dave and I headed toward a conex to secure our weapons, a major and a lieutenant colonel walked toward us. Both men were husky, athletic types. Lieutenant Colonel Wisneski could have been a football coach. Visions of Vince Lombardi came to mind. Major Schoder, bald and dignified, resembled a famous actor. As they approached, I whispered to Dave, "The Major looks just like--"

Before I could finish the sentence, Dave said, "Yeah, I know. Kojak." They greeted us and welcomed me to Tiger town. The major had an interesting resume. He'd been an Assistant Air Attaché to six countries, an instructor pilot in Washington, DC, a general's aide-de-camp and a T-33 and T-28 instructor at Webb AFB. He spoke French and Spanish.

Bernie and Maj. Schoder

Lieutenant Colonel Frank Wisneski, a former fighter pilot in the Air Defense Command (ADC), was relatively new to the position of Division ALO. Before a recent promotion, he was a major and the ALO at Miami Beach. When he attained the higher rank, he replaced Major Schoder as Division ALO, who would soon move to the 21st TASS at Nha Trang for the remainder of his tour. They welcomed us, and Lieutenant Colonel Wisneski told us to store our gear in one of the bedrooms and meet them in the lounge.

The entrance to the hooch, in the center of the building, opened to a wide bar. Sleeping quarters were located on either side of the lounge, enlisted men on the left wing, officers on the right. The place was tidy but rustic. I got a second look at the grounds when I realized there was no indoor plumbing. Buddha and Nam accompanied me to the three-hole facility. Steel drums and a large weapon canister, mounted on wooden scaffolding, captured rain water for the outdoor shower. Sand bags adorned the tin roofing on both the hooch and underground bunkers.

When I returned to the bar, Dave was sipping a beer with Lieutenant Colonel Wisneski, Major Schoder, and the flight scheduler, Captain Ted Olson, a short-timer with just a couple of months left on his tour. Ted graduated from the Air Force Academy and got a backseat F-4 assignment when he completed flight school. He upgraded to the front seat after a year, but before he could report to an F-4 squadron, got an O-2 assignment.

He told me, "I always wondered who it was I pissed off. I reported to Eglin and got checked out in the O-2, and when I checked in at FAC U, got the word I was going to fly the Bird Dog instead. I was convinced the guy who jerked my F-4 assignment followed me to Vietnam, intent on continuing to harass me. After a quickie check out in the O-1, I was sent to the Tums, assigned to the Cav Regiment."

Dave said he was leaving early in the morning for the 1st ROK Infantry Regiment, and asked what my agenda was going to be for the next few days. Lieutenant Colonel Wisneski said he wanted me to spend some time in the Tactical Operations Center (TOC), hanging out with our radio operators and meeting with some of the Korean officers. He nodded to Ted, who said, "Jake is going to arrive tomorrow afternoon and we'll start his checkout process. The next day Rod has a KEL mission scheduled in the morning and Bernie is going to be in the back seat. Then we'll send him up with Jake in the afternoon. If you want, we can book him another Miami Beach mission with Rod for Wednesday."

Dave said, "That sounds great, Ted. Fly his ass off. We've got several guys due any day and we need him qualified. Jake's checkout will be a piece of cake, but he needs all the air strikes we can give him. Look for a mission Thursday afternoon and we'll put him in the front seat."

"Roger that," Ted replied.

Holy smokes! These guys aren't screwing around!

Sergeant William Landry, and Airmen First Class Gary Lohr and Jim Start entered the lounge from the dining area, a large open area with several picnic tables, a refrigerator and a kitchen area. Sergeant Landry said, "Good evening, gentlemen. Would you happen to have a couple extra beers? Ken told us we had a new Tum on station and we'd like to greet him."

Lieutenant Colonel Wisneski slid a round of beers down the bar. I stood, introduced myself and they saluted me with raised Budweisers. "Welcome to Tiger Town, Lieutenant. We're glad you're here." I wondered if I was about to receive another Him. Small talk took place for an hour, we dined on a meal of chicken and ramen noodles, an entrée I would learn to love, then Dave and I hit the rack.

I drove Dave to the flight line the next morning, my first experience behind the wheel of a Jeep. He said he would see me in a couple of days and I watched him take off and fade out of sight, heading east toward Phu Cat Air Base.

Back at the hooch, I met Ken, who, along with the other radio operators, was assigned to the Tactical Air Control Party (TACP), part of the Air Force liaison with the ROKs. We drove about a mile to the TOC, an underground bunker constructed from railroad ties and covered with several feet of dirt. Airman Gary Lohr, one of our radio operators, manned the communication desk where all radio traffic, UHF, VHF and FM, was monitored. Our radio operators maintained a log book in which they noted all communications that took place between the command post and each airborne FAC.

When the ROK operations officer or our airborne FACs needed fighter support, our radio operators called the DASC in Nha Trang, and fighters were dispatched. The ROMADs always had the proper radio equipment at hand, regardless of where they were working: regimental headquarters; in the field during an offensive operation; or here at Tiger Town.

The bunker contained intelligence and operations officers that monitored the offensive and defensive activity of the three regiments. I met Captain Lim, an Intelligence Officer, who pointed out a scoreboard for an operation the ROK Cav Regiment was undertaking in the west sector of our AO. A tally on a chalk board depicted the current casualties: bad guys fifty-five, good guys zero.

Small, colored paper flags marked the locations of elements of each of the three regiments.

I was mesmerized by the loud, nonstop chatter. The Korean soldiers monitoring the land lines and airwaves, yelled into their phones and headsets. No casual conversations here, it was all business. Life and death business. I couldn't imagine working a ten or twelve hour shift in the place.

A call came in from Jake who was inbound from Qui Nhon, who said he was on his way and needed someone to pick him up. Ken and I went back to the hooch to get my flight gear, and when we got to the air strip, Jake was in sight on the eastern horizon. It was time for one more check ride.

We flew two and a half hours. It was the same profile Ace and the guys at the TASS used: plenty of navigation work, simulated air strikes, rocket practice and dozens of landings.

Jake directed me to a place close to Tiger Town called the Old French Fort for

target practice. He had no idea if it was the remains of a French structure or not, but it sounded good. The outline of a square foundation framed by hedgerows was all that remained on the valley floor. There was a pile of rocks inside the northern boundary that we used for a target.

I fired eight Willie Petes, some excellent, most acceptable and dropped a few smoke canisters out the window, none of which were close to the intended target. We headed for Tiger Town and the short, narrow runway. After a dozen short field landings and takeoffs, Jake said, "Let's park this baby and get a cold beer." I don't know that I dazzled Jake in the time we spent together, but I sure enjoyed flying with him.

When we got to the hooch Jake told me he was going to be spending more time at Tiger Town because Colonel Wis, that's what every officer called him, wanted to upgrade the facility. He needed a carpenter, and Jake was his guy. "I love woodworking, and the boss thinks we ought to have a classier bar. While you are flying with Rod in the morning, I'm going to design it and put together a list of materials. I can't wait to get started. The ROKs love hanging out with us, and they'll provide almost everything I need."

The bar became more crowded as afternoon faded to evening. Major Schoder and Colonel Wis were the first officers to join me and Jake. Colonel Wis asked Jake if I was going to make a good FAC. Jake nodded and said, "No sweat, Colonel Wis, he's a natural." Jake paused, winked at me and said, "I think. I'll have a better idea tomorrow."

Ted and two of the radio operators came in, followed by Sergeant Landry. The place was filling up. It was happy hour.

The hooch was unique. The officers and enlisted guys shared the same quarters and "Club." Jake and I wore flight suits, everyone else had on shorts and tee shirts. A few minutes later, two Korean officers walked in. It was Captain Lim, the intelligence officer I met earlier, and a chunky major who wore a flight suit. His name tag said Chung and the silver star that adorned his senior pilot's wings indicated his log book contained thousands of hours. They approached and Captain Lim introduced me.

"Major Chung, this is Lieutenant Hale, a 1st ROK Infantry Regiment FAC. He is new guy." The major shook my hand, gently nodded and said, "Ah, Lieutenant. It is pleasure to know you." The introduction seemed very formal. I met dozens of ROKs in Vietnam, officers and enlisted men, and not once did I hear anyone's first name mentioned. Something told me this time wouldn't be the last I'd see Major Chung.

In my sixteen month career, Ace was the first captain who told me to address him by his first name rather than rank, as did the captains at the TASS and the Tums. I noticed Ted and Jake called Major Schoder, Bill, but no one called Lieutenant Colonel Wisneski, Frank. I was a second lieutenant, a lower-than-dirt brown bar (gold insignia). In flight school I called first lieutenants, "Sir." I wondered if it would be okay for me to address Majors Schoder and Hadley by their first names. Probably. Was this the unique outfit it appeared to be? One filled with exciting, charismatic guys? No doubt about it. Was I in for an exciting adventure? I would have bet my good luck charm, the silver-winged tie tack, on it.

Rod McClellan

Jake chatted with Ted about the lighting he wanted to install in the bar. He was wound tight, excited about his project, ready to get started. I felt the same way, but for a different reason.

My first combat mission was upon me. Rod would pick me up at eight and we'd rendezvous with the fighters an hour later. The term "Known Enemy Location" was ominous to say the least, and I had no idea what to expect. All the professional training I received at Holly Field, FAC U and the TASS prepared me well, but it was all merely make-believe. When I left Ace at FAC U, he said to me, "If any of the guys in your outfit tell you they weren't scared before their first mission, they're pulling your chain."

I grabbed my gear and jumped out of Ken's Jeep when I heard the purr of the approaching Bird Dog. Rod was right on time. He taxied to the parking area, shut down the engine and got out of the plane. "Good morning, Bernie. You ready to launch?"

"Yes, sir," I replied.

He lit a smoke, walked around the plane, pulled the safety pins out of the rocket tubes and stuffed them in his flight suit. He told me the weather was going to be good, "A perfect morning to fly." He had me spread out my map, and gave me our target coordinates, which I noted on the chart.

Rod grinned and said, "Okay, One Four, let's saddle up."

I jumped in the back seat, stowed my AR-15 in the small compartment behind me, and fastened the shoulder harness. We were airborne within a couple of minutes, heading south toward our rendezvous point.

The thought of my dollar ride with Major Thomas came to mind. Here I was, stuffed in the back seat of an airplane, clueless about what would take place. The only thing I knew for certain, was that it was bound to be exciting.

An outstanding pilot, Rod talked nonstop, wanting me to hear and understand everything he was doing.

"Bernie, these known and suspected enemy locations seldom turn out to be hot targets. If bad guys are confirmed to be in a certain place, they're seldom there when we show up with fighters. The ROKs are constantly gathering intelligence, and go to great lengths not to be surprised when they send their troops into the field. When they suspect an enemy force to be in a certain area, they want us to work it over before exposing their soldiers. When working troops-in-contact, we always know exactly where the bad guys are; however, this morning we're just fishing, trolling for a nibble, hoping the fighter jocks stir up a little trouble."

We arrived at the target area at an altitude of 3,000 feet, made a wide, three-hundred-and-sixty degree circle and Rod asked me to tell him where I thought the target was located. I told him it was fifty meters south of a narrow stream close to a rectangular rocky area, and he agreed.

Rod said we had ten minutes before show time. "I've got the fighter's UHF frequency dialed in the radio and we ought to be hearing from them any minute. I know you've practiced this a thousand times, but pay attention to what I'm doing. Keep an eye out for air traffic and concentrate on what's taking place on the ground. Let me know if you see anything weird."

"Roger that," I replied, sweat began to slide down my back.

A moment later we got the call. "Tum Three One, Elect One Two, a flight of two Huns on station. How do you read? Over."

"You're loud and clear, Elect One Two. Say your ETA and lineup. Over."

"Elect is three zero minutes out, approaching from the north. We're loaded with snake, nape and twenty mike-mike."

"Roger that," Rod replied. "I'm an O-1, south of our target at two thousand feet, close to prominent rocky area. Our target is a known enemy location."

The fighter jock didn't acknowledge Rod's message on the radio; rather, he clicked the mic twice, a signal to let Rod know he understood. The radio remained silent for a few minutes, and I thought about how authentic the simulations were that Ace had me practice for hours on end.

Rod switched the radio wafer switch from UHF to intercom and said to me, "The terrain's relatively flat, Bernie, and we have no friendlies in the area. I'm going to put the Huns in a north to south, left hand pattern. If they take ground fire, they'll be heading feet wet when they pull off the target."

I didn't have time to respond before Elect Lead said, "Tally ho,Tum. Elect One Two has you in sight."

Rod answered with instructions to the fighters, "Roger that, Elect. Give me a north to south, left hand pattern. If you take any ground fire, Tuy Hoa is your closest base, and if you can't make it there, bail out feet wet. Give me hard bombs first, in pairs. I'll put in a mark when you're ready."

"Roger that, Tum. Elect is ready for your mark."

"Okay, Elect, here we go. Tum Three One's rolling in with a mark."

Again, I heard two acknowledging clicks.

Rod's Willie Pete penetrated the jungle, and the white phosphorous smoke began to slowly rise through the dense foliage. Rod cleared Elect Lead in hot and told him to hit his smoke.

I followed the F-100's approach and watched two five hundred pound bombs fall from the Hun, their retarding fins deployed, slowing the rate of descent, which gave the fighter pilot sufficient time to obtain safe separation from the impact.

When the weapons exploded, Rod made a sharp three-hundred-and-sixty degree turn to the right and I picked up Elect Two as he began his descent toward the target.

Rod keyed the mic and said, "Elect Two, you're cleared in hot. Hit twenty meters left of Lead's bombs."

"Roger that, Tum. Two's in hot, twenty left."

When he saw the impact, Rod yanked our Bird Dog into another steep turn. I spotted Elect Lead as Rod cleared him to release two bombs. Rod told him to make this pass twenty meters north of the previous impact. We weren't targeting a specific point on the ground, but as Rod told me earlier, we were trolling, hoping to stumble upon something exciting.

After three more passes in the same general vicinity, a dozen bombs had been expended, half of Elect's payload, with no results. Rod told the flight leader to hold high and dry and stand by for another mark.

"Roger that, Tum," replied the fighter pilot. "Elect's high and dry."

Rod flipped the radio to the intercom and told me he was going to move the fighters fifty meters west, closer to the rocky area. "It's less dense over there. Maybe we'll see something." Rod called the fighter jocks, who were no doubt getting a little bored.

"Elect Lead, I'm fifty meters west of your last target, rolling in with a mark."

"Roger that, Tum. I've got you in sight."

After each jet made an uneventful pass, we hit the jackpot.

Rod moved the target a few additional meters to the west and when lead's next pair of bombs hit the ground, a tremendous explosion erupted. The sky filled with thick, black smoke, trees and rocks. A shock wave hit our plane, and threw us violently to the right. Rod quickly righted the Bird Dog and keyed the mic.

"Shit hot!" he exclaimed. "Elect Two, you're cleared in hot! Hit Lead's bombs!"

Elect Two, suddenly exuberant, responded, "Roger that, Tum! Two's in hot from the north. I've got you in sight."

Rod spoke to me on the intercom, "Watch for ground fire, Hale!" That was it, one quick command. He was too busy to have a conversation. I was stunned, shocked by the noise and the impact of the shock wave.

The remainder of Elect's bombs didn't produce another secondary explosion, but the black smoke continued to rise to a height of more than a thousand feet. The Huns were out of hard bombs, so Rod had them drop napalm in the area of the secondary explosion. It was my first look at the long, silver canisters that tumbled in free-fall when dropped from the fighters. They ignited upon impact, spreading a blanket of fire the length of a football field. I felt the heat each time Rod made a low pass. The napalm cooked off more explosions, which caused small arms ammunition to ignite, streaking across the sky like bottle rockets.

Rod called the TOC at Tiger Town and requested another set of fighters. He wanted to be prepared for what could become a long mission.

Elect Lead told Rod the only ordnance they had left was twenty-mike-mike. Fighter pilots loved to shoot their guns and Rod knew Lead was eager to spray the area with his remaining weapon.

Rod asked the fighter jocks to expend their cannon fire on the area that was spewing black smoke, and told Elect Flight to save some twenty-mike-mike to cover us when we made a Bomb Damage Assessment (BDA).

Lead acknowledged and I watched the Huns streak down the chute, one after another, firing their guns as they moved the rudder from side to side, covering as much real estate as they could. After one pass, Rod told Elect to stand by for a BDA.

"Bernie, we're going to get right on the deck and see if we can see any damaged equipment, structures of any kind, or KBA (Killed by Air). I'll be jinking like crazy. Brace yourself and keep your eyes open."

At Holly Field we were told, when doing a BDA, to make quick, evasive turns, even if there was no visual sign of enemy fire. When I jinked in the peaceful airspace of Florida, I came nowhere close to the fierce manner in which Rod wrung out our Bird Dog. We were right on the tree tops going as fast as our little war bird would take us. My control stick and rudder pedals slammed against the stops as Rod made random, herky-jerky turns, a high-speed tilt-a-whirl run amok. We were a moving target, one I hoped would be hard to hit. I feared the wings would become tangled in the trees or simply fly off the Bird Dog. After three passes over the charred landscape, Rod called our fighters with a BDA.

"Elect One Two, we've got multiple secondary explosions, remnants of weapons, ammunition, and heavy smoke and foliage. If the ROKs uncover anything else, we'll be sure to pass it on. You guys did a great job."

The lead jock replied, "Thanks, Tum. Glad we could help."

Rod didn't have any time to relax. Airman Jim Start called from Tiger Town to tell him he had fighters on the way, "Tum Three One, you've got a flight of two

Huns en route from Tuy Hoa, call sign Bobcat One Eight. They should be there in one zero minutes."

"Roger that," Rod said. "Thanks for the help, Jim. You need to have another Tum ready to spell us if this thing gets exciting. We'll need to refuel in a couple of hours."

We had a few minutes to relax while we circled the smoldering mess. I was soaking wet, glad that Rod had opened the windows, letting cool air fill the cockpit. We flew at three thousand feet, both of us looking for signs of trouble. He told me he was going to have Bobcat target both sides of the area where we got the secondary explosion.

"We discovered a serious weapons cache," he said. "The ROKs are going to have a field day with this intelligence. They'll have an operation scheduled for Miami Beach before we get back to Tiger Town."

Our break didn't last long. Bobcat gave us a call, "Tum Three One, Bobcat One Eight is with you. We're a flight of two Huns loaded with snake, nape and guns. We see your smoke and fire, and we're ready to go to work."

Rod acknowledged Bobcat's transmission and gave him a quick briefing, "Bobcat One Eight, I'm an O-1 circling the smoke at three thousand feet. We've exposed a weapons storage area. No ground fire, just secondaries."

Bobcat Flight got the same instructions regarding headings and bailout information Rod had given Elect, and asked if he was ready for a mark. The fighter pilot told Rod he had him in sight and was ready for a Willie Pete. For thirty minutes, Rod moved the ordnance up the west side and down the east side of the weapons supplies we uncovered to no avail. It was a dry run.

We were running out of gas, and Rod called the mission off. "Bobcat One Eight, we're bingo fuel (enough gas to get home), and this party's over. When we get some troops on the ground, we'll share any BDA with you. We appreciate the quick response."

"Roger that. We'll always be there for you, Tum," came the sarcastic response from the fighter jock. He'd been sitting alert all morning waiting for the klaxon to ring, and when it did, I'm sure he expected something more exciting than a nonproductive trolling mission.

Rod asked me if I had any questions, which I didn't, but told him I was very impressed. The flight back to Tiger Town was quiet. I replayed the entire mission in my mind. The excitement of watching ordnance being delivered from high performance jet fighters on what may have been enemy troops overwhelmed me. The war stories I'd heard from the old heads at Holly Field, FAC U, and the TASS, had made a profound impression on me, but now, after experiencing it first hand, I had an understanding of what it was I would be doing for the next eleven months. Two hours ago, I didn't have a clue what a KEL mission might entail. Now I knew, and had a feeling my learning curve would be steep. I was in awe of the firepower I'd witnessed, and the calm manner in which Rod and the fighter jocks went about their business.

When we were a few minutes from Tiger Town, Rod called the command post and asked if someone would pick us up at the air strip. When we landed, Jake was waiting. I hadn't given one thought to the fact he and I were going to fly that afternoon. It was going to be a full day.

After Rod briefed Lieutenant Colonel Wis and Captain Lim on our mission, Jake and I headed for the air strip and another training flight. We flew around the perimeter of our AO again, "More familiarization," Jake said. He stressed the importance of knowing the lay of the land. We lit up the Old French Fort with eight Willie Petes, and shot a dozen touch and go landings. Finally, after five hours in the Bird Dog, it was time for a beer and a shower.

I was scheduled to ride in Rod's back seat in the morning. That evening, he, Jake, and Ted decided I might as well be in the front seat for the SEL mission. When it was mentioned, I was ecstatic, but the more I thought about it, I worried that Dave might be upset. He said I would fly my first strike mission with him, and he was my boss. I asked Jake if we should call Dave and ask him if it was okay.

Jake shook his head and said, "Dave will be glad you've got your first mission under your belt. Rod will let him know how you perform. Don't worry about it.

That was easy for Jake to say. I'd spent the last fifteen months in a strict, structured environment. Second lieutenants didn't have a vote on anything. We did what we were told at the given time for every scheduled activity and were never late. Our instructors at Reese evaluated each of our flights, and records were kept noting our progress. Ace did the same thing at FAC U, which gave the commanders at the TASS an idea of how we could handle the airplane. When it was decided I would work the fighters in the morning, without permission from a higher-ranking officer, I felt like one of the guys, a student no more.

Rod and I were going to Qui Nhon when we finished our strike, and Jake, too, would be there as we had a new guy arriving.

The early morning weather was perfect. We flew from Tiger Town to Qui Nhon, then south along the coast. When we passed Miami Beach, I turned west and flew inland twenty miles and we arrived at the rendezvous point thirty minutes early. I had plenty of time to plan the strike. I pointed out the target to Rod, which he confirmed. Not wanting to draw attention to our Bird Dog, we flew south, away from the target area. I explained to Rod every detail of how I planned to execute the mission.

"I'll run the fighters north to south, paralleling the ridge line, in a left hand orbit so they'll be heading feet wet when they pull off the target. If they have the same lineup we saw yesterday, I'll work the area with hard bombs, then nape and guns."

Rod said everything looked good and we punched holes in the sky at three thousand feet, waiting for the fighters to check in. I started feeling the nervous pangs of checkitis. In a few minutes I would direct the deployment of seven tons of explosives on what could turn out to be enemy soldiers, or a huge weapons cache like the strike I witnessed the previous morning. I directed two sets of A-1E fighters when I was a student at Holly Field, and that was three months ago. The A-1 jocks were students like I, and their airplanes carried dummy bombs that made a small puff of dust upon impact. Now I found myself in the big leagues, waiting for a fighter pilot to show up. *Man, I hope I don't screw this up.*

When our radio operators requested a mission, they gave the DASC the call sign of the FAC assigned to the mission. The radio transmission I received gave me goose bumps.

"Tum One Four, Limit Eight One, how do you read? Over."

The fighter jock could have been a disc jockey. His deep voice exuded confidence. Until this moment I'd been fairly relaxed. Now I thought I would puke on my jungle boots. I keyed the mic and said, "Limit Eight One, you're loud and clear. How do you read me? Over."

Rod's voice filled my headset, "Bernie, you're on the intercom. Talk to Limit on UHF."

Oh, great! What a way to start.

I felt my cheeks burn as I flipped the wafer switch to the right radio and repeated my message. I told Limit Eight One where I was and briefed him on our mission. The two Huns were loaded with seven-hundred-and-fifty pound high drag bombs (Mark 117s), nape and guns. When Limit Eight One had me and the target in sight and acknowledged the traffic pattern I wanted, my first mission began. I pulled the throttle to idle, dove toward the target and fired a Willie Pete. It was a few meters left of where I intended, but close enough, considering I was going to move the ordnance around. Working a real target for the first time, I began directing traffic. "Limit Lead, you're cleared in hot. Hit my smoke." The impact of the seven-hundred-and-fifty pound weapon was tremendous. We didn't get a secondary explosion, but splintered trees, rocks and smoke filled the air. I made a steep, climbing turn and picked up Limit Two as he was coming off the perch.

"Limit two, put your bomb ten meters right of Lead's. You're cleared in hot."

The wing man acknowledged, "Roger that, Tum. Ten right of lead. I'm in hot and have you in sight."

I gave him two clicks on the mic and for twenty minutes continued to move the weapons around the target area. When the Huns had expended their bombs, I told lead to hold high and dry and stand by. I switched to the intercom and talked to Rod.

"Rod, should I have Limit drop their nape?"

"Sure," came his reply. "Move 'em thirty meters east to the area that's more dense. Maybe you'll shake something up over there."

I was thrilled with how the mission had gone so far. Before the fighters showed up, I worried about saying or doing something stupid, embarrassing myself in front of Rod and the fighter jocks. Once I was speaking on the UHF, rather than the intercom, everything went well.

The rest of the mission was uneventful. Neither Limit Flight nor I saw any evidence of enemy activity. When their napalm and twenty-mike-mike was depleted, Limit Lead called.

"Tum One Four, Limit Flight's Winchester (out of ordnance). We're RTB (returning to base)."

I thanked Limit Lead for their good work, and headed toward Qui Nhon.

On the short flight to the coast, Rod evaluated my performance.

"Bernie, you did a good job, but you've got to pick up the pace. When one fighter releases a weapon, the next guy is a few seconds behind him and you've got to be quick with instructions. At times I could sense the fighter jocks thinking, 'When's this FAC going to tell us what he wants?' You've got to always have the next move on the tip of your tongue. When you've got troops in contact, you'll have to call the occasional time out, but with milk runs like these SELs, there's no excuse not to know what your next move will be. Always plan two or three moves ahead."

I replied, "I understand, Rod. Thanks for the help."

The speed with which the strike took place could never have been realistically simulated. I witnessed the hectic pace while riding in Rod's back seat the previous day, but watching and controlling a strike were two different things. It was a busy job having to monitor radio chatter, keep track of the Huns, scan the target area and surrounding real estate for signs of the enemy, search the sky for other aircraft and decide where to drop the next bomb.

Nine

Life at Qui Nhon

When I landed at Qui Nhon and taxied toward our revetments, I noticed a tall, wiry, first lieutenant standing next to Buddha, his arms extended upward. He usurped Buddha's authority, and sporting a broad grin, began directing me to a parking spot. I followed his hand signals, and when he crossed his extended arms, I braked to a stop, shut off the engine and the smiling pilot opened the door.

Pat Dowling & Bob Moore

"Hi, Bernie. I'm Pat Dowling and I'm glad to meet you. It's about time we got some new blood around here." Rod and I deplaned, stowed our gear in the conex, jumped in Pat's Jeep and headed for the compound. When we arrived, a grumpy MP waved us through the gate. We parked at the rear of the building and went straight to the chow hall for brunch.

While we ate, Pat looked at some names on a crinkled scratch pad, and let us know what was going to happen the next couple of days. "We're finally going to get some replacements.

Bill Lutz, a brown bar, is going to the 1st Regiment, and we're getting three first lieutenants. Larry Howerton, an academy classmate of mine who has been flying A-1s out of NKP (Nakhon Phanom/Naked Fanny) Thailand, is going to the Cav along with Bob Snyder, an F-4 driver. Steve Drummond, another F-4 jock, will join us in a couple of days and he'll be assigned to Miami Beach."

We left the chow hall and went up to our rooms. Rod headed for the shower, and Pat and I hung out on the balcony. Pat asked me where I went to college and I told him Montana, then posed the same question.

"I usually tell people I went to a small boy's school in the Midwest, but it was the Air Force Academy."

I'd been told a few times since reporting to Reese, the Air Force Academy grads, known as Zoomies, were either great guys or pompous jerks, no in-between. The jerks were referred to as "Ring Knockers." When given the opportunity to address a crowd, somehow their class rings happened to occasionally tap on the podium. I'd met three academy grads in the last few days and they were all super guys. I was four for four, counting Ralph Femrite, my classmate at Reese. I believed the animosity shown toward the Zoomies was jealousy. The majority of us would loved to have spent four years in Colorado Springs, Colorado.

Pat had been in-country four months before joining the Tums. He worked for the 9th ROK White Horse Division, located at Nha Trang. His call sign was Cutie Two Two. When the Tums became shorthanded and needed replacements, the TASS thought it would be prudent to send someone familiar with the Koreans, so Pat got the assignment.

Jake called us on the radio.

"I'm on my way to Nha Trang to pick up Larry Howerton, and Bob Moore is going to get the new Cav guy, Bob Snyder. Somebody has to get Lutz tomorrow. We'll figure that out tonight."

The land line rang. Pat nodded at me and pointed to the phone. I picked up the receiver and answered in the manner I'd been taught. "Tum Ops, Lieutenant Hale speaking, sir."

"Hale. Rog. How's it going?"

"Hi, Dave!" I exclaimed, happy to hear his voice. "I'm doing great."

"I'm at the regiment and just talked to Ted. He said you've had a busy couple of days. I'm glad you got to put in a strike."

"Yes, sir," I replied. "It's been hectic, but I enjoyed hanging out at Tiger Town and flying with Rod."

Dave told me he was going to be at the Qui Nhon airport in the morning. Ted had scheduled Dave and me an LZ prep mission.

"I'll call you at the hooch when I leave Phu Cat. Meet me at the runway."

"Roger that. I'll see you in the morning."

Pat told me I would be his roommate for one night, then he would go back to Phu Cat and Dave would spend a couple of days here.

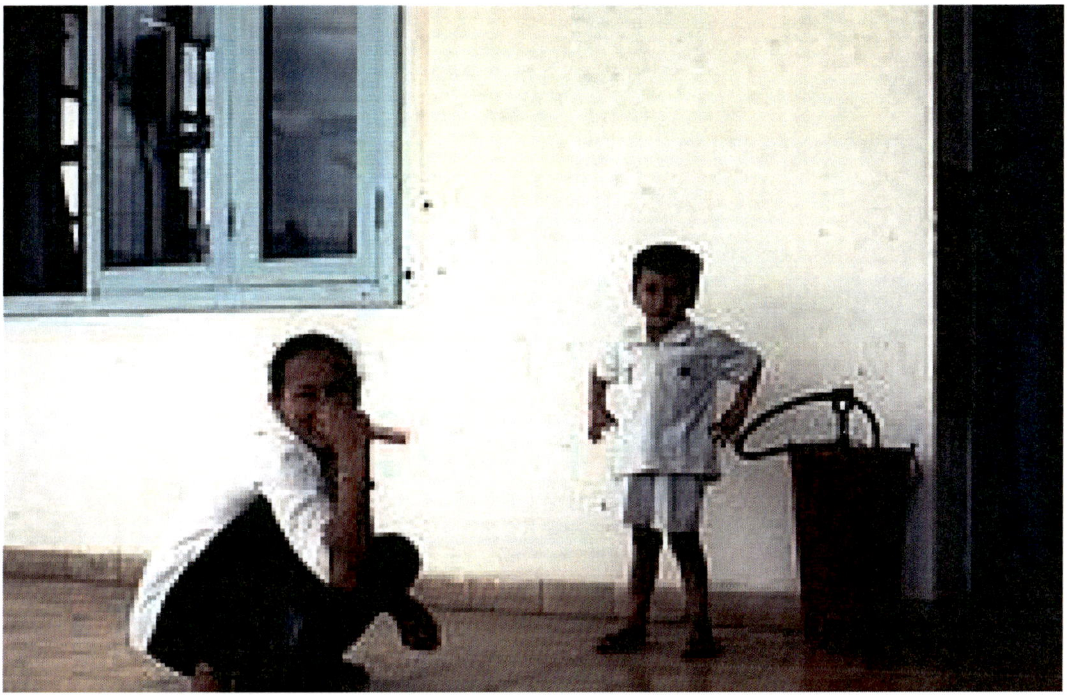

We walked the hallway and ran into a wrinkled woman changing linens. When she saw Pat, a broad grin lit up her face. He introduced me to mama-San as jung-Wi (lieutenant) Hale. She smiled, bowed at the waist, straightened up and said, "You no jung-Wi, you baby-San!" She was taken with my slight frame and teen-aged features. I told her I was glad to meet her and thanked her for doing my laundry on my I first visited to Qui Nhon.

The Dowling-induced grin never left her face.

"No problem, baby-San. Clean clothes every day."

Pat took off for the flight line on a taxi run and Rod and I were the only guys in the hooch. I loved the sound of silence. It had been a hectic eighteen days since I arrived in Vietnam. I'd logged fifty hours, not a huge sum by any means, but was whipped. I took a short nap and woke to the sounds of Tum FACs arriving.

Pat had returned from the flight line after picking up Jake and Larry. As I walked toward the balcony, I heard Larry explaining how he had ended up a Tum. He was confused and more than a bit angry about his new assignment.

Larry & Bernie

He wondered how personnel could tell him he was being sent to a Class B FAC mission, when he was told there was a shortage of A FACs, an assignment for which he was qualified because of his combat experience in the A-1 fighter.

He loved flying the 1945 vintage A-1 Skyraider, a single engine workhorse. Her payload and time aloft surpassed that of the F-100 and F-4 fighters. The bird wasn't bullet proof, but an abundance of steel plating protected her vital parts. Larry flew two different missions in the A-1. Search-and-rescue missions, with the call sign Sandy, and close air support sorties, using Spad and Firefly identifiers.

First Lieutenants Bob Snyder and Bob Moore arrived shortly after Jake and Larry. Snyder, a rakish six footer, sported an out of-regulation mustache. By the rules, facial hair could not extend past the end of one's lips. Our new Tum reminded me of one of the Three Musketeers. Like Ted, Bob thought he would fight the air war in the back seat of an F-4 Phantom.

Instead, he'd received orders sending him to Holly Field and a date with the Bird Dog. Bob and I went to the lounge and got a couple of beers, while he told me about his past two weeks.

He arrived in-country seven days after I did. We talked about the bus ride from Saigon to Bien Hoa and his short stay at the VOQ. He'd been assigned to the same room I slept in, the one across from the latrine and cold showers. A friend of his flew F-100s on the base, and he walked to the flight line to see if he could find him. While he was gone, a mortar attack hit the base and the VOQ took a direct hit. His duffle bag and clothes were destroyed. He had to get a new wardrobe, which delayed his arrival at FAC U.

A few hours after Bob arrived at Nha Trang for his FAC U checkout, the flight line took incoming rocket hits and one Bird Dog was destroyed. Later that evening, an alert sounded and he was told another attack was imminent. Weapons were issued to the transient guys, and he had to stand watch over the perimeter next to Ho Jo's. The attack wasn't long in duration and the flight line was spared further damage. There was, however, an injury. One of the guys with Bob received a scalp wound when he busted his head open jumping into the bunker when the alert siren went off. I made a mental note not to follow too close behind this Snyder guy. I thought of Ace when Bob told the story, and hoped he had survived the attacks.

Jake entered the lounge and said we were going to the Officer's Club. He went down the hall, woke Rod from his nap, and six of us, three old heads and three FNGs, walked down the stairs and across an open walkway to the Army Officer's Club. The place was packed with Army officers, none of whom gave us a second glance.

The club was unique in that it was composed of two structures, one on each side of an open garden area that held several round tables nestled among tropical foliage. The landscape designer was obviously the same guy who did the general's front yard. A long bar sat on one end of the open space, and a large, enclosed stage occupied the other. Jake told us three rookies that two or three times a month, there was a USO show at the club, usually Korean, Australian or Philippine musicians. Occasionally, Hollywood types showed up to visit with the troops.

Jake said, "Another reason the Army guys dislike us is because we've been known to take over the club on some of the nights they have entertainment.

Sometimes, we invite the musicians to join us on our balcony for a nightcap. We think it's the least we can do, considering they travel all this way to show us a good time."

I was glad there wasn't a show scheduled that night, as I had an early takeoff time in the morning and figured Dave would be early.

Pat and I woke before daybreak, ate breakfast at the mess hall and drove to the airport. I was a bit nervous considering the sun was barely above the horizon and we were unarmed in a neighborhood off limits from dusk to dawn. I felt better when we entered the perimeter of the Army Post, parked at the flight line and got our weapons and flight gear out of the conex. Pat jumped in a Bird Dog and took off for our regiment at Phu Cat. He was going to spend a few days with the Koreans while Dave and I flew out of Qui Nhon.

Dave touched down a few minutes after Pat's departure. We had plenty of time to locate our target and plan the strike. En-route to the target area, Dave told me the LZ prep missions were boring, but critical.

ROKs in the boonies.

"The ROKs give us these missions and expect us to nail the targeted area right on the money. They choose the location for one reason: elevation strategic to tactical advantage. They have a good idea where the bad guys are, and where they suspect them to go once the battle begins. The ROKs like to own the high ground. They don't pick flat, uncluttered landing zones in order to make it easy for the troops to egress from the choppers."

We were executing this strike at the request of the ROKs at Miami Beach (they were short on pilots), and the target coordinates were close to the area where Rod got the secondary explosions on my first mission. The Korean intelligence team had information that indicated bad guys were in the area. I identified the target, which Dave confirmed, and we were ready for the fighters to show up. I got my first close-up look at an F-4, when two Phantoms, call sign Cobra, arrived on station.

Each bird carried seven-hundred-and-fifty pound bombs, with Daisy Cutters, extended fuses that detonated the weapon above ground. The explosion cleared the landing zone of trees and foliage, which made landing and egress easier and safer for the helicopter pilots and ROK soldiers. We were on station for forty minutes and the mission went without a hitch. The pristine, jungle landscape was devastated.

I called the command post at Tiger Town and told Gary Lohr, the radio operator on duty, the mission was accomplished. The ROKs would soon be at work, planning an operation for the 26th ROK Infantry Regiment, at Miami Beach.

Dave and I headed back to Qui Nhon, stopping at the Old French Fort to fire the few Willie Pete's I had left after the strike. With a ten-cent grease pencil for a gun sight, we took every opportunity to practice firing rockets. Being accurate was a matter of touch, not technology. With practice, Robin Hood knew when the time was right to ever-so-gently release an arrow. With repetition, we, too, figured it out.

After lunch, Dave and I launched on our second mission. We toured our AO for a couple of hours, as it was time for me to start taking a turn with the daily Dawn Patrol flights and I was scheduled the next morning. Dave wanted to know if I could find my way around without getting lost. One of us had to be airborne every morning when the sun rose, looking for signs of enemy activity. Ted made the daily schedule and did his best to see that everyone shared in the Dawn Patrol experience.

Rather than return to Qui Nhon after our tour of the countryside, we went to Phu Cat Air Base to refuel and visit the 1st ROK Infantry Regiment, located a half mile from the flight line. Pat met us on the ramp and we drove through the security gate on the Air Force Base. We passed through the Korean check point and were waved through the gate by a smiling ROK security guard. Pat returned his snappy salute and we drove to our hooch where we were greeted by Swen, Harold, Charlie and Mike. I also got to meet our mama-San, Pom, a petite, young, pregnant girl perhaps eighteen. She had a black birth mark the size of a nickel nestled between her right eye and the bridge of her nose.

A dormitory contained eight single beds. A lounge with a bar, small refrigerator, five stools, three chairs and a round coffee table served as the dining area. There was a small, open area next to the bar that had a few chairs, a sofa and a round table used for reading and a card playing. The closest indoor plumbing was located on Phu Cat Air Base.

Our hooch was nestled in an area that contained several ROK Barracks, which could house up to 3,000 soldiers. Close-by were offices of the administrative, intelligence and operational officers. A helicopter pad and artillery battalion were located fifty yards south of our hooch. The 1st Regiment Tums were welcome tenants, living in a Korean village.

Captain Lim, the intelligence officer I met at Tiger Town, entered our lounge. He saw us drive in and said he wanted to spend more time with the new guy. Dave told him I was going to be spending plenty of time at the regiment. Pat offered him a soda.

"Captain Lim, do you want a Coke, do you want a Coke, do you want a Coke?" A broad grin lit up the Captain's face. He nodded, accepted the soda, and told me he looked forward to working with me. After a short visit he left, and Pat explained the odd conversation that took place when he offered Captain Lim something to drink.

"When I first met this guy, I offered him a soda, which he'd turn down. It was an extremely hot day and after a few minutes, I asked him again if he would like a cold drink.

Again, he refused my offer. I sensed he really wanted one and didn't understand his reluctance to take the plunge and drink a Coke. Several minutes passed and I tried again. This time, he nodded, accepted my offer and sucked it down. When he left, I asked Swen what the deal was."

Pat explained it was a Korean thing. When they enter someone's house, they won't accept a gift of any kind until it was offered three times.

Pat said, "When I understood the deal, I got the process over with in a hurry."

Dave and I walked a few yards to the Operations office, where I met Major Yoo, Dave's counterpart. As the Air Liaison Officer, it was Dave's responsibility to provide Major Yoo with whatever information he needed to assist the senior officer's staff as they planned their offensive operations. The major was very cordial, but I got the feeling he wasn't too keen on the idea of a second lieutenant giving him guidance on how to manage his business. Captain Lim, on the other hand, told me he looked forward to working with me.

We went back to our hooch and visited with the 1st Regiment ROMADs. Airmen Schaffer, Halderman and Amonett maintained the Jeeps and the four radios crammed in the back seat. Harold Schaefer grew up in Ohio and had twin boys. Mike Halderman was the fixit guy, handy with tools and always looking for something to work on. Charlie Amonett grew up in the northeast, and he appeared to be a little quirky. He showed me a cat he'd locked in a pet kennel and told me it was a stray who had bitten him a few days earlier. Charlie was keeping an eye on him, looking for signs of rabies. He liked to hang out with the ROKs, boxing with them and honing his Tae-Kwon-Do skills, a martial art practiced by every Korean soldier. These guys were not only prepared for hand-to-hand combat, they welcomed the opportunity to go toe-to-toe with the enemy. It was sport to them. The Koreans humored Charlie when it came to him participating in their athletic competition.

Dave and I returned to Qui Nhon late afternoon, and found the hooch crowded with Tums, new and veterans. Jake and Quis had flown all day with Larry Howerton, Bob Snyder, Steve Drummond and Bill Lutz, who, like Steve, showed up earlier than expected.

The guys at the TASS were getting FACs checked out and sent to the field as quickly as they could. I'd been a Tum for a week and when I arrived, every regiment was shorthanded. Now, it seemed, we had more warm bodies to share the workload.

I received a great surprise when Barry Moore, my buddy at Reese, showed up unexpectedly a few days later. An O-2 FAC, he was assigned to a small US Army outfit, advisors to an Army of the Republic of Vietnam (ARVN) unit in Cheo Reo, a small village an hour west of Qui Nhon. Barry was one of four Herb

FACs. They had two aircraft and a staff of nine to maintain their planes and radios, and coordinate operations with the Army advisors and ARVN troops.

When Barry was at the 21st TASS getting checked out, he asked about my whereabouts, and was told I was a Tum stationed at Qui Nhon. Barry could get away for the evening and flew to Qui Nhon hoping he would run into me. I was standing on the balcony with several of our guys, when he made his entrance.

"Hi, fellas. I'm a Herb FAC, stationed at Cheo Reo. I'm looking for the Lizard. Did I come to the right place?"

The room fell silent, the guys looking at one another, wondering who among us knew this guy or his buddy, Lizard. I'd recognized Barry's voice, and slowly turned, a huge grin on my face. "Holy smokes, Barry. What are you doing here?"

"Aha! I tracked you down, Lizard!"

I introduced Barry to the guys and after a few drinks, banter about the O-1 versus the O-2 began. Bob Snyder said, "The O-2 is a great airplane if you're going on a cross country flight, but if you're putting in an airstrike, it sucks. You can't see out of it, or turn on a dime like we can."

Barry responded, "Yeah, but we carry twice the Willie Petes and gas you guys do, and we have two engines."

The friendly exchange lasted a while, with no one willing to concede their airplane was, in any way, inferior to the other. We all had the same job to do, protect our ground troops. Barry had Vietnamese and U.S. Army advisors to support, and we had ROKs.

That night there was a USO show at the club, and we went en masse to hang out with our Army hosts. They were less than thrilled to see us enter the club. Not a nod or smile that acknowledged we were in this mess together, fighting the same war. We ordered drinks and something to eat. As we waited for the entertainment to begin, we continued to get acquainted with one another. Bill Lutz grew up in Mississippi. Like Bubba, the guy from Atlanta who gave me my nickname, Bill spoke with a heavy southern drawl.

Steve Drummond, husky and handsome, looked like a guy who might have grown up riding a surf board in California, which is exactly what he did. Bob Snyder's mustache was a thing of beauty. We hoped Colonel Wis wouldn't make him trim it to regulation size. Bob's appearance screamed for a nickname and before the night was over, one of the guys had dubbed him Snidley Whiplash. Like mine, it stuck. Larry Howerton's grin signaled mischief.

Eventually, an all-girl Philippine troupe took to the stand to whoops and hollers from the all-male audience. Thirty minutes into the performance, the leader of the band asked the audience if anyone happened to be having a birthday. Jake jumped to his feet and announced to all present, "Bernie is!" The Tums and Barry loved it.

Bernie and Bill

The Army contingent cringed. After all, it was their club. The sultry singer pleaded with me to join her on the stage, which brought another round of cat calls from the Air Force. With help from the lead singer, I sang a few bars of Chicago's *Does Anybody Really Know What Time It Is?* Shortly after my stage appearance we scampered back to our table and when the band took a break, Barry and I went back to our hooch. We both had an early wake-up call.

Up before dawn, we drove to the flight line and Buddha was waiting for us. My O-1 and Barry's O-2 were loaded with fuel and rockets, ready to launch. We performed our check list items, and taxied to the runway. We'd planned for me to take off first and get a three or four minute head start. He would catch up to me, we'd fly together for a few minutes, then go our separate ways. When we walked to our respective airplanes, Barry yelled across the tarmac, "Lizard, if I weren't a Herb FAC, I'd want to be a Tum. You guys are shit hot."

I smiled, nodded and gave him a thumbs up. I hoped I would see him again soon.

The sun appeared on the horizon as I taxied on the runway and began my takeoff roll. As I climbed through fifteen hundred feet, Barry caught up to me. He had his flaps and landing gear down, slowing his plane so we could fly a little formation. I stayed on his wing, and we flew together for several minutes. We were each in a Cessna war bird, one born in the forties, the other, shiny and new, flying together in a war zone, performing the same mission. Barry gently wiggled his wings, and we went our separate ways.

I flew past the Mansfield Peaks toward the northern boundary of our AO, then turned east to the coast and wove my way back and forth across the width of our territory. I saw several aircraft crisscrossing the landscape, but no signs of anything unusual or threatening. After two-and-a-half hours in the air, I returned to Qui Nhon.

Our fleet consisted of nine planes. One or two were always at the TASS undergoing routine maintenance, Tiger Town kept two, as did the 1st ROK Infantry Regiment, and the others flew out of Qui Nhon. On my way back to our compound, I passed a Jeep full of Tums on their way to the air strip. It looked like it could be a busy day.

The date was July 24th. Our Astronauts were on the moon, I'd been in-country twenty-days and a Tum for one week.

Ten

New Guys Step Up

When I got back to the hooch, mama-San greeted me with a nod and a toothy grin.

"Good morning, baby-San! How you today?"

"I'm fine, mama-San," I replied. I had the feeling between Lizard and baby-San, no one would ever call me Bernie again.

Dave and Bill Lutz were going over the flight plan for their morning mission. It was a familiarization ride for Bill and whatever else Jake had planned for the afternoon.

Ted goes home

There were daily requests from the ROKs for us to deal with known and suspected enemy locations and LZ preps. With Ted's departure Jake took over the role of scheduler. The new guys, one week junior to me, would get one tour of the landscape, then work airstrikes with the old heads.

Bob Moore was in the field with the ROKs working an operation for the Cav, and Chuck Hadley, the Cav ALO, was at their regiment. Pat was holding down 1st ROK Infantry Regiment duty while Dave dealt with me and Bill. Grier Cooper, the ALO at Miami Beach, planned to drive to Qui Nhon the next day to meet Steve, his new FAC. We 1st ROK Infantry Regiment FACs could fly from Phu Cat Air Base to Tiger Town and Qui Nhon, but the Cav and Miami Beach guys had to travel by Jeep on unkempt, and at times, treacherous roads.

I had the entire compound to myself. Everyone else would fly two, maybe three sorties today. My work day was over. I made sure mama-San had every piece of dirty laundry in my duffle bag and took a post-Dawn Patrol nap. When I woke, the place was empty, and for the first time since I left home, I wrote a few letters. Notes to Kay and mom were long overdue and would be appreciated.

I vowed to do a better job communicating.

Dave Rogers

Our four new guys and their instructors began showing up at our hooch around noon. After lunch, they headed for the flight line and their second flights of the day, this time with different Tums. We got to know one another quickly. Every waking moment we were together, hanging out at the hooch, the officer's club or flying with different guys. There wasn't a jerk in the bunch. The fighter jocks who had been turned into FACs weren't ecstatic about their new assignments, but they understood the needs of the Air Force.

The troops began showing up late in the afternoon. The last twosome to arrive was Dave Rogers and Steve Drummond, one of the F-4 jocks not too happy with his new assignment. Before they could pop a cold Schlitz, Bob Moore called from the ROK Cav Regiment operation site south and inland of Qui Nhon. He and his ROKs needed close air support. The ROKs, working with a group of U.S. Army soldiers, had uncovered a VC training complex that was a mockup of Phu Cat Air Base. Dave told Bob he and Steve were heading for the air strip and would be airborne in a few minutes.

When they arrived at the airstrip and were taxiing, Bob gave them a call. "Tum One Zero, Tum Two Three. Are you airborne?"

Dave replied, "Tum One Zero is taxiing to the runway now with Three Two in the backseat. We're cleared for takeoff."
"Good," Bob replied. "You've a set of A-1s on station two zero miles east of your location."

"Roger that," Dave replied. "We're on our way."

Dave was in a race with the setting sun and he and Steve went to work as soon as they rendezvoused with the A-1s. The fighter jocks had plenty of bombs, twenty mike-mike and nape. They expended the last of their ordnance. A flight of two F-100s, call sign Yellow Jacket showed up.

Dave asked Bob if he needed the Huns, and was told, "Hell yes, I need the Huns! If they're packin' nape, bring it on."

As it was getting dark, Dave described the target to the lead jet using certain fires to frame a reference point. He cleared Lead in hot and told him to light his afterburner when he pickled the nape, so Yellow Jacket Two could get a visual on the target. Lead's nape was right on the money, a shack. Bob was thrilled.

"Shit hot, Dave! Give us more of the same!"

Dave cleared two in hot and it was a disaster. He estimated the nape was at least thirty meters long and landed in an area close to the friendlies. Bob was quick to call off any more strikes until flares and a gunship were available

When the errant nape canisters ignited, the sky lit up with what Dave described as .50 cal machine gun fire. "The tracers were surreal, bright red jelly beans, floating up at us. They seemed to move side to side in slow motion"

Dave turned off the red and green navigation lights and headed for the coast and the bright lights of Qui Nhon. They loitered over the airport, not wanting to break contact with Bob, even though they would have been unable to return to the battle site because of the darkness. An 0-2 was on its way from to Tuy Hoa. After several minutes, Bob called to tell them the ROKs had the situation under control. Dave was surprised but relieved.

"Tum One Zero, Two Three here. Our guys and the Army troops have secured the area, thanks for the help. Drink a few beers for me, will you?"

"Roger that, Two Three."

Two clicks of the mic ended the conversation, and Dave and Steve headed for the runway.

The mood in the hooch was festive. Dave and Steve's war story mesmerized the crowd, especially us new guys. Larry Howerton had seen plenty of .50 cal up close in his role of A-1 pilot, and even he cringed as Dave described the scene.

In the early sixties, when the VC and NVA forces owned Binh Dinh Province, heavy weapons were prevalent. When General Westmoreland hired the ROKs in the mid sixties to clean out the bad guys in the Central Highlands, things changed. We received small arms fire, 7.62 mm rounds, deadly stuff but not nearly as fearsome as the Anti-Aircraft Artillery we called Triple A, weapons fired at our airmen working in higher risk areas, such as the Cambodian and Laotian borders, or the DMZ.

Most of the guys headed for the club, as there was a show scheduled, but Bill Lutz, the new 1st ROK Infantry Regiment FAC, and I hung out together on the balcony, waiting for Dave and Steve, who were taking their time showering and reliving their short, but harrowing, mission with Bob Moore. Bill, a Mississippi native who went to flight school in Georgia, and I were the same age and rank, both dark-haired, slim and happy to be working with the Tums. Bill was a Mississippi State alum, and a rabid football fan. He knew as much about Montana as I did Mississippi State, and was flabbergasted to think we had fewer than five or six thousand fans at our football games. I loved his southern accent and he was entertained by my Montana twang. The Air Force had introduced me to an exciting and diverse group of guys.

Dave showed up before Steve, and the three of us talked about our schedule. Dave and Bill were going to work a KEL site north of Phu Cat in the morning and remain at Phu Cat for a few days. I was going to fly to Phu Cat early, and Pat would take the plane back to Qui Nhon and fly with the new guys. I'd spend a few days with Bill, Dave, and the ROMADs. Rumor had it, there was going to be an offensive operation in the Qui Nhon area soon, and Dave said the ROKs might brief us on the plan.

It was incredible how often someone would say something stupid like, "Hey, have you heard the Air Force is going to send all the Bird Dogs home and we're going to be issued hot air balloons?"

When Steve arrived, we headed for the club to get something to eat. It was a sparse crowd, the entertainment was lousy, and thank goodness the lead singer didn't ask if anyone was having a birthday. There were two celebrities with a USO troupe, but weren't song and dance types. Sheila James, who played Zelda in *The Many Loves of Dobbie Gilles* sitcom, and Gary Vinson, one of Ernest Borgnine's sailors in *McHale's Navy*, joined us on the third floor for a nightcap.

Vinson, who'd been pounding down scotch nonstop at the club, asked how our inventory was holding out. He acted like it was his duty, as a big time Hollywood star, to entertain us lonely military guys. Tales of the bright lights were of little interest to us. As I listened to him do his best to impress us, I wished he could have traded places with Steve in Dave's back seat for a minute or two.

Sheila, on the other hand, got it. She'd heard enough of Vinson's babble, and asked me to show her the balcony. I jumped to attention, busting to get away from the standup comic. Their rooms were down the hall from ours and she had noticed the balcony when they checked in.

I told her I admired her work and she said the same thing to me. Gary Vinson would have never had that thought. Sheila stood on the balcony sipping cheap wine, enjoying the shimmering bay, as moving spotlights patrolled the beach. I noticed an empty beer can on the general's yard, something I'd not seen before.?

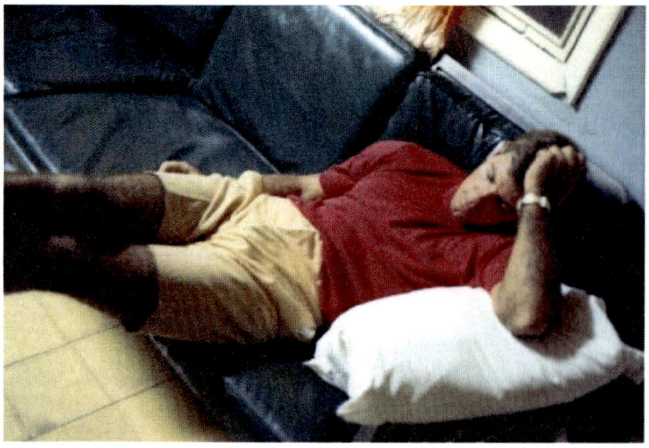

One tired Tum

Sheila and I didn't have a lot to talk about. I hoped she wouldn't want to discuss our participation in the war and it never came up. She talked about how beautiful the country was and what a good job her studio did in planning their itinerary with the USO.

When the wine and beer were gone, I walked her to her room and made a pass through the lounge. Steve was snoring on the couch and Larry and Vinson were doing their best to drink the last drop of scotch, which wasn't going to last long.

The Jeeps were full of pilots early the next morning. Mine was the only solo bird, and my mission was cake. All I had to do was deliver an O-1 to Pat at Phu Cat. The other guys were looking at two missions, directing fighters on LZ preps, or other targets of interest the ROKs wanted hit, known or suspected hot spots. I was on no schedule, so I watched the guys preflight their planes, and waited for them to get on their way, before I headed to Phu Cat.

The sprawling base was home to two squadrons of F-4s, AC-47 "Spooky" gunships, EC-47 electronic warfare birds, and C-7A Caribou, STOL aircraft that delivered life saving tactical supplies to troops in the boonies. The Air Force residents referred to the relatively new facility as Phu Cat Texas. As I slowly closed on the 10,000 foot runway, I wondered if I might see a golf course tucked in a far corner of the base.

Pat was waiting for me when I landed. He told me how to exit the base and enter the 1st ROK Regiment compound. He jumped in the Bird Dog and as he taxied toward the runway, yelled into the prop wash, "Remember about Captain Lim's Coke."

The guys met at the door of the regiment hooch and Harold showed me which single bed was mine. The beds were larger than a standard military cot, but smaller than what I remembered a single bed to be. The dormitory was tidy, but a tad mildewy. The latrine was outside.

Harold and Charlie were busy working on the radio Jeep, cleaning the four radios, inspecting the tires, making sure every detail was inspection ready. This was an everyday event. We never knew when the ROKs might blow the whistle and send a Chinook helicopter to whisk us away to a battle site. With Dave and Pat both airborne, I would be the guy to answer the bell. Dave's instructions were easy to understand, "Do whatever the ROKs tell you to do, Hale, and don't screw it up."

I enjoyed watching Harold pamper the radio Jeep. He reminded me of my high school buddy, Doug Bachman. No matter how lousy our Montana weather, his 1955 Ford never had a speck of dirt on it, in it or even under the hood. Harold asked me if I wanted to go for a shakedown cruise with him, and I jumped in the passenger's seat. We drove around the compound, waved at the Korean troops, and made a radio check with each piece of equipment, FM, VHF, HF and single side band. Harold talked to Ken at Tiger Town and every radio worked as advertised. He deemed his radio Jeep ready for combat.

Hiest knocks down a three

When we returned to the hooch a masculine, athletic looking guy, was shooting hoops on the basketball goal located twenty feet from our hooch. He was shirtless and wore a pair of gray shorts and tennis shoes. He smiled and grinned when we drove up. Harold returned his wave and said to me, "That's Captain Hiestand, an F-4 pilot in the 389th Fighter Squadron. He and Captain Rogers are pals. He hangs around here all the time. The Korean gate guards think he's one of us. You'll soon figure out he and Captain Rogers can be a bit mischievous."

I got out of the Jeep and walked over to meet the fighter jock. The fact that they were friends was an understatement. We exchanged pleasantries, and as we played several games of horse, Tom told me an incredible story.

He and Dave went to college together at the University of Portland and were roommates one year. They both enrolled in Air Force ROTC and underwent a flight instruction program like I did at the airport in Missoula. When they graduated, they both were stationed at Williams Air Force Base in Arizona, where they earned their silver wings. After Graduation, Tom became a T-37 instructor pilot, and Dave went to B-52 training at Castle Air Force Base in California.

Dave became one of seven first lieutenants chosen throughout the country to become B-52 aircraft commanders. The Strategic Air Command (SAC) wanted to know if a lieutenant could manage the responsibility of leading a B-52 combat crew carrying nuclear weapons. Would a lieutenant aircraft commander be able to earn the respect of a major or lieutenant colonel navigator? In Dave's case, it proved to be a slam dunk.

For five years, Dave and Tom didn't see or speak to one another. Their next meeting took place at the bar in the Phu Cat Air Base Officer's Club. Dave, a newcomer to Vietnam, was having a beer with the major he was going to replace as the 1st ROK Infantry Regiment ALO. Tom was at far end of the bar and Dave thought he heard Tom's voice. He peered around the crowded bar to see if it really was his buddy.

Bingo! It was his college roommate! Dave uttered some silly, college nickname just loud enough to get Tom's attention and their reunion began.

Tom kicked my ass on the basketball court and headed back to his squadron. I hung out with Harold, Charlie and Mike until we got a call from Dave letting us know he and Lutz were going to be landing soon. I picked them up at the flight line and we got back to the regiment just in time for lunch. I told Dave about meeting his buddy Tom, which he acknowledged with a belly laugh. "Hiest is a great guy. He'll be an honorary Tum one of these days if he doesn't piss me off." Another laugh told me these two guys were tight, best pals.

Bill stowed his gear next to mine, and we were ready to tackle the afternoon's agenda. Dave was intent on going over every detail involved in managing the regiment ALO responsibilities. The ROK officers would have preferred to have Dave on duty every day, but that wasn't practical. His underlings had to take a turn every now and then.

We started with a trip to the Phu Cat BX. Swen had an account at the facility and made sure the troops always had enough groceries. The Koreans at Tiger Town had a BX facility, but it lacked volume and options. Like we cared for mama-San at Qui Nhon, Dave wanted us to always share with the ROKs. Out of his own pocket, he filled a shopping cart with cigarettes, razor blades, shaving cream, magazines, candy and sodas. When we loaded the stuff in our Jeep he said, "These guys come up with some crazy, off the wall stuff they want, and we need to hook them up if we can."

When we got back to the hooch, we unloaded the loot in a special ROK pantry and headed out on foot to see if we could meet Colonel Kim, the Regiment Commander. Dave understood the Koreans and it didn't take us long to understand their strict discipline and respect for rank. Dave knew if he presented his junior officers to the Korean higher-ups in a manner that indicated he trusted us we just might be held in esteem by the ROKs. They didn't have to like us lieutenants or even speak to us, but Dave felt it necessary to give his troops every chance to be accepted by the big shots.

We went to Major Yoo's office and he remembered me from my prior visit and was very cordial. Dave told him he wanted to introduce his two new brave FACs to Colonel Kim, and hoped that would be possible. Bill and I looked at one another with looks that asked the question, *we're brave?*

Major Yoo picked up a land line and screamed Korean gibberish into the phone. The enlisted clerk at whom the Major was screaming made it happen. We walked to an adjacent building and were led into the Colonel's office. It was obvious, the Colonel was glad to see Dave.

"Ah, Captain Rogers, welcome. I am happy to see you."

With a gentle nod, Dave replied, "Thank you Colonel Kim. Sir, I am happy to present Lieutenants Hale and Lutz, 1st ROK Infantry Regiment Tum FACs."

The Colonel shook our hands firmly, and told us he was happy to know us. Dave knew, and I sensed, the meeting was over. We weren't invited to sit and chit chat. The colonel was a busy man and Major Yoo led us out of the office and sent us on our way.

When we got out of earshot Dave said, "You guys were shit hot! Colonel Kim likes you. It's time for hoops, let's go."

Following his lead, Bill and I picked up the pace and jogged back to our hooch.

We changed into our sneakers and tee shirts, and played a game of three-on-three, officers versus enlisted. Jungle rules applied. No foul unless a drop of blood hit the ground. Mike Halderman stood over six feet tall, but was no match for Dave's speed and athleticism. Bill and I figured out early that all we had to do was toss the ball to Dave and get out of the way.

A welcome timeout occurred when the Korean gate guard drove up and told Dave there was an army officer at the gate asking to see him. The driver parked in front of our hooch and out stepped a major, sporting a broad grin. He didn't have a clue who we were, at that moment we were simply basketball players.

"Gentlemen, I'm Major Koprivica. Captain Dave Rogers worked an air strike for me in support of the--"

Knowing where this conversation was going, Dave interrupted the major, offered his hand and said, "I'm Dave Rogers, Major. Let's go get a beer."

He led the way to our bar and snatched four beers from the cooler. Dave raised his Schlitz in a salute and said, "Welcome to the 1st ROK Infantry Regiment, Major."

Our guest told us his story.

"I was commanding the tanks that were blocking the end of a valley where the ROKs were conducting their operation. The squeeze was on the bad guys. When your last napalm canisters ignited, the enemy opened up on you like crazy. It was .50 cal, and I don't know how they missed you. Tracers filled the sky, and with a slight adjustment, we were able to train our big guns on the bad guy's location. We and your ROKs had their ass. I'm finishing up my second tour, and I've worked with many FACs. I've never seen one of you guys take that much of a pounding and survive. I wanted to track you down and thank you for the great hustle you gave us."

Bill and I listened to Dave give his version of the battle and both of them agreed that it was an outstanding team effort. The major said he was in a hurry and as much as he wanted another beer, had to get on the road. We stood to walk him to the front of our hooch and he paused where our three radio operators were hanging out, no doubt listening to the major talk about his and Dave's mission.

The major shook everyone's hand on the way out and thanked the ROMADs for keeping the radios up and running.

Dave served everyone a cold beer, then said, "I don't have to tell you guys how the troops on the ground, Korean, US Army or ARVN appreciate our teamwork when the cheese is binding. It's pretty neat that this guy took the time to look us up. Even though you weren't on this mission, you guys can be proud."

He didn't mention one word about himself or Steve and the part they played in protecting the ground troops.

The sun began to set on my first night at the 1st ROK Regiment. Pom fixed our evening meal, then left the Korean compound. Everyone chipped in and cleaned up the kitchen. Swen and the radio operators retired to the lounge and started a card game. Dave, Bill and I stayed in the bar and planned the schedule for the next couple of days. The three of us were going to return to Qui Nhon. Dave told me and Bill we were going to fly together back to Qui Nhon and we could flip a coin to determine who got the front seat. Dave would follow when Pat returned to the regiment.

Dave mentioned Major Koprivica's mission and the importance of being able to work air strikes at any time, day or night. He asked us, "How many Fac assignments did you have in your class?" I told him we had ten at Reese and Bill said a dozen.

"How many were O-1s?"

"I was the only one," I said. "There were two OV-10s and the rest were O-2s."

Bill's ratio was about the same.

"There you have it guys. The O-2 is coming, the Bird Dog is a goner. We won't get any OV's because they need to be in the high-risk border areas; but, the Skymaster is loaded with avionics and is an all-weather plane. The Air Force paid Cessna a boat load of cash to build these things and we'll sure as hell fly 'em. I'm convinced the O-1 is the superior FAC bird, but the O-2 drivers would argue with me."

Bill asked Dave how soon he thought the transition would take place and whether or not we would get a local checkout in the O-2 and stay with the Tums.

"I don't have a clue," he said, "but it'll be before you guys go home. That's just my opinion."

When I saw Dave check his watch, I figured it was time for us to hit the rack. It sounded like the card game was going to continue for a while.

The regiment plumbing, a relief tube and outhouse were located halfway between the hooch and basketball court. A single, underpowered light bulb illuminated an uneven, wooden walkway that led to the rudimentary facilities. Dave advised his two rookies to go together the first few trips to get used to the bumpy steps.

Dave warned us, "It's darker than dark, guys. Don't fall and bust your ass."

Bill and I walked side-by-side at a slow pace, testing the strength of each wooden plank. We didn't hold hands, but I thought about it. Bill whispered even though there was no reason to do so. I guess he thought it was the thing to do.

"Why didn't Dave or one of the guys give us a flashlight?"

I replied, also in a whisper, "I think they're giving us the business, Bill. This is some kind of fraternity bull shit."

A sudden explosion sent both of us clamoring for a piece of quivering earth to grab hold of. The deafening bam that knocked us down was the beginning of a reaction created when a Korean artilleryman, fifty yards from our outhouse, pulled the lanyard of a 155 mm howitzer aimed at a known or suspected enemy force on the west side of the base. The weapon was more than a loud noise; rather, a sudden and extreme release of high pressure, an instantly accelerating mass. The 155 mm projectile moved up the howitzer barrel and out its muzzle. This movement was accompanied by a recoil that drove everything associated with the howitzer in the opposite direction of the projectile. The bam that petrified us announced to the experienced veterans instantaneous displacement. We new guys, however, didn't have a clue about what was going on. Every molecule within range expanded and retracted. A loud, ominous *whhhooossshh* announced molecular equilibrium was returning. We two rookies, however, continued for a few moments to struggle with our balance. The earth moved under our feet.

When we wobbled to the hooch, our first move was to the cooler. We popped a beer and sat down in the bar. Dave was playing cards with the guys in the lounge. Bill and I were both thinking the same thing, *How could he have known someone would fire that damn thing at that moment?*

Bill said, "Lizard, that's the damnedest thing I've ever experienced. Both of us go to the can at the same time and almost get blown up halfway back to the hooch."

The card party was over. The guys broke up and we knew they were in on the deal. I believed the fix was in and so did Bill, but Dave having the juice to ask the Koreans to fire a howitzer at his whim, was hard to believe. The last thing he said when we slipped into bed, was "You guys always need to check your six."

That was an old fighter pilot adage emphasizing the importance of a fighter jock always knowing if an airborne foe was lurking directly behind him.

The big gun fired randomly throughout the night. With each report, I felt a bond with the bam and subsequent tingling sensation of molecular equilibrium. A good night's sleep, however, was out of the question.

The next morning, Bill won the coin toss and I jumped in the back seat. Dave wanted us to fly over every square mile of our AO. He stressed the importance of knowing every landmark on our turf. We wrapped up our sortie with a target practice session for Bill at the Old French Fort. I dropped a few smoke cans from the back seat, but was glad I hadn't been trying to identify a target. Bill made a few landings at Qui Nhon, all excellent.

After we parked, we ran into Grier Cooper and Steve, who were waiting for Buddha to check the oil in their airplane and top off the gas. We had a few minutes to talk to them and it was the first time Bill and I had the chance to meet Grier. A camera, one with a long telephoto lens, dangled from his shoulder. Like every other Tum, he was cordial, and seemed to be genuinely happy to have me and Bill, a couple of second lieutenants, on the team.

I told Grier I'd met Ted Gamlin, one of his ROMADs, at Miami Beach when I first visited Tiger Town. Ted was working at Tiger Town and we all played volley ball, enlisted versus officers, of course. Yes, jungle rules applied. Ted was distinguished, sporting horn-rimmed glasses. He'd been a ham radio operator as a kid and didn't even have to go to Air Force radio school. He asked the instructor if he could take the final exam and aced it.

Ted said it was hard for the guys to get from Miami Beach to Qui Nhon or Tiger Town. They seldom travelled the roads outside their compound because the roads were considered unsafe. They flagged down northbound choppers and asked if they could hop a ride to Qui Nhon or Tiger Town. Coop had arrived the previous day in the Miami Beach Jeep.

When Buddha extended his right index finger and twirled it over his head, a signal their plane was ready to take off, Coop said, "We'll see you guys in a couple of hours."

Grier Cooper and Rod McClellan were the only two pilots at Miami Beach and one of them had to be at regiment headquarters day and night. Steve, having some F-4 experience wouldn't take long to get qualified, and Coop had two more Tums in the pipeline, Second Lieutenant Chuck Engle and Captain Jim Cross, a Gooney Bird pilot.

Dave and Pat were in the same situation at the 1st ROK Regiment. Since they were the only qualified pilots, one of them was stuck at the regiment around the clock. Pat and Dave were pushing me and Bill and there was also another 2nd Lieutenant en route from FAC U. Joe Smith would join us within a month.

The ROK Cav Regiment had three qualified pilots, the most in any regiment. Major Hadley, the ALO, had Bob Moore and Quis, both captains and experienced FACs. Quis was going to return home in a month and Bob would be right behind him. Larry Howerton, with his recent fighter experience, would be a quick study and Second Lieutenant Dohrman Crawford was scheduled to arrive in September.

There wasn't any written test to pass or specific number of missions to fly with an experienced FAC before putting in a solo strike. The ALOs made the call with guidance from Jake and the other veterans who flew with the new guys. I flew combat missions with Rod, Dave and Jake. They each had an opinion how I would perform under pressure. It was certain that not one of us would be cleared to fly solo missions until every seasoned veteran agreed we wouldn't kill ourselves, a friendly on the ground, or a fighter jock in the air.

There were eight combat qualified Tums and three of them were always on duty at their respective regiments. The five that were available to fly stayed on the go, flying six or seven hours a day, sitting in the back seat watching rookies control fighters. After a full day they were ready for a cold beverage and so were their students. Some of the guys chose to stay in our hooch and eat at the mess hall, while others wanted to go to the O-Club and irritate the Army guys, especially on the nights they hosted USO shows.

Early one evening, when the guys were getting ready to take the short walk to the club, Jake asked me to tell him one more time the name of my home town. He had a hard time remembering "Missoula." When I told him for the umpteenth time, he snapped his fingers and said, "By golly, I'll never forget it again! We're going to change the words of the Oklahoma fight song, and chant our way to the club." When we assembled on the walkway, Jake began humming the Okie fight song and the guys picked it up right away.

When we began our short trek Jake began chanting, "Zoo la zoo la, zoo la zoo la, zoo la zoo la, zoo la ZOO ZOO ZOO!"

I cringed and hoped there weren't any Oklahoma fans in the audience. The ironic thing about the Army officer's disdain for us was that we would have flown through hell's back yard to save their ass, just as we would for our Korean soldiers. The Army officers we lived with were known as Rear Echelon Mother Fuckers (REMFs) and didn't know any better. They pushed paper, not the elements of war. Major Koprivica would have straightened them out in a heartbeat, but he was living in the boonies with his tanks and troops. He thought we Air Force types were pretty shit hot.

The committee of Dave, Jake and Rod cleared me to direct fighters after eight dual missions. My first solo strike was a KEL, with Elect Two One my lead F-100. Our target was in a steep valley in the Phu Cat Mountains, not far from the coast. I was on station thirty minutes before our rendezvous time, pinpointed the target and flew east, feet wet.

"Tum One Four, Liter Two One's on station. How do you read? Over."

"Liter Two One, Tum One Four reads you loud and clear. I'm an O-1 on the coast ten miles north of Phu Cat."

"Roger that, Tum. I've got you in sight. We're ready for you."

With that simple radio transmission, my nervous anticipation vanished. Not once did I think about my backseat being empty. My head was on a swivel. I never lost sight of the F-100s and constantly searched for signs of ground fire or enemy activity. I hoped for a secondary explosion with each bomb that the F-100s dropped, but the mission proved to be a dry run. It was, however, well executed. Ace would have approved. Me working a set of fighters without a senior FAC in the back seat was certainly not a big deal. With all the training I'd received at Holly Field, then with Ace and now with these seasoned Tums, if I couldn't do it now I never would.

I was finished for the day. The others, Bill, Steve, Larry and Snidely, were going to fly twice. The ROKs always had several known and suspected enemy locations they wanted hit with air power and one of the regiments was always planning an offensive operation and needed landing zone prep work done. When Pat and Bill finished their second flight of the day, Pat returned to Phu Cat.

Eleven

The ROKs Take a Hit

Dave arrived from the regiment late in the afternoon and wanted to spend some time with me and Bill. To get away from the noise of eight rowdy pilots discussing the missions they'd flown, we hid out in one of the bedrooms. Our boss had a tragic story to share with us.

Unbeknownst to the ROKs, who'd maintained a threat-free environment in the port city of Qui Nhon for three years, a local VC force had established an underwater demolition team. Recently, on the north end of Qui Nhon, along an estuary known as the Mud Flats, the VC made their move. They stayed hidden under water when the tide was in, breathing through bamboo air tubes. When the tide was out, they targeted power barges moored in the bay to provide electrical power to the military installations in Qui Nhon.

A Korean squad was dispatched to uncover and destroy the upstart force. Five ROK soldiers were ambushed, their bodies dismembered and displayed in the local area, an act of terror to intimidate the locals. The ROKs were furious.

In the summer of 1965, when the first US Army combat units arrived in Vietnam, virtually the entire Binh Dinh Provence was controlled by North Vietnamese Army and Viet Cong forces. The Tiger Division deployed to Vietnam in the fall of 1965 and came ashore in Qui Nhon. They joined forces with the US Army's 1st Cavalry and an ARVN unit.

Their mission was to clear the Province of enemy forces. The ROKs provided security for Lane Army Air Field and the 161st Helicopter Assault Company. They went into the field together, fought as one, and when I arrived in Qui Nhon the area was secure, or so I thought. The five Korean soldiers were butchered a half mile from where our Bird Dogs were parked.

Captain Lim told Dave that a Korean major general (two star) and several senior officers stationed at the Headquarters of the Republic of Korea Force, Vietnam, in Nha Trang, had flown to Tiger Town. The speculation was that a few high ranking officers had been relieved of their duties and additional demotions were likely to follow. The Korean generals were humiliated and more officers would likely suffer their wrath.

Dave, being the 1st ROK Infantry Regiment ALO, would be advised of every move the ROKs would make in planning a retaliatory strike and the wheels were already turning.

Dave didn't have any specifics on the timing of an offensive strike, but he had already made a plan for our regiment. He gave me and Bill the scoop.

"Captain Lim told me there will be a major attack beginning tomorrow and the ROKs are going to set up a site on a hill overlooking Qui Nhon and the Mud Flats. Bernie, you and Harold are going to man the TOC. Pat is going to be in the air, and I'm going to monitor everything on the ground. I'll communicate with Major Yoo and be available to spell Pat if he needs a break. I'll be staying in Qui Nhon and there will always be a Bird Dog on the ramp loaded with gas and Willie Petes, ready to launch. Bernie, If the mission goes on for two or three days, you, Pat and I will swap roles. Everybody will get in on the action. Harold will drive the radio jeep to the TOC tomorrow morning. Any questions?"

Bill and I looked at one another and slowly moved our heads from side to side. In unison we said, "No, sir."

Aussie Band

Dave replied, "Shit hot. Let's go see what the guys are doing. I'm hungry."

As we walked to the balcony, I thought about Dave's briefing. It was like I'd just listened to a coach give his team a game plan and pep talk. He understood every eventuality that could take place and instilled in his players the confidence needed to execute the plays. The balcony was packed and the beer flowed. Jake let us know there was a show at the club, an Aussie band.

All the new guys were describing the missions they'd flown. I thought Dave might let everyone know about the upcoming operation that would take place a short distance from where we were standing, but he didn't bring it up. Everyone would know about it soon enough. Larry launched an empty Schlitz can toward the general's yard, but it hit one of several electrical cables and fell short.

We formed up and chanted our way to the club, ordered burgers and beers, and watched the Aussies put on their show, which was outstanding. The USO had booked a real looker who hit it big a few years ago as the "Dodge Girl," a spokeswoman for their line of cars.

Maintaining our grip on the Army-sponsored talent, the USO folks joined us on the balcony after the show. Listening to the Aussie accent was a treat. The guys were enjoying our company and I was not surprised when the Dodge Girl took a shine to Dave.

Somehow, Army Captain Miriam McKinney, the general's drop-dead gorgeous aide-de-camp, appeared on our balcony. She trumped the Dodge Girl by a mile. Larry discovered her room was on our floor, at the far end of the hall and invited her to join us for a drink. None of us had ever seen her. Leave it to Larry.

Captain McKinney had a few beers and left. It wasn't that she didn't like our company, it was obvious she did, but the captain knew it would be professional suicide to get caught mingling with the enemy. I was glad Larry didn't launch a beer can at the general's hooch while she was with us. It wasn't easy, but Dave convinced the Dodge Girl we fly boys had to get some sleep.

I was up early, eager to get to the TOC in Qui Nhon. Our radio operators in Tiger Town and the 1st ROK Infantry Regiment had been in contact with each other and the DASC in Nha Trang. All parties understood the importance of having fighter support available for our ROKs as long as they needed it and it was the DASC's responsibility to have fighters readily available for Pat. Captain Lim, Lieutenant Youn and Harold arrived early and Dave and I were there to greet them.

Bernie and Harold's operation

Harold checked all his radios and I confirmed with Airman Montague in Tiger Town, what we were told earlier that the DASC would have plenty of fighters available. Navy SEALs were in our corner, though we never saw one of them. Their mission was to monitor the perimeter of the Mud Flats and intercept bad guys trying to evade the ROKs. Our Naval liaison officer, Lieutenant Mike Nelson, arrived in his own Jeep. Korean Marines, stationed in I-Corps, were also part of the offensive force and a formidable one it was.

I was in awe of the Koreans. Their tenacity, discipline, respect for one another and commitment to their mission was overwhelming. They wouldn't have fought any harder had they been on their homeland. On a contrasting note,

Airman Montague had been told by the on-duty Korean Operations Officer that an ARVN unit was supposed to fortify the eastern perimeter, but they never showed up. They were content to have us and the ROKs fight their battle for them. I wondered if that attitude prevailed throughout their entire country.

The artillery troops went to work before dawn the next morning. It was a substantial wakeup call. Harold and I leapt out of our cots. Dozens of flares were launched, lighting up the Mud Flats and the surrounding territory. The ROKs didn't give us specific instructions or requests, but Harold and I knew we'd better be ready to go to work.

Lieutenant Youn appeared at our Jeep sporting a broad, toothy grin. He looked like Bucky Beaver, the Ipana toothpaste character I remembered from my childhood. The lieutenant was dressed for battle: holstered .38 pistol, knife, jungle boots and AR-15 automatic rifle. He didn't say one word, just nodded a few times. I called the hooch and told Pat the game was on and he'd better get an early breakfast and be ready to launch soon. I expected we'd be ordering a set of fighters before long.

Other than the sound of flares being fired I heard nothing. When the sun peeked above the horizon, the artillery guys silenced their Howitzers and all was calm, mysteriously quiet. Harold chattered nonstop, as did the radio guys in Colonel Kim's command center. I had Beanie-Weenies and pound cake for breakfast, my last meal for a while.

The battle began mid morning. Artillery kicked it off with multiple howitzer salvos to the north and the ROKs requested air support. Suddenly a flight of two F-100s arrived overhead. The ROKs, in the tent next to our Jeep, gave us target coordinates which were passed to Pat. He identified the target area and fired a Willie Pete. The ROKs confirmed the target, and the fight was on.

Huey helicopters swarmed about, inserting troops. A flight of F-100s circled above the battle site, waiting their turn to put their weapons on Pat's targets. An occasional lull in the action gave the ROKs time to analyze what was taking place. As the battle moved around the area, strategic adjustments were made and new targets were identified. The moments of brief downtime allowed Pat to fly to the air strip in Qui Nhon, not always to refuel, but to fill the rocket tubes with Willie Petes.

Pat was in the air ten hours and fired sixty-four rockets. He didn't have any idea how many sets of fighters he controlled, but said most of them were F-100s out of Tuy Hoa. He had one set of AT-37s show up. They were the attack version of the Tweet we flew at flight school. They didn't carry as much ordnance as the bigger jets, but were very accurate. While South Vietnamese pilots could fly this small fighter, a USAF pilot was required to be in each flight.

At times communication could be a problem. During the strike Dave saw two Tweets flying directly at one another, a midair collision waiting to happen. He couldn't hear the radio chatter, but the Vietnamese pilot who was flying the wrong direction continued straight ahead. The Air Force Tweet driver obviously sent him home.

All afternoon Dave was prepared to give Pat a breather but he refused. He would finish what he started. When I had the opportunity to talk to Pat he told me it wasn't necessarily a dangerous mission, but a very rewarding one. He said, "Today I felt like I did more for the war effort than any other day."

As the sun began to fade, Lieutenant Youn approached Colonel Kim's tent and I noticed his muddy uniform. He spent several minutes with Captain Lim and a few other officers, then walked over to our Jeep. He hadn't said more than a handful of words to me since we met, but now his hair was on fire. He couldn't speak fast enough in his clipped English.

"Lieutenant Hale, I have story. Today we have three VC prisoners. Need to know where VC hide. Maybe in Mud Flat caves, we not know. I go with VC in helicopter. Ask where VC hide. VC no tell. OOH, OOH (rhymes with coo)! One VC pushed out! One more VC pushed out! Other VC show Korean soldier where is cave."

At this point, with eyes bulging, on the verge of hyperventilating, I thought he might pass out he was so excited.

"I take Korean soldiers in cave. I see VC. VC have hand bomb! OOH, OOH! Much danger!"

With an extended thumb and index finger he created a pistol and mimicked his fatal shots. With a sense of urgency, he fired his make believe weapon twice. He took a deep breath, and exclaimed, "Lieutenant Hale, I kill VC."

Harold and I were speechless. The phrase "OOH, OOH, much danger" became part of our vocabulary.

The howitzers were quiet all night. Early in the morning, Captain Lim told us the Koreans would stay one, maybe two more days. They had gathered extensive intelligence and planned to thoroughly sanitize the area. Harold and I had to be with them if an airstrike was requested.

Dave, Pat and Jake drove to the operation site in the afternoon. The Korean brass couldn't have been more gracious in thanking Pat for the outstanding job he did in destroying every target the Koreans identified. Pat's performance earned him the Distinguished Flying Cross.

Harold and I were told we could return to Phu Cat the following day, but the drama of the Mud Flats mission wasn't over for Dave. He was told by the ROKs he had to attend a meeting at the Mud Flats three days after the operation concluded and he briefed me on the get-together.

"Hale, this is incredible. A four star general from PACAF (Pacific Air Forces) flew in from Hawaii and met with me, a couple of Korean Generals and a handful of colonels. This tall, square-jawed guy was full of himself. He wore fatigues that were starched stiff, spit-shined boots, and get this--on his belt he had two pistols adorned with pearl-handled grips.

The issue that brought the general all the way from Waikiki was his understanding that this specific region had been sanitized two weeks before by ARVN forces. I explained to the general that VC soldiers lived among Qui Nhon residents, and the only way to deal with them was to ask the ROKs to eliminate them, which would be an endless struggle. They weren't going away. This is one screwed up war we got ourselves into, Bernie."

I enjoyed camping out with Harold and the Koreans. I learned how demanding the ROKs could be when their troops were threatened and the importance of being aware of everything that was going on at any moment. Harold and I were an integral part of the team and I looked forward to my next operation.

"Listen here, General..."

Twelve

"Saddle Up Cowboys"

It was late September and with three exceptions all our FACs were qualified, which made Jake's life as the scheduler much easier. We had three new second lieutenants and one captain in the pipeline. They were the last Bird Dog pilots to be assigned to the Tums. Dave's prediction would come true in October, when our first O-2 was scheduled to arrive. Colonel Wis assigned a second lieutenant to each regiment. Dohrman Crawford went to the ROK Cav Regiment, Joe Smith to the 1st ROK Infantry Regiment and Chuck Engle to the 26th ROK Regiment at Miami Beach along with Captain Jim Cross, a former C-47 pilot.

The first of these newcomers to arrive was Dohrman. He'd gone from the TASS to Tiger Town and bypassed Qui Nhon. He was close to getting qualified and moving to the Cav. Colonel Wis liked for each of us to visit Tiger Town occasionally, as he was all about teamwork and camaraderie. It was at Jake's bar I met Dohrm.

I entered the hooch late one afternoon, skirted around the bar and walked down the hallway, looking for a place to stash my gear. I planned to stay two nights. Jake was to schedule a mission for me each day before I returned to Qui Nhon. I tossed my bag in an empty room and walked back to the bar.

Jake, Colonel Wis, Ken, Jim and Gary, three of our radio operators, occupied the place. Jake got me a beer and the guys welcomed me back to Tiger Town. Dohrm stood and introduced himself. His dark hair curled a bit and a genuine grin lit up his face. He said he was glad to finally meet the Lizard. Dohrm and I traded *"Where ya from? Where'd ya go to flight school?"* stories and compared notes on our experiences at FAC U and the TASS. I asked if he flew with Ace, and he said he hadn't. Everyone who spent any time at Phan Rang eventually mentioned the Officer's Club on the hill, where one could see the air strikes that took place almost every evening. With Jake, Colonel Wis and the enlisted guys listening intently to every word, Dohrm told a story he swore came from a reliable source.

"A group of Army officers got drunk and rowdy. When the club's officer, an Air Force captain, realized their inebriated and obnoxious condition was out of control, told them to leave and never come back. Well, come back they did. With their commanding officer, a colonel, driving a Jeep that pulled a howitzer loaded with a 105 mm artillery shell.

The colonel drove up the steps to the entrance of the club and stuck the nose of the howitzer in the door. He told everyone present he would blow the fucking place off the hill if his soldiers weren't invited back in. You could have heard a Kleenex hit the floor. One of two majors, both F-100 jocks, eased over to the club's officer, who looked like he was about to faint, and whispered in his ear, 'Captain, check out the colonel's eyes. I think it would be in everyone's best interest, especially yours, if you would buy our Army guests a round of drinks.' The club officer nodded and asked the colonel what his men would like to drink."

It wasn't long until I heard Dohrm serenade the crowd with a chorus of *Mary Ann Burns*, one of many bawdy songs in his repertoire. He wasn't full of beer, rather, intent on having a good time. That was a priority for Dohrm. I asked Jake if I could take Dohrm on my flight in the morning and he said it would be a good idea because it was an Agent Orange mission. We didn't have that many opportunities to work with the C-123 defoliation pilots. I asked Dohrm if he wanted to tag along and he said, "Hell yes, I want to go!"

In the morning we met with Jake and he gave us a briefing on our mission. Highway 19 was a major supply route from Qui Nhon to Pleiku. Military convoys were commonplace on the mountainous road and there was always the threat of an ambush. We were going to define a stretch of terrain that ran east to west in an area not far from the ROK Cav Regiment.

The C-123 Providers were twin engine military airlift planes manufactured by Fairchild and their missions required precise teamwork. The C-123s, known as Ranch Hands, flew in flights of three at tree top levels so their defoliant would be highly concentrated when it covered the jungle surface. Consequently, they were susceptible to ground fire. A second FAC flew behind the flight of C-123s and if their aircraft received enemy fire, he would mark the area with a smoke can. There was always a set of fighters on station ready to defend the helpless C-123s. Snidley Whiplash would be on station with me and Dohrm.

My job was to mark the start and stop coordinates for the Ranch Hands. In order for me to be able to mark the stop point before the first Ranch Hand reached the finish line, I had to be going as fast as I could. When flying level, our max speed was no more than ninety knots, not nearly enough to win the race to the finish line. I climbed to four thousand feet and when we saw the Ranch Hands on the horizon, I put our Bird Dog in a steep dive with full power and we hauled ass to the first set of coordinates. When we reached the start point, I fired a Willie Pete and heard the lead Ranch Hand announce to his flight of three C-123s in a cool, calm, Clint Eastwood-like, command, "Saddle up, cowboys."

We flew to the end of the targeted area as fast as our O-1 would go and I fired a Willie Pete as the C-123s approached the end of their mission. When they flew through my smoke, their work was over.

Neither Snidley nor the Ranch Hands took any enemy ground fire, but we Tums had a flight of F-100s circling above prepared to defend our unarmed brothers.

Dohrm and I had a great time flying together and I asked Jake if we could fly the Dawn Patrol in the morning and then go to Qui Nhon.

"Dohrm's going to be heading to the Cav soon and he may never get a chance to see our digs at Qui Nhon. Besides, he needs to meet the rest of the guys."

Jake agreed and early the next morning I jumped in the back seat and we toured our AO looking for signs of trouble. We landed in Qui Nhon three hours later.

Dohrm was scheduled to fly a second mission, a KEL, with Rod…his last flight. He was going home. Every time I flew with Rod I was at ease, just like with Ace.

I hated to see Rod leave because he was a great guy and instrumental in my early training, but I was happy he was going home. We planned to send him off with a rousing farewell at the club.

I had the rest of the day off. Mama-San worked on my laundry and I wrote home to let mom and Kay know I was doing fine. Kay would be happy to know her banana bread was everyone's favorite. Dave was in charge of getting our mail and we all shared our care packages.

Mail Call

An MP walked by my room, stopped and said, "Three Koreans are at the gate asking to see Lieutenant Hale. Is he here?"

"That's me, I'll be right down."

I slipped into a flight suit, walked down to the gate and met Captain Lim and two enlisted men I didn't know. The guard let them enter the compound and when they got out of their Jeep, I felt faint. I knew I was in trouble because Captain Lim was carrying a Sears and Roebuck catalog. Like we always did with mama-San, we spoiled the Koreans by buying them toiletries, candy, sodas and cigarettes, but this shopping list was a doozie.

"Ah, Lieutenant Hale. I am happy to see you," said my friend, Captain Lim.

He introduced me to his driver and the other soldier, then explained his mission.

"Lieutenant Hale, General Jo (a Tiger Town big shot) has special request for you."

Captain Lim opened the catalogue to the first of two pages marked with a note pad and pointed to a Hammond Organ. Not a child's toy or small keyboard, this was an instrument that appeared to be like the one in Lawrence Welk's orchestra. The captain had a look of glee on his face and quickly flipped to the second bookmark. It was a color TV. No small portable set, but a large wooden console, like the ones that could fill up a small living room. They came in pine, oak and maple.

The general wanted maple.

I thought Captain Lim had finished, but he said, "One more thing, Lieutenant Hale." His driver handed Captain Lim a magazine. When I saw what it was, I thought, *Oh no, it's a girlie magazine, the XXX kind. The general's going to want me to order a subscription.*

Captain Lim spoke as he pointed to the back cover. The full page advertisement offered inflatable dolls. "Lieutenant Hale, General Jo like American blonde woman very much." The dolls came in red heads, brunettes, and of course, the general's favorite.

There was no way I could fill the general's order. The blonde doll perhaps, but it would have to ship to me and the guys would never believe it was for a Korean general. I was toast. I had to say something to these three ROKs who were giving me the Cheshire Cat routine.

"Captain Lim, it is not possible to ship anything like a TV or organ to Vietnam. The items would have to be crated and I don't know how I would pay for the shipping and..."

He interrupted me, "No problem, Lieutenant Hale," as he dug into his uniform pocket. "I have U.S. dollars for you. Sears send to Korea, not Vietnam."

If the gate guard would have seen the wad of greenbacks he flashed, I would have gone straight to jail. I could see the headlines, 'Air Force pilot turned black-marketeer sent to Leavenworth for thirty years.'

I walked to the gate and told the guard I was going to take my guests up to our quarters for a soda. When we got upstairs, I passed sodas around (they didn't make me ask three times) and did my best to convince them I would do anything for my Korean friends, but didn't know how to place the order for the general. Captain Lim was not going to accept my explanation, so I finally said, "Captain Lim, Captain Rogers will be here tonight. He will know what to do."

"Ah, Lieutenant Hale. Thank you, thank you. I will visit you and Captain Rogers tomorrow."

When Dave arrived that evening, I filled him in on what happened.

"You told him what?" Rogers bellowed.

"I had to tell him something, Rog. It's the Korean rank thing. I'm a lowly second lieutenant and he's a captain. I told him I had no idea how to make it happen, but he wouldn't take no for an answer."

As I knew he would, Dave convinced Captain Lim we couldn't do business with Sears while in Vietnam.

Thank goodness the blowup blonde was never mentioned.

Thirteen

Cave Mission

When the day's flying and debriefing were over, Jake called everyone to happy hour on the balcony and the beginning of Rod's retirement party. After a few drinks, we walked to the club for dinner and ordered champagne for our departing Tum. We were not treated to a USO show, so we didn't hang around long after we ate. The atmosphere was much more cordial and lively on our balcony. Jake quieted the crowd and shouted,

"Lets say goodbye to Tum Three One!"

The crowd screamed, "Goodbye, ass hole!"

Jake bellowed, "Lets say goodbye to the ass hole!"

The crowd yelled, "Goodbye Tum Three One! Himmm, himmm, fuuuck himmm!"

The ritual of the Him, like a tired Bob Hope joke, never failed to bring the house down. I hoped the general's windows were shut.

Dave and I both had early wakeup calls, so we wanted to hit the rack. Dave was leaving early for an operation in the northern part of our AO and he wanted me to be on station in case the ROKs needed an airstrike. Charlie Amonett would be his ROMAD.

When Dave and I snuck out of the balcony, Dohrm was serenading the crowd with a chorus of *The Balls of O'Leary* in an Irish accent that would have watered Saint Patrick's eyes.

My midmorning flight to the Phu Cat Mountains was uneventful, but Dave and Charlie didn't have it so easy. When one of the three regiments went into the field to conduct an offensive operation, a Tum Fac and a ROMAD went with them. The ROMAD drove our MRC-108 radio Jeep into the bowels of an Army Chinook (Hook) helicopter.

Twin 60 foot rotors, each powered by a 3,750 horse power turbo shaft engine, powered these war birds. They were flown by baby-faced Army warrant officers and they supported troop movements and delivered supplies throughout Vietnam. A loadmaster secured our Jeep with chains, and we sat in our vehicle, white-knuckled, unable to see outside the chopper or communicate over the roar of the engines.

Most of the landings were on flat terrain but occasionally the pilot had to offload equipment, troops, or in our case a Jeep, on uneven ground. In this instance, the landing zone was so narrow there wasn't enough room for the pilot to place both the forward and aft landing gear on firm ground, a challenge for the best of pilots. That was the case for this chopper pilot who was taking Dave and Charlie to the ROK's operation site. To make matters worse, they began taking small arms fire.

The helicopter pilot and his crew maintained their composure despite the pinging sounds made by bullets bouncing off the chopper. They focused on offloading their passengers and Jeep so they could quickly get out of harm's way. While the flight crew seemed to have ice water in their veins, Charlie panicked and attempted to back the Jeep out of the chopper. Fortunately, the pilot had not told the loadmaster to release the tie-downs on the vehicle, or my buddies would have taken a potentially fatal ride down a steep hillside. It took the pilot a few tries, but he made a safe touchdown.

They set up their camp next to the Korean TOC and began preparing for action. The Phu Cat Mountains were beautiful and majestic, but treacherous. Steep, thick jungle terrain hindered the ROK's mobility and provided a safe haven for the bad guys. I located Dave's position and flew east toward the coast, so not to draw attention to me or the Koreans, even though the enemy had to know something was up because of the activity that took place the last few days when the ROKs were moving in.

I'd been in the air thirty minutes when Dave called to tell me Charlie had requested a set of fighters, and a flight of two F-100s were on their way. Their call sign was Limit and their ETA was two zero minutes out. Dave gave me the coordinates for our target, which I quickly identified. It was in a small ravine surrounded with steep, jungle-covered mountains.

Limit flight checked in right on time.

"Tum One Four, Limit Two One. How do you read? Over."

I responded to his radio call and gave him my location. I made visual contact and copied his lineup of 750 pound Mark 117s, nape and guns. I briefed him on our mission.

"Limit Two One, we have friendlies two klicks south of your current position. They're on the high ground on a plateau and the bad guys are due north of the friendlies. Your pattern will be east to west. If you take ground fire, bail out south over the friendlies if you can't make it to Phu Cat. Let me know when you identify the friendlies and we'll get started."

The fighter jock told me he saw the general location of our friendlies and took up an east to west pattern. I flipped the radio toggle switch and told Dave we were ready to put in a mark.

Dave replied, "Roger that, One Four. Stand by."

I acknowledged and waited for clearance to put in a Willie Pete. Dave was conferring with the ROKs. There were good and bad guys moving around in the same real estate and we had to make sure we knew who was who. When Dave confirmed the coordinates he cleared me to put in a mark and said he wanted single bombs first.

"Limit Two One, Tum One Four is in with a mark. Give us single bombs first."

Limit acknowledged, "Roger that Tum, I've got you in sight."

I pulled the throttle back, dove toward the target, centered my grease pencil mark on the target and fired a Willie Pete. It was right on the nose and as I pulled up looking for Limit Lead, Dave said, "Tum One Four hold your fighters."

I acknowledged and told Limit Lead to hold at altitude. Something was wrong. My Willie Pete was dead on the coordinates I'd been given.

I was surprised when Dave told me I had missed the target by a large margin. I read back the coordinates, which Dave confirmed, and verified the target by comparing the terrain to that on my map. It was an easy match because of two tall peaks a short distance away. They stuck out on my map like flashing lights.

I radioed Dave, "Tum One Zero, Tum One Four, I've confirmed the coordinates. Your guys are wrong. Ask them where they want the air support in relationship to my mark and be advised, the dense foliage opens up to a rocky area about a klick north of my mark. Perhaps they could use that landmark for a reference, over."

"Roger that," Dave replied. "Stand by."

"Limit One Two, Tum One Four, over."

"Go ahead Tum."

"Limit One Two, we're having trouble confirming the location of the friendlies. Stand by for another mark."

Lead responded with two clicks of his mic as Dave called.

"Tum One Four, One Zero. Give us a mark thirty meters due north of your smoke."

I replied, "Roger that. I'm in with a mark."

As I dove toward the jungle floor, I talked to the lead Hun, "Limit One Two, Tum One Four is rolling in with a mark."

Two clicks on the mic told me the fighter jock understood and could see me.

I estimated thirty meters from the first Willie Pete, fired a smoke rocket and crossed my fingers. We struck out again. Dave told me it was not a good mark.

"One Four, our guys are struggling. This mark is too close to the friendlies. Stand by."

I called our fighter jock. "Limit One Two, Tum One Four, stand by for confirmation. Over."

"We understand, Tum," Limit Lead replied.

I spoke to Dave, "I've got an idea, One Zero. I'm going to plot the coordinates of the rocky area that's about a klick north of the mark the ROKs just refused. If they will clear me to fire on it, we might be able to establish a starting place. What do you think?"

Dave replied, "Anything is better than what we're doing now. Stand by."

I told Limit Lead we might be going farther north and he replied, "No sweat. We can stay with you for another hour."

I flew toward the rocky area and it appeared be a small cave opening. I noted the coordinates, gave them to Dave and said, "Rog, this might be the jackpot. I hope the ROKs will let us hit it."

The ROKs approved the strike, I put in a Willie Pete on the target and when Limit One Two dropped a seven-hundred-and-fifty pound bomb on the rocky surface, everybody went nuts. Obviously that was the area they wanted hit all along.

Dave screamed in his mic, "One Four, that's it! That's our target!"

Immediately, small arms fire erupted from a densely wooded area northeast of the rocky surface. Limit One Two saw the ground fire I did and I cleared him in hot. Both Hun drivers expended twenty-mike-mike on the source of the incoming rounds, which was quickly silenced. My heart pounded and I was jinking like crazy. Rod would have been proud.

I moved Limit's bombs around the rocky area, which exposed a cave entrance. Korean soldiers, engaged with an enemy force south of the caves, were advancing rapidly. By the time Limit Flight was bingo fuel the ROKs had control of the area. I had plenty of fuel and buzzed Dave, Charlie and the ROKs at the TOC on my way home. It wasn't a textbook operation, but we got the job done and no friendlies were harmed. I was in the air two hours and thirty minutes.

Dave and Charlie stayed with the ROKs two more days, but additional air strikes weren't required. Our troops were active and captured several POWs, one a young VC woman, another a seasoned NVA soldier. The caves contained medical supplies, cots, sewing machines, bags of rice, weapons and ammunition.

Fourteen

Bloody October

I always felt if I was destined to be severely injured, it would take place not in an aircraft, but while on an operation with the ROKs. My training at Snake School taught me that the jungle was unforgiving. Combine the natural hazards inherent in that environment with a shooting war, and it's not a warm and fuzzy place to hang out.

On the evening of October 12th, 1969, Sergeant Ted Gamlin was in the field with Captain Grier Cooper and the ROK 26th regiment at Miami Beach. Their TOC was located on a hill east of, and not far from, Tuy Hoa. As darkness engulfed the operation site, an unrelenting mortar barrage began. Several Koreans and Coop were seriously injured. Ted received shrapnel wounds, but was able to assist in the rescue of the wounded.

Ted had line of sight radio contact to the base at Tuy Hoa which enabled him to use the VHF and FM radios to communicate with Dust Off, an Army helicopter unit, whose mission was rescue. Ted directed the choppers to their location, but the landing zone was too hot for Dust Off to land. Ted illuminated an alternate landing site with flares and directed the chopper pilot down. Ted carried several seriously wounded Koreans to safety and once the chopper landed, stacked them like cordwood on the floor of the Huey helicopter.

When Ted thought he had all the wounded aboard and the Huey began elevating for takeoff, he turned and saw Coop standing nearby in a state of shock. Blood flowed from his ears, nose and chest. Ted signaled for the pilot to stand by and tossed Coop onto the bodies in the chopper. Dust Off made an uneventful takeoff and Coop survived. Several ROKs did not.

When Coop arrived at the hospital at Cam Ranh Bay, we Tums were safe in our Army compound, winding down after the day's flying when the phone rang. Dave answered and Colonel Wis gave him the bad news, "All I can tell you is Coop and Ted's TOC took a major hit early this evening and they're both wounded. Coop's in the Cam Ranh hospital and Ted is being treated at their regiment. Several ROKs were injured, but I don't know if there were any fatalities. There's nothing you guys can do. I'll call when I have more news."

We were stunned. Steve Drummond wanted to get in a Jeep and drive to Miami Beach to be with his regiment, but like Ted told me when we met at Tiger Town, the road to and from Qui Nhon was dangerous, especially at night. Had it been daylight, we might have been able to assist somehow, but all we could do was wait to hear from Colonel Wis.

The morning news was good. Both Ted and Coop would recover, but Coop was on his way to a medical facility in the Philippines. Colonel Wis told Dave one of the ROMADs at Miami Beach would deliver Coop's belongings and Dave was instructed to have a crate constructed for shipment.

The next day, Dave and I packed all of Coop's stuff in two duffle bags, taking special care to secure his photography equipment. Knowing Coop had been given a good chance to fully recover was encouraging, but the act of packing and shipping the belongings of a wounded comrade was sobering.

Colonel Wis recommended Ted receive the Silver Star for his heroic actions. It was later upgraded to the Air Force Cross, our country's second highest military award. The synopsis from the "Combat Leadership website" reads:

The President of the United States of America, authorized by Title 10,Section 8742, United States Code, awards the Air Force Cross to Sergeant Theodore R. Gamlin, United States Air Force for extraordinary heroism as a radio operator in operations in Southeast Asia. Sergeant Gamlin was trying to coordinate the evacuation of several wounded soldiers in the Vietnamese jungle on the evening of October 12, 1969. He'd been hit by enemy gun fire himself, but disregarded his wounds to help others. After Sergeant Gamlin had made contact with the rescuers, he went to the landing site and illuminated it so the pilot would know precisely where to land. When the helicopter landed, Sergeant Gamlin helped carry the wounded soldiers to it. He refused to leave with them, choosing to fight side-by-side with those remaining for the rest of the night.

In attendance for the awards ceremony at the Pentagon were General Russell, Vice Chief of Staff; General Holloway, commander of SAC; and most important to Ted, Lieutenant Colonel Frank Wisneski.

With Coop recuperating in the Philippines, the guys at Miami Beach had their hands full. Steve Drummond was the only qualified Tum. Their two new guys, Chuck Engle and Jim Cross, had just arrived.

Second Lieutenant Chuck Engle was right out of flight school. He had the chiseled body of a wrestler, thick black hair, ebony eyes and a dark complexion one would expect from a guy who grew up on an Indian reservation. Chuck made it clear he wanted to fly all day, every day. He was an excellent pilot, perhaps a little reckless, but the guy was born to fly.

Chuck Engel (left) and Jim Cross

Captain Jim Cross came to us from a C-47 Gooney Bird assignment. He was a heavyset, cordial guy, very quiet and reserved. He grew up in Ohio and was fascinated by politics. He never took to the soap box, but it was obvious he longed for a career in that arena.

Colonel Wis made sure Steve and the guys at Miami Beach had support from the other outfits, and Jake's mission was to get Chuck and Jim qualified as soon as possible. Dohrm was checked out and flying combat missions in support of the Cav. Our two new guys, Chuck and Jim, along with Second Lieutenant Joe Smith, who had yet to arrive at the 1st Regiment, were the last O-1 pilots we would have. I flew two flights with Chuck, and told anyone who would listen to me that he was ready to solo. I went up with Jim only once and didn't have a feel for how he was progressing.

Nineteen days after Coop, Ted and the Miami Beach ROKs were pounded with mortars, another event took place that left Colonel Wis somewhat stressed.

Fifteen

Evicted

When Dave and I happened to be in Qui Nhon at the same time we always seemed to end up bunking together in the room next to the lounge. This given night was no exception. The guys who weren't spending time at their respective regiments or at Tiger Town with Colonel Wis and his staff started to arrive late in the afternoon. Tales of the day's missions were swapped, letters read and written, showers and naps taken.

When we were refreshed, the allure of a stage show drew us to the club. The burgers were okay. The entertainment? Not so much. We didn't, however, hit the rack early. For days Larry had struggled with not being able to launch a beer can with the accuracy he wanted. He was a fighter pilot and anything less than a shack was unacceptable. That evening, he figured out that an inch of beer left in the bottom of a Schlitz can served as ballast and was the answer to an accurate toss. For the first time, the general's yard took a few solid hits. To make matters worse Captain McKinney was enticed to visit the Tums for a nightcap.

OOH, OOH. Much danger!

A predawn, rapid-fire pounding on our door startled us. The accepted methods of rousing a Tum out of a sound sleep were shaving cream in the face, chest hairs yanked or water sprayed from a portable fire extinguisher known as the red persuader. Simply beating on a door wasn't much fun.

We both bolted straight up and Dave exclaimed, "Holy smokes, come on in!"

The door flew open and slammed against the wall. A tall, thin, fair-skinned Army major flanked by two powerfully built MPs stepped across the threshold.

I thought, *this is not going to be good.* The major squinted, his beady eyes moved back and forth between me and Dave, sizing us up. With starched fatigues, brass sparkling, the leather on his jungle boots spit shined, he was ready for a parade.

I thought about Major Koprivica, the Army guy who tracked down Dave to thank him for the air support that saved him and his troops from injury or death. He was a real soldier. This clown was content to spend every day supervising a clerk shuffling paper from a wire inbox to a waiting outbox.

Feeling in control and believing his prey to be intimidated, he yelled, "Who's in charge here?"

As though we had rehearsed for this moment, Dave and I pointed at one another and said in unison, "He is."

A few silent seconds passed and the major's face turned bright red. His jaw clenched, exacerbating the shape of his pointed, dimpled chin. He couldn't think of anything to say. "You... You... You guys have no respect for military protocol! You're an embarrassment to the Armed Forces!"

This REMF was no doubt thrilled about being able to tell the general he had our ass. However, he would first have to compose himself, get his heartbeat down a smidgeon from two hundred beats a minute. He wanted to kill us.

The major exploded. "You fuckers are outta here! You've got forty-eight hours to pack your stuff and haul ass. If you don't depart the compound by then you'll be forcibly removed!"

With that he executed a snappy about face and marched out of our room followed by his minions. One scowled, looking for a fight, the other suppressed a snicker.

I said, "Holy smokes. What are we going to do now, Boss?"

"I don't know, Hale, but we'll think of something."

Quis, Jake and Larry appeared at our door. Quis asked, "What was *that* all about?"

Dave said, "Quis, it appears we've worn out our welcome. We've been evicted."

I made a pot of coffee and thought about what our plight might be. *I suppose Colonel Wis could bust us for behavior unbecoming of Air Force Officers. We certainly didn't show the major any respect or remorse for our behavior regarding the issue with the General's quarters. I'm a second lieutenant, the lowest rank there is. Maybe I'd wear sergeant's stripes and be a clerk. That would make mom happy. Colonel Wis couldn't put us in a brig because we didn't have one. Threatening to send us to Vietnam wouldn't work.*

The other guys were quiet, too, and I broke the silence.

"Dave, the major said we have two days to pack our stuff. Who knows what stuff's ours?"

"It doesn't matter, Hale," he replied. "We're going to take everything that isn't nailed down. I'm going to call Colonel Wis and break the news, so we can make a plan."

Dave reached for the phone and rang the hooch at Tiger Town. Ken Montague answered, "Tum operations. Airman Montague speaking, sir."

"Hi, Ken. Captain Rogers here. Is Colonel Wis available?"

"Stand by, sir," he replied.

The five of us were silent, eyes darting from one to another, young brothers about to confess a dastardly deed to our father.

Colonel Wis answered the phone, "Good morning, Dave. What's up?"

"You're not going to believe this, Colonel Wis."

"I'd believe anything," he replied. "Who got arrested?"

"Well, sir, you might say we all did. We've been evicted and have two days to get out."

"You've got to be shitting me!" he exclaimed.

"No, sir, I'm not."

Several seconds passed without a word spoken: the father contemplating an appropriate response, volcanic eruption or measured calm. Colonel Wis chose the later and said, "I'll call you back."

Dave heard from Colonel Wis at noon.

"You guys are moving to Phu Cat," he said. "I talked to Colonel Harry Trimble, the wing commander, and he arranged for six rooms in the VOQ. Each room will sleep four, so you'll have plenty of room."

Relieved, Dave said, "Thanks, Colonel Wis. I'll fly to Phu Cat this afternoon and get a truck. We'll be out of here tomorrow."

Saying goodbye to mama-San was heartbreaking. When she noticed the guys packing and taking things off the walls, she came to my room with a bewildered look on he face and asked if we were leaving.

"Baby-San, GIs di di mau?" That was Vietnamese for go or leaving.

"Yes, mama-San, we di di mau tomorrow"

She began sobbing and said, "Please baby-San, GIs no go."

I hoped the Army guys who got our rooms would treat her as well as we had.

Once we knew Phu Cat Air Base was going to be our home, any embarrassment or guilt we felt about being tossed out like no-count derelicts vanished. We were ecstatic, thrilled to be leaving the Army compound.

Dave arrived at the Air Force motor pool two hours later and told the clerk he needed a truck and would return it the next afternoon. The clerk looked at his military driver's license and said, "Sir, you don't have a stamp on your license authorizing you to drive a truck. I can't give you one until you pass a test."

Dave tapped the Korean shoulder patch on his flight suit and said, "Sergeant I report directly to the commanding general of the Korean Capitol Division, the guys that keep this base safe at night. I have to move some classified equipment for the general and I don't have time to take a chicken-shit test in order to drive a truck. I majored in forestry and drove logging trucks all over Oregon. I'll make you a deal. You stamp my license and I'll take you for a ride in a combat aircraft, the O-1 Bird Dog."

The clerk asked, "Is that one of those puddle jumper things?"

"It sure is. You'll love it! It's exciting. We'll fly over the tree tops, maybe see some VC."

The sergeant looked around the office in a clandestine manner and said in a soft voice, "Captain, I'm going to sign you off, but I'll pass on the plane ride. Take good care of those Koreans, sir."

Obviously, the clerk didn't want to get in a "puddle jumper" with Dave.

Dave arrived back in Qui Nhon late that afternoon and the next morning, with Quis helping the three of us began hauling everything we could down the stairs.

The most important items went first: six air conditioners (we left the external covers in the windows); the refrigerator; a sofa; four chairs; one bookcase; two fans; a coffee table; three end tables and the phone and radios, which actually belonged to us.

Dave decided the lowest ranking officer would ride in the back of the truck and protect our booty while he and Quis rode in the cab. *Oh, great. I've got to ride shotgun and this stuff is precious cargo.*

Two men and a truck

A skinny hundred-and-thirty pounder wasn't going to frighten anyone, but I would keep my AR-15 automatic rifle in my lap and my .38 pistol on my hip, a certain deterrent to mischief. I sat in a chair facing aft as we pulled out of the compound. Mama-San, bowed with her hands held together under her chin, sobbed and pleaded with me to stay,

"GI no go. Please no go." She grabbed onto the rear bumper and I reached down and gently removed her hands. As we eased away, I said one last time, "We beaucoup love you, mama-San."

We left her in tears.

When we exited the gate, the guard gave us a snappy salute and nodded with a grin. I wondered if it was because we were leaving his turf, or if he thought our high jinx were, in a way, entertaining. The thought of getting stopped at the gate and questioned about our payload never entered our minds. We would have come up with something.

We made our way through the crowded city. The locals watched threateningly as we crawled our way through the congestion. When we got on Highway 1A North, I hoped the traffic would be less dense and we could keep moving. We passed through several small villages. Bicycles, motor scooters, pedestrians and military vehicles clogged the road.

Only once did the congestion force us to stop and I got very nervous. I couldn't see Quis or Dave and hoped we wouldn't be stuck long. *Here it comes, I'm going to die defending a few air conditioners and a cheap Army refrigerator.* As I moved my head from side to side looking for trouble, a lone Korean soldier surprised me. He tossed his duffle bag on our truck and jumped on.

He had a large grin on his face and nodded up and down several times, a gesture I perceived to be a "thank you." I was ecstatic! Dave and Quis took care of their little buddy! They found me a bodyguard. He must have noticed the Korean logo on Quis' shoulder patch and asked the guys if he could have a lift.

I kept track of our progress by following the terrain features and villages on my map and knew when we turned off the highway we had but a few miles to drive to the village of Phu Cat, next to the base. When we slowed, for some reason, my traveling companion grabbed his gear and jumped off the back of the truck. He walked a few yards, turned, smiled and flashed the peace sign. We spoke not one word to each other, yet formed a sort of bond. He got a free ride to Phu Cat and I was saved from possible death at the hands of VC pirates.

We drove a short distance to the gate at Phu Cat Air Base and continued to the VOQ, our new quarters. I jumped out of the truck when Dave stopped and said, "Thanks, guys for picking up the ROK soldier. I was thrilled when he hopped on board."

They looked at each other, then turned to me with wrinkled eye brows as if to ask,

"What are you talking about?"

They had no idea the enterprising Korean soldier had hopped a free ride to Phu Cat.

Ya gotta love the ROKs.

Sixteen

New Digs and Sky Pigs

Bernie and Pat teaching mama-San Frisbee

We had six rooms in the VOQ, three on each side of a hallway. Each room had two sets of bunk beds, two chests of drawers, a refrigerator, a sink, a built-in closet and three or four metal chairs with vinyl covered seats and backs. A latrine with a six-head shower room was at the end of the hall. A second story mirrored our floor and was reserved for visitors. Our mama-San was a petite young girl and her smile told me we would get along fine. The chow hall was in walking distance from our

hooch and conveniently located across the street was the Officer's Club. The 1st ROK Infantry Regiment was less than a mile away. It was perfect. Dave and I chose two rooms for us 1st Regiment guys, Quis did the same for the Cav troops and the last two were reserved for our Miami Beach FACs.
After the three of us tossed our gear in our rooms, we unloaded the truck at our regiment and drove it back to the motor pool. It was getting late in the afternoon and the guys who flew morning and afternoon missions at Qui Nhon were beginning to land at Phu Cat. Three guys volunteered to drive our Jeeps from Qui Nhon to Phu Cat. Dohrm flew in from Tiger Town and he and Snidley Whiplash chose one of the Cav rooms. Pat, who was on duty at our regiment, met the arriving guys at the runway and escorted them to our new digs.
The 12th Tactical Fighter Wing at Phu Cat had two squadrons of F-4s, the 389th and 480th. Dave's friend, Tom Hiestand, was assigned to the 389th and Dave went by their squadron and left a message for him. It read, "If you don't show up at the club tonight you don't have a hair on your ass."

Dave didn't sign the note. He didn't have to, Hiest knew who it was.

The club had a long L-shaped bar, and a portion of the dining room could be sealed off for special occasions. Several different aircraft were stationed at Phu Cat and each squadron's plaque adorned the walls. There were transports, electronic warfare birds, Agent Orange Ranch Hands, two different gunships, helicopters and the guys who ruled the roost...the F-4 jocks with the radio call sign Cobra. Above the bar hung wooden letters that dwarfed the squadron plaques. They spelled out C O B R A S L A I R.

Hiest and two of his buddies, Mike Swanic and Rick Kadar, were in the club when we got all our guys rounded up and settled in for our first night at Phu Cat. We were going to enjoy getting to know the F-4 drivers because we had worked air strikes with them and now would have the opportunity to get acquainted. Mike was an aircraft commander and Rick a Weapons Systems Operator (WSO). They sat in the rear cockpit and jammed signals from enemy radar sites and helped the pilot scan the skies for MIGs and enemy ground fire. Rick, like most WSOs was a pilot, qualified to fly the F-4. Some WSOs were navigators. The WSOs were called the Guy in Back (GIB).

When I arrived at Qui Nhon, I felt guilty because the setting on the bay seemed so pristine, peaceful and seemingly out of harm's way. It didn't take me or the other guys long to figure out we would never be considered peers by our Army hosts. However, we weren't miserable because we had each other. I wish Larry would have discovered the secret of the beer can ballast months ago. We would have gotten evicted sooner.

Living on an Air Force base with fellow airmen was a breath of fresh air. We had our own barracks, a lively club a stone's throw from our quarters and were surrounded by guys who knew who we were and the strength of our commitment. Every plaque on the wall represented a group willing to give their all for the mission. The Army general in Qui Nhon was enjoying a quiet evening in his cabaña and the Tums were having New Year's Eve in Time Square. We met Steve "Choo Choo" Train and Bob Strang, second lieutenants like me, Dohrm and Bill. These guys flew the twin engine C-7 Caribou, a STOL aircraft. They delivered ground troops, paratroopers, ammunition and supplies to rudimentary landing fields used by special forces units.

Dave and Hiest acted like long lost pals even though they'd seen each other every time Dave worked at the regiment. Dohrm, Bill and I were sipping Green Stingers

(Creme De Menthe and brandy) and trading flight school and war stories with the Caribou drivers. Hiest noticed our cocktail of choice, crawled over the bar, and with a grease pencil wrote on the drink menu, "Green Doofers 25 cents." He said that sounded more masculine. The club staff never erased it.

We met several guys during our first outing at the club and unlike our former "peers," they welcomed us with open arms and seemed pleased to have a FAC outfit on their base.

When the club manager suggested we call it an evening, not one Tum questioned his authority. We did, however, make sure that when the club opened the next day, the wooden sign at the end of the bar read, C L A I R S B R A.

The game was on.

Our getting the heave-ho couldn't have come at a better time. We had an unknown number of O-2s arriving soon and the Army Air Field at Qui Nhon was already overcrowded. If we added four or five pilots to our ranks we might not have had enough rooms at the hooch and I couldn't see the Army going out of their way to accommodate us with more bunks.

Pat and Bill in the office

Colonel Wis not only got us a great place to live, he was able to convince Colonel Trimble we needed an office. There was a fifteen by twenty-five foot structure under construction on the flight line. We helped complete the finish work and moved our pilfered loot in the new office a few weeks after our arrival. Colonel Wis told us we might take over the flight scheduling from Tiger Town. We also would monitor the flight hours on our fleet of Bird Dogs and scheduled

Steve and Bernie

them to be flown to Nha Trang for periodic maintenance.

Dave and Colonel Wis were the only Tums who had met Colonel Trimble, the wing commander. The meeting took place to discuss an issue with the 1st ROK Infantry Regiment. Colonel Trimble had been told a few of the ROKs had stolen some goods from the BX, a charge vehemently denied by Dave and Colonel Kim, the Korean Regiment Commander. The issue was never resolved and Colonel Trimble continued to hold a grudge. Dave said the colonel talked down to the Koreans, which infuriated them.

Everyone referred to the wing commander as "Shit Hot Harry." Dohrm and I understood the moniker when one morning, while waiting for Snidley to join us at our Jeep, the Colonel had his driver stop his shiny staff car in front of us. We saw the car coming, came to attention and saluted. Colonel Trimble rolled down the passenger side window, halfheartedly returned our salutes, and asked, "You guys FACs?"

We answered in unison, "Yes, sir."

Digesting our reply, he extended his right thumb, clenched his fingers into a fist and replied, "Shit hot!"

He asked another question, "Those your Jeeps?"

"Yes, sir," we responded.

His thumb snapped to attention, "Shit hot!"

"Is that Korean writing on your Jeeps?" he asked.

"Yes, sir."

Again his thumb came to life, "Shit hot!"

He was out of questions and his final remark was "Fly safe boys. Shit hot!"

We watched his Air Force blue automobile drive toward the chow hall. The colonel held his right arm out the window, thumb extended.

I said to Dohrm, "I've got it figured out."

"What's that?" Dohrm asked.

"Shit hot's got 'shit hot' tattooed on his right thumb nail."

Dohrm busted out in a broad grin, promptly extended his thumb, made a fist and replied "Shit hot, Lizard!"

Bob Snyder joined us for a trip to the flight line and thought we were pulling his leg when we told him about our introduction to the wing commander. It was, indeed, a hard story to swallow.

Colonel Trimble, a slight, handsome man with a long face and brilliant white teeth, strutted with an air of confidence. Wing commanders could act that way. The consensus seemed to be that he ran a tight ship, which wasn't necessarily a bad thing, except he insisted on maintaining some foolish rules. For example, he demanded tennis players wear white shirts, shorts and tennis shoes. I didn't really care because I didn't play, but Pat did. He was on the varsity tennis and basketball teams at the Air Force Academy and thought it was a stupid rule. Since our commander, Colonel Wis, spent virtually all his time at Tiger Town, Colonel Trimble wanted to know who the next ranking Tum was.

The SRO

Major Chuck Hadley, the ROK Cav Regiment ALO, was that guy. Dave should have been the officer chosen to be Colonel Trimble's contact since he would never leave Phu Cat Air Base except to spend time at the 1st ROK Infantry Regiment, walking distance from our hooch, but Colonel Trimble wouldn't hear of it. He demanded to have the senior officer identified as his direct contact. Consequently, Charles Hadley no longer went by Chuck. He was now our Senior Ranking Officer and we referred to him as the SRO (pronounced *shro)*.

It's not that the SRO took this title seriously, he didn't. However, he knew it would be a mistake to get on the wrong side of Colonel Trimble. His first test took place a couple of weeks after we moved in. There was a show scheduled at the Officer's Club and everyone looked forward to it as it was not often the club booked entertainment. The club officer and his staff cleared out all the dining room tables and packed the place with chairs. The folding walls that sealed off the party room were opened to make more room for chairs.

Every seat was taken and guys pushed and shoved to find standing room. If the base Fire Marshall had poked his head in the door, he would have closed the place down. The two F-4 squadrons had the largest number of attendees and occupied the best seats. A dozen Tums sat in the back rows close to the exit. We'd never seen the handful of guys that sat in front of us. They were transient flight crews.

The six entertainers, four male musicians and two scantily clad female singers, were young, Oriental and not very good. The drinks flowed, the crowd grew restless and so did Steve Drummond, Tum Three Two. The strangers in front of us grew increasingly obnoxious with each arriving gin and tonic. When they stood up and began chanting Show us your tits!" Steve told the strangers to sit down and shut up. They did, but one tempestuous pilot couldn't stay in his seat, which happened to be the one in front of Steve. He stood up, tapped the short, stalky, captain on the shoulder and repeated his order to sit down.

The SRO, sitting close enough to the confrontation to realize what was going on, told both of them to sit down and relax or they would get the boot. Steve said, "SRO, I'm going to give this jerk the boot right now."

It was a good thing the Tums and strangers were sitting at the entrance of the club.

Both teams made it outside without drawing attention to the higher ranking officers seated close to the stage. The SRO, who was taller than both combatants, stepped between them and said, "Our Wing Commander isn't here, but you know good and well some of his minions are. Trimble will have your ass. This is the worst stage show I've seen in my life and you idiots are willing to fight about it. Bob Hope and Raquel Welch maybe, but not these bums."

Bill chimed in, "SRO is right, Steve. Let's get the hell out of here."

Dohrm and Snidley offered the same opinion and we headed back to our rooms. Steve laughed about it and said in his best Marlon Brando voice, "I coulda been a contendah."

My only comment was, "Steve, that cheese ball would have been toast. You're a real bull dog."

Like so many nicknames, this one stuck. Steve became Bull Dog overnight.

Colonel Wis called us in our office early one morning with news we'd been anticipating for weeks. The first O-2 Skymaster--also referred to as the Oscar Deuce--would arrive this afternoon. He told us Colonel Trimble wanted every Tum who wasn't flying to be standing tall when the O-2 arrived. Base Operations understood they were to let us know when the O-2 was ten miles out.

Pat, who manned the office as the day's duty officer, said, "It's too bad we don't have our Mess Dress Uniforms (tuxedo-like formal wear) with us." His opinion of the O-2 was that it was a great cross country bird.

Snidley Whiplash walked in and when Pat gave him the news Snidley said, "There goes the neighborhood."

As the guys came in to get their aircraft assignments, Pat gave them the word about our new Tum and the need to be available to greet the O-2 jock when he arrived.

Dohrm believed, "No one in an O-2 could do the job for the ROKs as well as we O-1 drivers because their visibility and maneuverability sucks."

Larry, our A-1 fighter jock said, "I'm not interested because it doesn't have a stick." Every plane he'd flown except the T-41, our first trainer, had a control stick in the cockpit, not a yoke.

Dave said, "It's simple. The aircraft wasn't designed for our mission. I'm glad I don't have to fly it."

Bill Lutz didn't sugarcoat his opinion, "I don't care if we get the O-2 or not. I'm repulsed by the thought of it replacing the Bird Dog."

Resentment filled the air.

A dozen of us stood on the hot tarmac waiting the arrival of the Tum's first Oscar Deuce. Several airmen, crew chiefs and maintenance workers, huddled around the ramp anxious to see the new aircraft. I scanned the ramp looking for a brass band and was relieved not to hear a tuba warming up.

All eyes swiveled to the south when the aircraft approached the runway. I wondered if Shit Hot Harry had told the tower operator to hold all incoming traffic so not to disrupt the ceremony. When the Skymaster landed and turned off the runway, a crew chief waved his arms and led the newcomer to a parking spot. Colonel Trimble and his four-man entourage approached the aircraft when the pilot shut off the engines.

When the pilot opened the door and stepped onto the ramp, my jaw dropped and I yelled, "Murph!"

Colonel Trimble and the crowd turned in my direction as Lieutenant John Murphy, UPT Class 69-05, Reese Air Force Base, Texas, found me in the crowd and screamed, "Lizard!"

The wing commander interrupted our reunion to make a short speech telling Murph and the crowd how pleased the staff of the 12th Tactical Fighter Wing was to welcome the first O-2 Skymaster and Lieutenant John Murphy to Phu Cat Air Base. When the embarrassing ordeal was over, I introduced Murph to the Tums and we went to our hooch to get him settled in. He was going to the ROK Cav Regiment and would bunk with Dohrm, Snidley and the SRO.

Murph had been stationed at a small base at Da Lat in the Central Highlands, due west of Cam Ranh Bay. He never met a stranger and was fun to be around. He talked about the CIA often and told us he was going to spend his post-Air Force career working for the spooks. We thought, *Yeah, right.*

Several of us escorted Murph to the club and told him he had to buy us drinks as long as we wanted. He had no idea when the next O-2 would show up but told us he couldn't wait to show us what a great job the Oscar Deuce was going to do for the ROKs. None of us believed a word of it.

We dined at the club and retired to our hooch. It turned out to be a long night. Murph listened to everyone who wanted to throw verbal stones at his aircraft and handled it well. There was no way to settle the debate except performance, and we all looked forward to flying with Murph when he worked with fighters. The banter continued into the wee hours and at one point someone made the observation that this hooch was a real zoo.

The last two guys to go to bed were Dohrm and Bill, as they had a surprise for Murph. Dohrm made a stencil out of a piece of cardboard. He and Bill crept onto the flight line when everyone was asleep, armed with the stencil and a small can of red paint. When Murphy saw his airplane the next morning he was livid. A silhouette of a bright red pig adorned the fuselage of Murph's Skymaster.

Dohrm could have decorated the O-2 with anything, but chose the pig because they're fat, ugly, and not very agile. Murph admitted as much after he settled down.

From that moment, we no longer lived in a hooch or VOQ--we lived in the Zoo, site of much mischief.

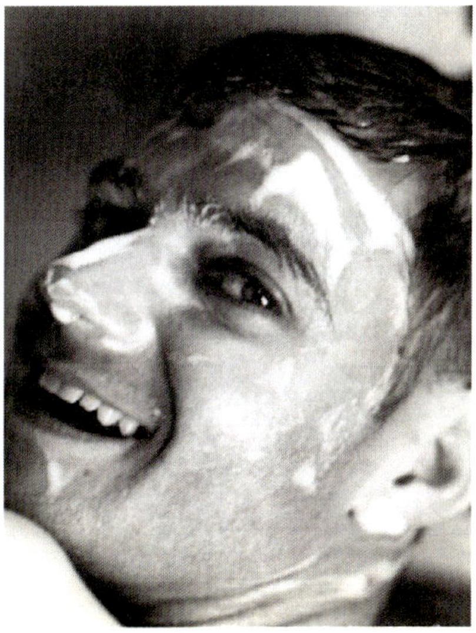

Shaving cream in the face!

Ron takes a hit with a smoke bomb!

The weapons of choice were the Red Persuader, portable fire extinguishers that hung in the hallway, and smoke grenades for outside use only! However, one night two captains, a Tum and an F-4 jock, ignited a green smoke can in a mop bucket and rolled it inside the room inhabited by me and Bill Lutz. Thankfully, we were at the club at the time.

Every square foot of our room was covered with red powder. From the ceiling to the floor and even in our dressers. Mama-San wanted to kill us. Every piece of clothing and bedding had to be washed. The perpetrators remained anonymous for months.

As it turns out, it was Hiest and the Miami Beach ALO, Ron Tribo, who were the ones behind the mischief. They went to the flight line and grabbed a smoke bomb out of Sky Pig. Had the smoke burned through the steel mop bucket, the whole base may have gone up in flames.

Boys will be boys.

Seventeen

The Bird Dog Express

Dohrm's wife, Sue, kept us stocked with Parodi (pa-road-ee) cigars and chocolate chip cookies. What a combination! The cookies were scrumptious. The Parodies were three inches long, black, gnarly, nasty and came in a five-pack.

They sucked.

Dohrm had been on an operation in the An Khe pass area for three days when he called our office with a request.

"Tum Ops, Tum Two Five, how do you read? Over."

Dave answered the call, "You're loud and clear Two Five. How's life in the boonies?"

Dohrm replied, "It's been exciting out here. The ROKs are kicking some major ass, but it seems to be slowing down. How about a mail and cigar drop? There might be a few cookies hidden in my sock drawer, too."

Dave told Dohrm I would be landing soon and we would fly to his operation site with mail and goodies.

I finished my uneventful two hour VR mission at noon and an hour later Dave and I were airborne, on our way with important provisions for our fellow Tum. I was in the back seat tasked with dropping the loot on Dohrm's campsite.

Dave called Dohrm and got his coordinates. He plotted a course that would take us to the operation site and as we approached, Dave called with an ETA. "Tum Two Five, Tum One Zero will be on station in five minutes."

"Roger that One Zero. We're on the high ground and you'll see the rusted carcass of a Huey helicopter that's been destroyed by strafe. It's thirty meters north of our location, you can't miss us. Your approach will be clear but stay out of the tall grass covering our hill. I marked our tent with a message to help you pinpoint us."

Dave told Dohrm he saw the tent and descended to an altitude ten feet above the grass. I opened the window and gripped the nylon mail bag that held what cookies were left after I found them in Dohrm's room, three boxes of Parodies and a handful of mail from Sue and Dohrm's mom.

When we were within sight of Dohrm's position I gripped the package tight and held it out the window. I concentrated on the speed of our plane, getting a feel for how much I would have to lead Dohrm's tent. Dave and I saw the message Dohrm had mentioned at the same moment and burst out laughing. Written on top of the tent in red duct tape were the words, "HO CHI MINH IS QUEER!"

My drop was a shack, it landed right beside the radio Jeep. The drop would have been a complete success had Dave not clipped ten inches off Dohrm's fifteen foot whip antenna with our left wing.

Late that afternoon, while Dohrm was cooking steak and eggs, the ROKs began taking incoming fire and Dohrm made a frantic radio call, "Tum FAC, Tum FAC, any Tum. This is Tum Two Five. How do you read? Over."

Those of us who heard Dohrm's call knew he was in trouble and thought of Coop and Ted's ordeal at Miami Beach. Pat answered Dohrm's call, "You're loud and clear Two Five. This is Tum One Two, over."

"One Two, Steve (Rideout, Dohrm's ROMAD) and I are taking incoming. We're getting mortared"

Pat asked, "Where are you guys?"

"We're under the fuckin' Jeep and the sign I put up is coming down if I get out of here alive!"

When there was a lull in the action Dohrm grabbed the HF radio and beat a trail to the ROK's command post a hundred feet up the hill. He stayed there all night and worked two gunships, an AC-119 Stinger and an AC-47A Spooky. There were no casualties or injuries.

A supply chopper arrived at the operation site with much needed supplies, primarily ammunition for the ROKs, C-rations (individual canned, precooked meals) for the troops, and cold beer for Dohrm and Steve.

There happened to be a U.S. Army Colonel on site observing the ROK's performance and he seemed puzzled and a bit disgruntled as he watched Dohrm and Steve offload their personal supplies. Only Dohrm could figure out how to have steak and eggs and a cold beer while in the boonies. He was one hell of a scrounger and set the standard for camping-out in the jungle.

Eighteen

Jungle Fighter Pilots

Major Chung, the Korean pilot I met when first visiting Tiger Town, loved hanging out with the Tums. While he spent the majority of his time at Tiger Town, we did see more of him after our move to Phu Cat, since he could easily catch a ride in a Jeep or chopper to visit the Koreans at the 1st ROK Infantry Regiment. He was a hard drinker, the life of every party and was especially fond of Dohrm. He called him Lieutenant Crawf, the only nickname I'd heard from a Korean.

There was always an empty bunk in the Zoo and Major Chung spent several nights with us. One morning I showed up early at our operations hooch and found someone asleep on our green vinyl sofa, an open copy of *Sports Illustrated* spread over his face. As I approached, I could tell who it was by the pilot's wings on his flight suit. Major Chung sensed my presence, peeked out from a corner of the magazine and said in a pained voice, "OOH, OOH. Lieutenant Hale, I have major overhanger."

Dohrm told me a story about Major Chung and Lieutenant Im, a junior lieutenant learning the ropes while on an operation with the ROK Cav Division. The weather was lousy, socked in, and the ROKs were engaged with an enemy force in a steep valley. Lieutenant Im, perhaps wanting to impress his senior officers, demanded an immediate air strike. Dohrm had fighters loitering overhead, waiting for a break in the overcast sky and he did his best to make the young lieutenant understand it was not possible for the fighters or the FAC, Snidley Whiplash, to enter the valley. Lieutenant Im could have been talking on the radio to soldiers on the valley floor who told him the visibility was fine, which it could have been, but only at the lower altitude.

Dohrm said to Lieutenant Im, "We cannot have airstrike. Clouds too low, mountains too high, fighters fly too fast."

The Lieutenant didn't get it, "We must have air strike, we must have air strike now!" Being of equal rank, the Korean officer could get frisky with Dohrm.

Major Chung stood nearby, silent, impassive, his arms folded across his chest. As the lieutenant ranted, Major Chung stepped forward between the two lieutenants. He motioned to Dohrm that he would speak and barked a command at the junior officer.

Lieutenant Im snapped to attention and stood deathly still. Major Chung chewed him out, shaking a finger in his face. He then stepped back and punched him in the mouth, knocking him to the ground. Without saying a word the bloodied lieutenant jumped up and snapped to attention. Major Chung continued his conversation with the startled lieutenant. He didn't scream, rather, seemed to be telling him he had argued enough with Lieutenant Crawf. When he finished...*wham,* down the lieutenant went again, and like the first time, he hopped up, stood at attention and saluted.

Dohrm stood with his mouth agape. Major Chung turned and in a calm, matter-of-fact voice said, "Lieutenant Crawf, I have told Lieutenant Im we cannot have air strike."

On one of my visits to Tiger Town, Major Chung said he wanted to fly with me. I assumed he'd jump in the back seat and check me out, see if I was a good pilot. When we arrived at the air strip he said, "I sit in front seat. Fire rockets."

I asked him if he'd shot Willie Petes before, and grinning like a kid with his first BB gun, he answered, "Today is first time."

I knew he'd flown with Dave and Colonel Wis and I'd never heard anything derogatory about his ability to fly safely. If he truly was an F-86 fighter pilot like everyone said, I had nothing to worry about. Launching rockets was a piece of cake.

After we performed the preflight inspection, I showed the major how we pulled the red safety pins on the rocket tubes, then stowed them in my flight suit. With my student sitting in the front seat, I pointed out the cotter pin on the control stick, a safety mechanism that locked the firing trigger. There was a panel on the right side of the console that contained eight toggle switches, one for each rocket. When a switch was toggled, the rocket was armed, ready to fire. I gave him my black grease pencil and an explanation of how our sophisticated bomb sight worked.

"Major Chung, when we are straight and level, with no G-forces on our aircraft, mark an X on the windscreen where the horizon line appears. When you pull the throttle back and begin your descent, arm a rocket, put your X on the target you've chosen and gently squeeze the trigger."

I stressed repeatedly the importance of arming one rocket at a time and only when the aircraft was in a nose-low attitude.

The Major knew our geography well. We flew over the ROK Cav Regiment, east to Phu Cat and the 1st ROK Infantry Regiment, south to Qui Nhon, and then it was time for rocket practice. He was a good pilot, aggressive like fighter jocks and FACs, but safe. I gave him a description of the Old French Fort and the lesson began. I steered him to the area of our target, which he recognized when it came into sight.

"Lieutenant Hale, I see Old French Fort," he said. "Very good, Major Chung," I replied. "Do you see the pile of rocks inside the fort? That's your target."

"Roger that," he replied. "I see rocks."

So far, so good, I thought.

I briefed him on the procedures we'd use on each rocket pass, "Major Chung, I'm going to walk you through each step you make in firing a rocket. I want you to acknowledge every command. Do you understand?"

"Roger that, Lieutenant Hale."

I had him make a three-hundred-and-sixty degree turn toward the target. We were a quarter of a mile away, which gave him plenty of time to line up. When it was time for him to descend to the target, I told him to retard the throttle and unfasten the cotter pin on the stick.

"Roger," he replied.

When the Bird Dog was in a nose-low attitude, I had him prepare to arm and fire a rocket.

"Okay, Major Chung, it's time to fire the rocket. Flip one toggle switch, arm your rocket." "Roger, Lieutenant Hale. Rocket is armed."

"Very good, Major. Now put your grease pencil mark on the pile of rocks and gently squeeze the trigger." *WHOOSH!* The Willie Pete left the rail and made a sharp turn to the right, missing the target by a wide margin. He shanked it!

Major Chung exclaimed, "OOH, OOH! I push rudder pedal, Lieutenant Hale."

No shit, Major.

He was a quick study and improved with each rocket pass. He never scored a shack, but could have easily worked a set of fighters.

He did, however, violate our most important rule. After firing seven rockets the aggressive fighter pilot attitude in him surfaced. Rather than wait for me to tell him when to arm and fire the last rocket, he chose to do so before putting our plane in a nose low attitude. He was full of adrenalin and his excitement caused him to make a serious mistake. As I watched the Willie Pete scream toward the village of Qui Nhon at the speed of sound, I imagined it to be my career vanishing before my eyes. The wayward missile winging eastward didn't seem to be an issue for Major Chung. I, however, felt faint. I prayed it would pass over Qui Nhon and land in the South China Sea. I watched it disappear and never saw a puffy white cloud appear on the horizon. It was my lucky day.

Oblivious to the serious mistake he had committed, Major Chung keyed the intercom and exclaimed in a loud voice, "OOH, OOH! Lieutenant Hale, we are Jungle Fighter Pilots!"

When I returned to Phu Cat and entered our operations office, I told the guys what Major Chung said and Dave asked, "What the hell does that mean?

"I don't have a clue," I said, "but if Major Chung says we're Jungle Fighter Pilots, that's what we are."

The handful of guys in the office looked around at one another, trying to make sense of what I told them. Dave concurred with me and said, "Hale's right. We're Jungle Fighter Pilots."

That evening Dohrm sketched what turned out to be the shoulder patch we proudly wore on our flight suits. There was a seamstress in the BX and we had our unique patches in a couple of days. We loved having a nickname that puzzled the other pilots.

Major Chung, Jungle Fighter Pilot

Nineteen

Tales of the Fall

Now that we had branded ourselves Jungle Fighter Pilots, a cocky camaraderie swept through our unit as fall brought a wave of change amidst storms that threatened to dampen our mood.

Anyone who wanted to box with the ROKs and practice the ancient art of Tae Kwon Do with Korean masters had to be crazy. Airman First Class Charlie Amonett, the ROMAD who panicked while off-loading a jeep from a Chinook helicopter on Dave's operation, was that guy. He was a husky fellow with the thickest, blackest head of hair I'd ever seen. The Koreans never seriously injured Charlie during their matches and he always came back to the regiment with a grin on his puffed up face.

I went into the field with Charlie only once. He and I hopped a ride in a UH-1 Huey helicopter and flew to the site of an operation in the Phu Cat Mountains, five miles north of our regiment and two from the South China Sea. We were to relieve Dave and Harold who had been with the Koreans four days. Our plan was to remain on site until the operation concluded, then fly back home in a Chinook helicopter.

The ROKs pounded the countryside day and night with artillery. Pat and Bill supported me and Charlie with airstrikes. And in the four days Charlie and I were in the boonies, we received no incoming mortar fire.

Our last evening on the hill, Lieutenant Nu walked from the ROK operations tent a quarter of a mile down the steep hill to our tent. Perhaps he thought that I, like Dohrm, maintained a stash of beer when I worked an operation. He, and most of the ROKs, enjoyed visiting with us. It was good practice for their English skills, which was important for their advancement through the ranks.

Lieutenant Nu briefed us on the operation and told us it was very successful. There were no casualties for the good guys and they had inflicted heavy losses on the enemy. He was in a mood to philosophize about the war and the Korean's role in the conflict.

"Lieutenant Hale, Korean soldiers love American G.I., we very good friends for long, long time. We honored to fight enemy soldier with you." He paused for a moment composing a thought. "I have plan. You Americans go home. Your country send Korean soldier weapons, tanks, airplanes, supplies and money for all things we need to fight VC and NVA soldiers. We kill enemy soldiers in Laos and Cambodia. VC no have supplies. We defeat North Vietnamese Army. Then Korean soldier go to China and defeat China Army. Then we go to North Korea and defeat North Korea Army. Then Korean soldier walk home to our country. Korean soldier very strong, very brave. Can do, but need beaucoup money from America. You like idea, Lieutenant Hale?"

I thought, *How about these guys? They aren't afraid of anybody and understand there's only one way to fight a war.*

"Yes, sir," I answered. "Korean soldiers are very brave and we are glad you are fighting with us. I will tell Captain Rogers your plan. He will be happy."

The ROKs didn't release us until the afternoon of our fourth day. Charlie made a radio call requesting a Hook and we quickly folded our tent. By the time our transportation showed up, the sun was falling into the horizon. The flight time to Phu Cat was at least thirty minutes, so it would be nearly dark when we touched down.

Charlie slowly drove our jeep up the ramp and the loadmaster quickly secured it with chains. As always, we sat in the Jeep. After only thirty minutes, the pilot reduced the power and began our descent. The landing zone at the regiment was concrete and I anticipated a soft landing. A soft landing it was, but as Charlie backed down the ramp I was shocked. We weren't at the regiment. The young pilot had landed on a wide open dirt area the size of a soccer field. I had no idea where we were. I sprinted up the ramp to the cockpit and told the young warrant officer he was supposed to take us to Phu Cat. He said, "This is where I was told to drop you. It's the end of the line, lieutenant. Get your ass off my aircraft. Highway 1A is just beyond the old Buddah shrine just east of us."

With that, he was off in a cloud of dust. When I located the shrine I knew where we were, but it was disconcerting knowing it would soon be dark. Charlie and I, packing four radios in our jeep made a luscious target.

"Haul some serious ass, Charlie. I know you're Korean-trained in the art of hand-to-hand combat, but I don't want to have to see you in action."

Thirty minutes after we turned off Highway 1A, the bright lights of Phu Cat Air Base lit up the horizon.

***

Captains Bob Butler and Ron Tribo arrived within a few days of one another. Bob arrived first.

He flew the Lockheed C-141 Starlifter before receiving his O-2 assignment and had been stationed at Da Lat with Murph.

Da Lat was a garden spot high in the mountains. The runway was 3,000 feet long and the field elevation 5,000 feet. The high altitude and relatively short runway was a challenge for the O-2 drivers because airplanes don't perform well at high altitudes due to thinner air. For that reason alone, the bulky O-2s should have never been stationed there. The pilots reduced their Willie Petes from fourteen to eight and didn't fill the gas tanks to keep the weight down.

At Da Lat, the Sky Pig really was a pig.

Bob would have arrived a few weeks earlier, but was delayed by a brush with death. Accompanied by a young Army sergeant, Bob launched on a VR mission and when things unexpectedly went south. As he rolled down the short runway he realized the acceleration was not quite what it should be.

Ron and Bernie

He did, however, become airborne at the usual spot on the runway. Shortly after takeoff, Bob knew he was in trouble because the Skymaster was not performing as it should. He mushed through the sky and turned to avoid steep terrain and give his plane a chance to pick up some airspeed. It didn't work.

Bob declared an emergency and turned back toward the runway. He didn't make it. He ran out of airspeed and altitude and crashed in a muddy rice paddy a quarter of a mile from the runway. An Army helicopter pilot who had taken off a few minutes before Bob, heard the emergency transmission and turned around to help him. He picked Bob and his Army passenger up and they landed on the runway seven minutes after they took off. They received no serious injuries and the cause of the accident was deemed to be fuel contamination. Two Oscar Deuces had been lost in the past six months. The following week, the Da Lat O-2s were sent elsewhere.

Ron Tribo came to us from SAC. He was a tanker pilot, one of the guys who flew the Boeing KC-135 Stratotanker whose mission was in-flight refueling. Colonel Wis assigned Ron to the 26th ROK Division at Miami Beach to replace Grier Cooper, who was still recovering from the shrapnel wounds he received in early October. We didn't get to see much of Ron when he arrived because, as the ALO, he was pressed to learn the geography of his AO, get acquainted with the Korean officers with whom he would work and bond with his two combat-ready pilots, Chuck Engle and Jim Cross.

I flew with each of them when they first arrived. Jim was calm, analytical, deliberate on the controls, never in a hurry. Chuck, on the other hand, flew the Bird Dog in a reckless manner. He jerked the plane around like a motocross racer on a short, winding track. Still, however, he always managed to stay in total control of the aircraft.

We all carried our AR-15 automatic rifles when we flew, but Chuck packed a second weapon, the M79 grenade launcher, a shotgun on steroids. He loved to fly and couldn't get enough of it.

His recklessness left me with the impression he might have a death wish. Chuck didn't revel in mischief like most of us. He was always a very serious guy.

One day Dohrm had an opportunity to trick him good. All of us struggled at times keeping up with three radios and the intercom. Failure to move the wafer switch on the radio panel to the proper radio was always embarrassing. One afternoon, Dohrm was airborne and heard Chuck make a transmission that should have been to Phu Cat tower, but instead, it went out over our VHF frequency and all airborne Tums heard it. Dohrm answered Chuck's call and played the part of the tower operator. The conversation went something like this:

"Phu Cat Tower, Tum Three One is a mile out for landing, over."

"Tum Three One, Phu Cat, maintain your position and make right hand, three-hundred-and-sixty degree turns."

After flying in circles for fifteen minutes, Chuck called again on the wrong radio to request landing instructions. This time Dohrm said, "Roger Tum One Three, continue to hold your position and now make left three-sixties."

Chuck, always serious and extremely confident, figured out he'd been had and was embarrassed and pissed. He switched to the proper radio and talked to the tower operator.

Engle wasn't the kind of guy who would say something like, "Dohrm, ya bastard! You really got me that time. Come on, I'll buy you a beer."

***

Sven, the Noncommissioned Officer who managed the airmen in the 1st ROK Infantry Regiment, headed home early in November and was replaced by Sergeant Rumker, a short, jolly, roly-poly guy. When he became accustomed to the casual attitude which Dave promoted, he began asking if he could get a ride in the O-1. Everyone enjoyed Sergean Rumker's spunk and he turned out to be a great scrounger, a real asset to the regiment.

Dave began calling him "Rummy" and one morning told him to pack a lunch, as he was going to take him on a routine VR mission. Rummy was like a kid getting to go to the circus. "My dad will not believe this!" he exclaimed as he headed for the flight line with two sandwiches packed in a paper bag and a camera bobbing around his neck.

Shortly after they were airborne, the mission turned out to be far from a milk run. Dave got a call from Harold , the radio operator who was working a 1st ROK Infantry Regiment operation in the Phu Cat Mountains with Bill Lutz, Tum One One. Harold gave Dave their coordinates and told him the ROKs were in contact with bad guys and a flight of two F-4s were on the way from Phu Cat.

Dave told Rummy to strap in tight and headed for Bill's location. The terrain was rocky, a steep ridge paralleled a narrow valley. Dave gave Cobra Lead the canned briefing: the location of the friendlies and bad guys; where to head if they were hit; the order in which he wanted their ordnance dropped; then the strike was on. Dave put in a Willie Pete, Bill confirmed it to be on target and cleared Cobra Lead in hot. The fighter jock pickled two bombs that hit exactly where Dave had wanted. As the pilot pulled out of his dive he took ground fire and began to lose hydraulic fluid. The fighter pilot declared an emergency and told Dave he was heading for Phu Cat and Cobra Two, Lead's wingman, wanted to escort him home. He requested permission to salvo his ten five hundred pounders. The fighter jock didn't want to land with bombs hanging on the rails. Dave told Bill to order another set of fighters and cleared Cobra Two to salvo his ordnance, which the pilot did at the base of a granite wall. The mountain erupted in a hail of rocks. Dave found himself flying formation with boulders the size of Volkswagens.

He jinked his Bird Dog as though he was taking ground fire from enemy gunners.

The granite barrage ended as quickly as it started and the only casualty was Rummy's lunch sack. The violent ride resulted in a case of nausea for Dave's passenger and he thought it prudent to puke in his paper bag rather than in the plane. He blew the flimsy thing apart.

Another set of F-4s showed up momentarily and the mission was accomplished. There were no more plane rides for Rummy.

***

On a cloudy, nasty day with just enough ceiling and visibility for the Tums to fly safely, five pilots decided to do a little formation flying. The flight of three planes contained two O-1s and one O-2. They used "Parodi Flight" for their call sign.

Frequently, the Koreans fired flares from their 105 Howitzers during night surveillance missions. They slowly floated to the ground, suspended by small parachutes three or four feet in diameter. At Dohrm's request the ROKs gave him a few chutes.

The F-4s, like all fighter jets, deployed drag cutes upon landing to save wear and tear on the brakes. Upon touchdown, some of the fighter jocks would ask the tower operator if they "had a good chute." Dohrm believed the guys in the cockpit could merely look in their rear view mirrors and see if the chute had deployed. He also said a chute opening at the high landing speed would be felt by the pilots in the cockpit. In his vernacular the fighter jocks were simply "shining their ass" by making an unnecessary radio call.

Dohrm was in the front seat with Bill in the back of Parodi Lead. Bull Dog and Snidley were Parodi Two, and Murph, flying Sky Pig, was Parodi Three. When the flight was ready, Dohrm called the tower.

"Phu Cat tower, Parodi Flight, two O-1s and an O-2 are read to taxi. Over."

"Parodi Flight, Phu Cat, you're cleared to taxi and take off to runway three three."

"Roger that, Tower. We'll RTB in fifteen minutes and will be requesting an overhead pattern."

"Roger that Parodi Lead. See you soon," replied the tower operator.

The two Bird Dogs took off together and Murph waited a minute to let them get out of his way. When he caught up to the two Bird Dogs, he dropped the flaps and lowered the gear to create drag. The O-1 cruised at ninety knots, a hundred slower than the O-2.

When their joy ride was over, and the three-ship formation, led by Dohrm, approached the tower, Parodi Lead called the tower and requested permission to land.

"Phu Cat tower, Parodi Flight inbound for landing, requesting an overhead pattern."

"Overhead pattern approved," came the reply. "You're cleared to land."

The chutes were attached with a grenade pin to the radio antenna that stretched from the vertical stabilizer to the top of the wing. When the back-seater in the O-1 tossed the chute out the rear window, it would slide back, catch on the vertical stabilizer and blow in the wind like a real drag chute, a brilliant piece of engineering.

Murph assumed the lead position so he could land first and get out of the way of the slower Bird Dogs. As Parodi Flight approached the runway, the tower called to tell the guys to depart the airspace because a flight of F-4s were approaching the hold line and would be allowed to take off when they were ready.

The lead fighter jock replied to the tower, "Phu Cat tower, Cobra Flight will hold for the fighters in the pitch." They wanted to see what the Tums were up to.

The plan worked as advertised. When each member of Parodi Flight touched down, the back seaters tossed out the chutes and they worked perfectly. Dohrm, struggling to keep from laughing, asked of the tower, "Phu Cat Tower, do I have a good chute?"

The fighter jocks holding for takeoff loved it. Parodi Flight was the talk of the club that night. Colonel Trimble told the SRO the stunt could have resulted in serious damage had one of our chutes been sucked into an F-4 air intake. The SRO, as he always did, agreed with the colonel and told him it would never happen again.

***

I was scheduled to fly a KEL mission early one November morning and was excited when my fighters checked in with me.

"Tum One Four, Spad Two Zero with you. We're a flight of two, over."

For the first time in my tour I was going to work with A-1E Douglas Skyraiders. Lead and his wingman were carrying Mark 82 five hundred pound bombs, twenty-mike-mike, rockets the size of our Willie Petes loaded with High Explosive (HE) warheads and napalm.

The A-1 flew under two call signs: Spad for offensive air strikes and Sandy for rescue operations. The Navy purchased this WWII vintage aircraft about the time the Army was taking delivery of the Bird Dog. There was a good chance we pilots were going into combat flying airplanes older than we were.

I briefed the fighter jocks on our mission and told them I was going to move their ordnance around, trolling for bad guys. I let them know the target area was a free fire zone, no friendlies close by. The terrain was rugged, the foliage thick. I put them in a north-to-south left hand pattern so they would be turning toward the coast in case they were hit.

The pattern these guys flew was substantially different from that of the F-100s and F-4s. Their dive angle was forty-five degrees, much steeper than the fighter jets.

The mission was a yawner for three or four passes, then it got exciting. I was following Lead down the chute, waiting for him to pickle his next bomb when Spad Two, on the downwind leg, called with a warning.

"Tum One Four and Spad Lead, you guys are getting hosed from your six."

Lead, near the target, salvoed his bomb right away, jinking wildly as he climbed to altitude. When the bomb went off, a huge secondary explosion erupted, followed by several more. Rocks, dirt, trees and dust filled the air. I, too, jinked like crazy as I turned off the target. I asked Spad Two if he could maneuver to the hot spot and he replied, "Roger that, Tum" and I cleared him to hit the area with five hundred pound bombs. They were right on the money. The lead aircraft, made a tight three-hundred-and sixty degree turn and followed with napalm. Then both fighter jocks sprayed twenty-mic-mic around the entire area. We saw no additional ground fire from the bad guys, and trolled around the area dropping bombs for several minutes, but failed to get any secondaries.

When the A-1s headed home I called the TOC at Tiger Town and gave them a BDA of multiple secondaries. I couldn't confirm any KBA but the fighters were on top of the bad guys in a heartbeat. No one escaped their wrath.

We FACs needed more A-1s as it was an outstanding platform for close air support, superior to the Huns and F-4s. That opinion, of course, was up for debate.

***

When I was ten years old I watched television on a black and white screen not much bigger than the laptop on which I'm typing. My favorite show, *You'll Never Get Rich,* featured Phil Silvers as Master Sergeant Bilko, who was in charge of the motor pool at Fort Baxter in Roseville, Kansas. The clever noncommissioned officer had a knack for coming up with whatever he or his underlings needed to make their lives easier or weasel out of trouble. Not long after I arrived in Vietnam, I realized Mr. Silver's military character was based on truth.

When Dave and I went to get a plywood box made for Coop's personal belongings, we saw more three-quarter inch plywood than a Montana saw mill could produce in a week. Every hooch in Vietnam had a small lounge, and if the one we had in Tiger was typical, they all needed to be remodeled. Whoever had a stash of plywood could demand a high price. Not money. Stuff.

Jake, our resident carpenter, was remodeling the bar at Tiger Town and Dave and Dohrm helped him acquire materials by performing the "Clipboard Caper." Dohrm said the clipboard was the most important piece of equipment in the Air

Force next to airplanes and bombs. "Anyone brandishing a clipboard had to be someone with authority," he said.

They strolled the aisles of the Army Supply Depot in Qui Nhon. Dave played the role of an aide to a high ranking officer, and Dohrm, the junior officer, his assistant. Dave nodded when he saw something he thought Jake could use and Dohrm made a note on his clipboard. A clerk accompanied them. They needed to get a few pallets of plywood, nails, sandpaper, glue and what turned out to be the most valuable acquisition of all--several gallons of pink paint. The guys had no idea why the gaudy paint was there, but Dohrm made a big deal out of it. He said, "Captain Rogers, the colonel will *love it.*"

New mattresses

They thanked the clerk for being so helpful and headed back to Phu Cat in a truck provided by Dave's buddy, the guy in the Air Force motor pool who hooked him up with the truck we used during our eviction.

We didn't need much paint for our lounge, however, we sure were glad it was pink because it proved to be our most valuable asset.

One afternoon a couple of Huey helicopter pilots dropped off some ROKs at our regiment and walked into our hooch looking for a couple of cokes, something that was routine. They were stationed at Lane Army Airfield close to Tiger Town and often worked with the Koreans. These guys flipped over the color of our hooch and made us an unbelievable offer. For enough pink paint to cover their hooch, they would give us a Jeep. No kidding, a jeep. They delivered it in a CH-47 chopper, and for a case of beer our ROKs painted Korean lettering on it.

In addition, Dave was able to get new mattresses for our three regiments. All it took was a pallet of plywood, a case of steaks and the deal clincher--one gallon of pink paint. The allure of the unique paint fascinated us. We never knew why it was in the Army Supply Depot in the first place.

Sergeant Bilko would have been proud.

***

The first time I visited Tiger Town I was given a bottle of large, rectangular pills and Jake told me to take one a day.

"They're horse pills," said Jake. "If you gag one down every day you won't get malaria and will never be constipated."

Being a pharmacist's son, I knew the importance of obeying the doctor's orders and never failed to take my malaria pill, even when I was in the boonies with the Koreans.

While I always took my horse pills, there were a few good men who did not. Bud Leithiser, a classmate of mine at Reese, was assigned to the 9th ROK Division, 28th Regiment at Phu Hiep five miles south of Tuy Hoa and close to our 26th ROK Regiment at Miami Beach.

That fall, Barry got word to me that Bud was very ill with malaria, hospitalized at Cam Ranh Bay. Quite often we had to take an aircraft to the TASS at Nha Trang for periodic maintenance and I told Col Wis I needed to be the next guy to ferry a bird to Nha Trang. Two days later, I was on my way south in an O-1 that needed a tune up.

Bud had been so sick he couldn't fly or ride a jeep the short distance to Cam Ranh Bay and the Koreans arranged a medevac helicopter to pick him up. Bud didn't know how long he'd been asleep but when he woke up he saw George Harrison, AKA Tuco El Crude, a classmate of ours, in the other bed. He, too, had the dreaded disease.

While at Reese, George went with Rob Nuss, one of our classmates, to the theater to see one of the Clint Eastwood spaghetti westerns that were popular then. One of the bad guys was a dirty, surly, disgusting Mexican named Tuco El Crude, and Rob thought it appropriate for George. Bud thought he was hallucinating, but when George pulled out a medicine bottle full of gin and tonic, he knew only Tuco El Crude could pull something like that off.

When I got there, I missed seeing Tuco. He had been discharged and Bud had the room all to himself. I was shocked, wouldn't have recognized him had it not been for his name on the door. His eyes were bright red, not a trace of white cornea, his face swollen. He shivered with fever and was in and out of consciousness. I sat on his bed for several minutes, then left. He didn't know I was there.

When Murph first arrived at Phu Cat, I asked about Bud and he told me he had recovered and was flying again.

I assumed he was taking his daily horse pill.

***

Doctors Patrick and Steven were two of several Flight Surgeons on the base who took care of our medical issues. For the most part, we were a healthy group and didn't visit their clinic often. When we did, they always asked if we were taking our malaria pills.

They were required to fly a certain number of flights each month with the flying squadrons on the base to maintain their flying status. Those F-4 flights were legitimate and duly noted on the squadron's flight log. The occasional trips they made with the Tums, however, were off the record.

Colonel Trimble, the wing commander, would not have approved of one of his Flight Surgeons flying around in an O-1.

Doc Patrick had a nurse friend in Qui Nhon and occasionally he would ask us to fly him the thirty miles and drop him off so he could spend some time with her.

Doc Steve would occasionally stop by our hooch and see if there was any chance of us taking him up for a ride. He was enthralled with our little airplane, a huge step down from the F-4 and enjoyed getting an occasional flying lesson.

We were happy to accommodate the docs. For our travel service and flight lessons, they wrote us prescriptions for grain alcohol, which enhanced a certain concoction we occasionally mixed up when a special event called for a party. We went to the Weapons Supply Storage facility and got a styrofoam container, in which shipped seven-hundred-and-fifty pound bombs. They were about eight feet long and made a great punch bowl. We filled it with several different brands of whisky, a little scotch, a case or two of beer, gallons of mixed fruit juices and a generous portion of the doc's grain. To honor the Koreans of the Tiger Division we called it "Tiger Piss."

Then there was the occasional horseplay-induced cut or scrape that required attention. One such incident took place while I was tending the store at the regiment and missed what was a real doozie of a party at the Zoo.

The guys were enticed to see how much Mateus wine they could consume in one evening. Apparently it was a substantial amount as the details of what happened were fuzzy. The story I got when I returned to Phu Cat was that a few wine bottles were broken and the floor was very slippery.

Bill Lutz crashed and burned. He was tripped or pushed, no one remembers the details, and fell face first into some shards of glass. First person accounts of the accident reveal he hit the floor nose first, a blessing as it could have been his eyes that absorbed the blow. His nose was mangled and gushed blood. Dohrm and Snidley poured him in a Jeep and raced to the clinic. Doc Steve said Bill was so inebriated he couldn't give him an anesthetic to numb the suturing he had to perform. Dohrm said, "It's okay, Doc. He won't mind."

Before the procedure was finished Bill had been given a nickname. "Snootz" was a combination of snoot and Lutz. As he was cleaning up the mess, Doc Steve said to no one in particular, "I wonder if it's too late for me to transfer to the Coast Guard?"

Yes, our outstanding Flight Surgeons took good care of us, and we took good care of them.

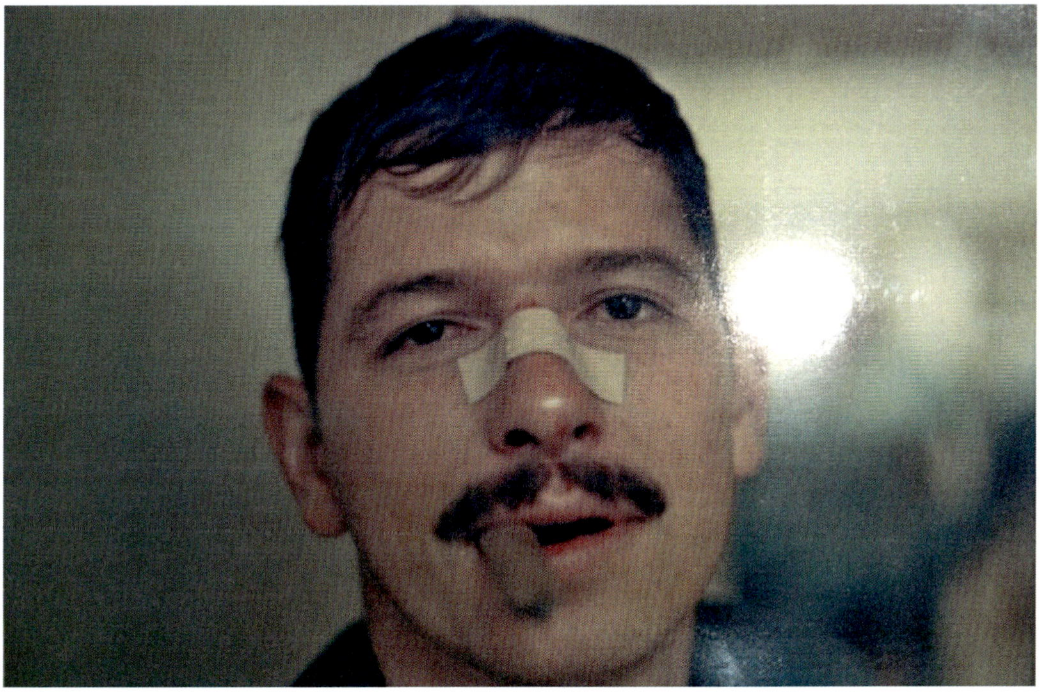

Twenty

The Dreaded Short Round

The most terrifying mission I flew took place in late December, six months after I arrived in-country. I'd just finished completing my early morning mission, the daily Dawn Patrol, and was on final approach for landing when Dave radioed and told me to hightail it to his location in the Phu Cat Mountains. He was in the boonies with our 1st ROK Infantry Regiment and needed me to work a TIC mission.

I arrived on the scene within a few minutes and rendezvoused with a set of fighters who were ready to go to work. I briefed the fighters, a set of F-100s, on what was taking place, confirmed the locations of the friendlies and the bad guys, and we began to do what we were trained to do--kill the enemy.

I wasn't afraid because there was a firefight taking place and I was in the middle of it, but a radio call I received from Dave seconds after Bobcat Lead released his first salvo of five hundred pound bombs stunned me, took my breath away. I was petrified. I had never felt real fear until that moment.

"Tum One Four, hold the fighters!" screamed Dave. "We've hit the friendlies!"

I told the two F-100 jocks to hold high and dry and I waited. And waited. And waited for Dave to let me know what was going on.

I thought, *were there any fatalities? Did I misunderstand Dave's radio transmission clearing me to hit the white cloud created by my Willie Pete? Was the operation in jeopardy because I'd made a mistake? Were there women and children in Seoul Korea whose fathers and husbands wouldn't be coming home?*

The thought of me having a short round incident (friendly casualty) had never occurred to me.

In going over what happened, I knew I made the right decision when I told Dave we had to move the ROKs back because they were too close to the coordinates they wanted us to hit. Something had gone terribly wrong and I had no idea how I could have made a fatal mistake.

Time passed at a rate too slow to measure. I made a radio call to Bobcat Lead telling him we had an issue on the ground and asked how long they could stay with me.

The Hun driver said he had thirty-five minutes for me, then he would have to RTB.

I relayed his message to Dave and told him to order another set of fighters if there was a chance of continuing the strike. He assured me the strike would go on and said he'd get us all the fighter support we needed. I told Dave I'd been airborne for over three hours and we might need to get another Tum in the air as I would soon need to refuel.

Dave called a moment later. "Tum One Four, One Zero here. You're not going to believe this."

I replied, "Boss, I'll believe anything. Please tell me there are no casualties."

"Bern, there are several broken bones and lacerations, but no deaths reported so far. These guys had the balls to send one grunt with a smoke bomb fifty meters down the hill and pop it. You got tricked. They wanted the ordnance right on top of them and that's what you gave 'em. The wounded have been evacuated, and the ROKs are ready to start over. The original target is good, the friendlies are at a safe distance and ready for action. Gimme a smoke and we'll start over."

I was stunned, ecstatic. I couldn't believe no one was killed. I thought, *These guys never cease to amaze me.*

"Bobcat Lead, Tum One Four. I'm ready to give you a mark. Let's kick some ass."

The fighter jock replied, "Roger that, Tum. We're ready to light 'em up. Standing by for your mark."

For thirty minutes Bobcat Flight and I put bombs, nape and twenty-mike-mike exactly where Dave asked for it. What began as a potential disaster turned out to be a successful mission for the ROKs. We didn't need additional fighter support.

Four hours and fifteen minutes after I launched on a routine Dawn Patrol mission, I landed at Phu Cat, bypassed breakfast at the chow hall and went straight to bed.

***

One of the more interesting going away parties we had began on the flight line and ended in the Officer's Club.

Bill Schoder and Chuck Quisenberry were scheduled to return home the same day and they wanted to fly their last flight together. With Bill in the back seat and Quis in the front, they took off for a two hour VR mission.

The previous day Dave and Snootz went to the base fire department and asked the fire chief if he could have one of his firefighters drive a fire truck to the parking area on the ramp to welcome two dignitaries. The request was approved and we

spread the word that everyone who could be there needed to show up for the welcome. Dave called Colonel Wis and asked him if he would fly from Tiger Town to Phu Cat and take part in the surprise that was planned and he said he wouldn't miss it.

When Quis called the tower and requested permission to land, we all took our places, actors in a play. I was one of many extras loitering in the revetment where Quis would park. Pat and Bob were perched on top of a revetment, movie cameras ready to record the event. Colonel Wis, holding a bottle of champagne in each hand, played the part of a ground crew member directing a pilot to the right parking space.

As Quis slowly approached the revetment, the fire truck raced forward at a high rate of speed, siren wailing, horn honking. Dave and Snootz, imitating firefighters, clung to the speeding truck with all their strength, firemen hats strapped to their chins. When the truck stopped near the O-1, Dave and Snootz jumped from the truck, fire hoses in hand, waiting for the real firefighter to turn on the water. *WHOOSH!* The pressure of the water was so strong Quis and Bill struggled to get out of the cockpit. In a matter of seconds they were drenched. The soaked radios were written off as battle damage.

The party that took place that night included several departing Tums. In addition to Bill and Quis, Pat and Bob Moore were leaving in a week and since there were no

more O-1 pilots to check out, or bars to remodel, Jake was going to Bien Hoa where he would spend a couple of months traveling around Vietnam making sure we FACs were following guidelines set forth by brilliant administrators in the Pentagon, the White House or the TASS. A good example was a directive that stated "Hence forth Bird Dog pilots will wear parachutes." Not only could we not get out of a Bird Dog while wearing one, with a chute on there wasn't enough room to move the control stick through its full range of motion. Brilliant.

We tried to give each departing Tum a cheesy plaque wishing him good luck with his next assignment. The plaque we had made for Jake read, "This Plaque Intentionally Left Blank."

***

January ended on a high note. I flew to Hawaii the last day of the month for a week of R&R. The aircraft was full of airmen, soldiers and sailors eager for a brief respite from the war and the opportunity to spend time with spouses or girlfriends. Bill and Dave chose to go to Australia for their vacation and Steve opted to visit Hong Kong where he bought me the first quality camera I'd owned and a Seiko watch.

We landed in Hawaii at Hickham Air Force Base. A row of blue busses waited for us to retrieve our luggage and whisked us to a rainbow-colored hotel in the heart of Honolulu where we rendezvoused with our spouses. For two days, Kay and I hung out at the beach, walked for miles around the city and behaved as tourists, exactly what we were supposed to do.

On the third day we checked out of our hotel and flew to Kauai, the most northern of the islands. We toured during the day and watched surfers in the late afternoon and evening from the balcony of an open air restaurant next to our seaside hotel.

It was a fabulous vacation, one that flew by in a flash. I was pleased and somewhat surprised that there were no antiwar demonstrations taking place in either location Kay and I visited. I credit that with the fact the military presence was huge and firmly ingrained in the Hawaiian environment.

Twenty-One

We Meet The New Boss

The O-2 pilots continued to roll in and the Bird Dog jocks began to roll out. Russ Stewart, Jerry Shirley and Jules Shockley were assigned to the ROK Cav Regiment; Gary Dickers, an Air Force Academy graduate, went to the 26th ROK Infantry Regiment at Miami Beach. Bob Pavelko, another Air Force Academy graduate and Ted Barna, my classmate at Reese, joined me at the 1st ROK Infantry Regiment. All lieutenants, the O-2 was the first assignment for each of those guys.

Snootz and Jerry Shirley

Colonel Wis departed three days after his replacement, Lieutenant Colonel Clent Houston, arrived. When Colonel Wis finished briefing our new boss on our mission and introduced him to the high ranking ROKs with whom he would work every day, he was given a grandiose farewell by his staff and Korean officers at Tiger Town.

Dave and I met our new boss a week later. We flew to Tiger Town to visit Lieutenant Colonel Houston for a couple of days. We spent an afternoon reiterating the preparation he had received from Colonel Wis: our organization; the tremendous respect we had for the ROKs; the skill of our FACs and the importance of our mission. He seemed impressed.

Dohrm's Cav Regiment was deployed west of Tiger Town and he was going to get airborne early the next day in case they needed an air strike. He wanted me to ride in his back seat and Dave thought that was a good idea so he could spend some one-on-one time with our new boss.

Russ & Dohrm at the CAV Regiment

The colonel had been an F-100 pilot, which was a good thing because he understood the fighter pilot attitude--aggressive. The bad news was he'd spent the previous twelve years in the Pentagon working in the procurement area. Someone in the assignments department must have decided, because of his extended non-flying assignment, he would be safe flying something that flew low and slow like the O-2, but that wasn't the case. Our highest ranking O-2 pilots, Captains Ron "Treebs" Trebo and Bob "Smutler" Butler were quick to realize that our new commander was a threat to himself and anyone who flew with him. They convinced Lieutenant Colonel Houston that Smutler should move to Tiger Town, fulfill a vacant administrative slot, and fly the colonel wherever he needed to go.

Award ceremony for Dave. (From left) Ted Barna, Korean Captain, Dave, Lt. Col. Houston

Our new boss was a quiet, kind, meek gentleman, unlike the typical fighter pilot or FAC. He had seven kids and didn't drink or smoke as he was of the Mormon faith. I had the feeling he wouldn't visit Phu Cat often, but hoped he would surprise me and engage with his troops the way Colonel Wis did. It didn't take long for one of the guys to tag him Casper Milquetoast, a character in The Timid Soul comic strip.

I flew with Dohrm every chance I got, which was not too often since we were in different regiments. Airman Ken Montague drove me to the air strip and it wasn't long before we heard the Bird Dog approaching. The wind sock, buffeted by a gusting wind, indicated we were in for a bumpy ride. Concertina wire identified the southern border of the compound and mines were planted between the wire and a steep fifteen foot drop-off from the runway.

Dohrm touched down, taxied clear of the fifty foot wide PSP runway and came to a stop near our Jeep, prop wash filling the air with red dust. The door flopped open and Dohrm greeted me, "Welcome aboard, Lizard."

I squeezed into the back seat, fastened my lap belt, plugged my headset into the radio and said, "I'm strapped in, Dohrm. Let's go."

We taxied to the runway and were airborne in a matter of seconds heading northwest toward An Khe, a small village on Highway 19, a major supply route from the port at Qui Nhon to Pleiku, home to a major Army complex. Dohrm's ROK Cav Regiment was deployed on an operation in the An Khe area and his mission was to support them if they needed help.

Snidley Whiplash was in the sticks with the Cav ROKs, and Dohrm called him when we got close, "Tum Two Three, Tum Two Five. How do you read? Over."

"You're loud and clear Two Five. I hope you're close because we just made contact with bad guys two klicks north and one east of An Khe. We're going to call for a set of fighters. Over."

Dohrm replied, "Lizard's in the back seat, Snidley, so you're in good hands. We'll be in your neighborhood soon."

In a few minutes Snidley called Dohrm to tell him he had a set of F-4s on the way from Phu Cat and gave him the target coordinates and the radio frequency the F-4 drivers would use to contact him.

The call came soon, "Tum Two Five, Cobra Lead, a flight of two F-4s, how do you read? Over."

"Loud and clear," came Dohrm's reply.

My job was to look for ground fire, other airplanes and helicopters. I was Dohrm's wing man.

An hour after the fighters showed up, the show was over. Snidley told Dohrm the ROKs had the situation under control. The enemy force that prompted the air strike was small and was dispatched quickly. Dohrm and Snidley, working closely with the ROKs on the ground, managed the mission without a hitch.

We headed back to Tiger Town and Dohrm's introduction to Lieutenant Colonel Houston. The turbulence was fierce, it was one bumpy ride.

When we approached Tiger Town, Gary "Snickers" Dickers called Tum Operations and told Ken Montagne he was inbound for landing and needed to be picked up.

He was making the trip to meet the new boss.

When Gary finished his conversation with Ken, Dohrm responded. "Snickers, be advised there is a tree at the far end of the runway that eats O-2s and the turbulence is brutal. Be careful."

Gary didn't reply. Not a word. Not even two clicks on the mic. He was speechless.

Dohrm said to me, "Bern, you'd better tighten your harness, this could be a rough landing."

"No sweat," I responded. "This is no hill for a Jungle Fighter Pilot. You'll nail it."

When we turned on final approach I noticed the wind sock indicated a direct cross wind of at least twenty-five knots, a challenge when landing on a narrow runway. Dohrm pointed the Bird Dog into the wind and we crabbed down final approach offset from the runway heading by at least ten degrees. As he approached touchdown, Dohrm smoothly applied right rudder and left aileron, which aligned us with the runway in a perfect slip configuration, left wing low. He then executed a textbook touchdown. The left landing gear touched down, followed by the right, then the tail wheel.

As I reached down and grabbed the handle to release my shoulder harness, Dohrm yelled, "We're going off!". The plane jerked abruptly to the left, sending us off the runway and over the steep drop off. Dohrm had no room to ground loop the plane to a stop and we didn't have enough airspeed to generate lift and fly. It's true that in dire situations, the passage of time slows to a crawl. My life didn't pass before my eyes, nor did I contemplate death. There was only one thought. *This is going to hurt.*

We struck the ground squarely on the nose and teetered for a moment, a lawn dart grasping for purchase and failing. We toppled to a rest upside down, both of us dangling in our harnesses, our wounded bird engulfed in fine, red, crystalline dust. I released my lap belt, landed on my head and crawled through the broken window, intent on getting away from the aircraft in case a fire broke out. There was no reason for me to worry, for in the few seconds that passed from touchdown to impact, Dohrm shut off the flow of fuel to the engine and turned off the ignition and electronics.

Free of the aircraft, I stood up and promptly fell down. I got up, fell down again and began crawling away from the wreckage.

Dohrm called out to me, "Lizard, I can't get out!"

I scrambled back to the plane on my hands and knees and found the door jammed. Dohrm had released his harness and with him pushing and me pulling, we got the door open. We stood up and promptly fell down. We did so again and crawled away from the plane. Fuel trickled from the right wing, but not close to the hot engine. Three Willie Petes, jarred from their firing tubes, littered the area. I wondered where the mines were buried.

When Snickers approached and saw the wreckage, he called the TOC and told Ken there was an O-1 on its back. Fearing the worst, and unable to contact anyone in the hooch, Ken left his post with a trainee and began sprinting toward Tum headquarters, hoping to find someone with a Jeep. When he got there he found everyone outside playing volleyball. After he told the guys what was going on, he gathered a few first aid kits, a portable radio and jumped in one of two Jeeps. Ken was the first guy to get to us. He was a mess, soaked to the bone with sweat having ran a mile to the hooch.

Lieutenant Colonel Houston and Sergeant Landry arrived in the second Jeep followed by a parade of Koreans. I thought, *wow, nothing draws a crowd like an accident.*

It seemed as though our commander was very concerned, not so much about his two pilots, but rather how he was going to explain a broken airplane to the staff weenies at the TASS. In a frantic state, he paced around the wreck, eyes darting back and forth from the plane to me, Dohrm, Dickers, Ken and the ROKs.

"How did this happen?" he asked of no one in particular.

Dohrm answered, "We had a break failure, sir."

When Dohrm applied the brakes, the right pedal failed and went all the way to the floorboard. The left brake grabbed and pulled us left, off the runway. There was nothing he could have done to prevent the accident.

Our new boss turned to Dickers and said, "Lieutenant get these guys to Phu Cat right away. They need to get to a flight surgeon and have their blood alcohol tested ASAP."

He then turned to us, "There will be an accident investigation team here soon, so no one can touch or move the aircraft. Leave it alone."

The colonel studied us for a moment and said, "You guys need to get haircuts before the investigation begins. Do it tomorrow."

He wasn't yelling at us or blaming the accident on Dohrm. He didn't have a clue how to deal with two fellow pilots who had just been in an accident and were still somewhat shocked. The right brake didn't work. It was that simple.

"Damn you Lizard, you were supposed to wake me before we landed."

Had I released my lap belt when we touched down on the runway like I planned, I could have been impaled on the control stick when we struck the ground.

Then, both the colonel and I would have had something really important to worry about.

We got our maps and weapons out of the Bird Dog, stepped into Snickers' O-2 and headed for Phu Cat. One of our guys met us at the airplane and took us to the infirmary where we were met by Doc Steve. He knew why we were there and once he saw that we were okay, grinned and said, "Yes, I'm going to give you some mission whisky, but not until we take care of business."

The doc drew blood samples, treated our cuts and bruises, poured us a healthy shot of grain alcohol and sent us on our way. It took us five minutes to get to the club.

Word of our mishap spread rapidly, and we didn't buy a drink all night.

The next day Joe Smith, one of our 1st Regiment FACs, told Dave he flew the airplane before Dohrm and failed to report the fact he ran off the runway at Phu Cat. Every pilot knew that a "hard landing" was to be reported so maintenance could inspect the plane. Nobody could explain why the damaged hydraulic line didn't fail when Dohrm stopped to pick me up at Tiger Town.

Joe ignored a procedural directive and worse, failed to look out for a fellow pilot, an inexcusable act. Dave told him to pack his stuff and sent him to the TASS at Nha Trang to be reassigned. Dohrm and I were angry and disappointed in Joe, but neither one of us attempted to confront him. He knew he screwed up.

Twenty-Two

Suddenly Short

One day in mid-February I flew with Bull Dog to a garden spot called LZ English, a thirty minute flight from Phu Cat. He'd been assigned Temporary Duty (TDY) to lend support to the 173rd Army Airborne Division.

The runway was reminiscent of a roller coaster littered with pot holes and the door to the operations hooch was marked with bullet holes. I told my buddy I would miss him and hauled ass back to Phu Cat.

Steve received incoming mortar rounds occasionally, and from a ringside seat got to watch AC-119 gunships hose down the hillsides at night. Bob Hope was never going to be booked at LZ English.

Steve's short TDY was the first of several temporary moves that affected our diminishing O-1 fleet. I flew eighteen missions in February and ten of them were in an O-2. I didn't work an airstrike but got plenty of Skymaster stick time. I had five months to go on my tour and there was no way I would finish it here. I was a Tum short timer who didn't know where he was going to end up.

***

The best flight I had in February was a mission on which I was merely a passenger. Tom Hiestand was the aircraft commander and he was flying an F-4 Phantom.

There were a few F-4 WSOs who liked to go up with us on their days off and fly the Bird Dog. Dave asked Hiest if he thought we FACs could get a ride in the F-4. Their Squadron Operations Officer, Lieutenant Colonel Dusty Schoen, thought it would be a good idea and our request was approved. I was confident an F-4 assignment was in my future and was excited to fly with Hiest.

F-4 Phantom

In order for us to make the flight we had to sit alert and wait for a mission. We didn't sit in the alert shack and play pool with the F-4 jocks. We had to sit in the back seat of an aircraft, strapped in and ready to go. When the klaxon went off announcing a mission, there would be no time for Hiest to mess around getting me strapped in the aircraft. We walked to the parachute shop, where I got a chute and G-suit and we went to Tom's assigned aircraft. He put me in the back seat, strapped me in, plugged in my radio and oxygen connections, explained the ejection sequence and left me there while he went back to the alert shack.

It was the middle of the afternoon and thank goodness it was a cool day. I had no idea when or if we would get a mission. I looked forward to watching a FAC put in an airstrike from the vantage point of a fighter.

Thirty minutes after Hiest strapped me in, the shrill blare of the klaxon startled me. My heart raced as I watched Hiest and his wingman sprint toward me. Tom took the ladder rungs two at a time, hopped in the front seat, strapped in, engaged the radio and told Cobra Two he was ready to taxi. "Roger that, Lead. Two's ready to taxi," came the reply, and Hiest pulled out of the revetment like a NASCAR driver leaving the pits at Daytona.

We launched on our way to the Laotian border and a rendezvous with Covey Two Four, our FAC. When the DASC sent an order for a set of fighters from Phu Cat, they gave Hiest's squadron the details of the mission, including the FAC's call sign and the target coordinates.

When we cleared Phu Cat airspace and leveled off, Hiest said, "Shake the stick, Lizard. You've got the airplane."

I did so and in my best fighter pilot voice, replied, "Roger that, I've got the airplane."

I flew in a loose formation while Hiest briefed me on the mission. We were headed west where Covey Two Four had a TIC situation. The weather, however, was going south rapidly. It was a thirty minute ride to the target area and when I handed the airplane back to him, Hiest began a descent into the target area. It was obvious a low ceiling was going to be an issue. Covey Two Four knew he wasn't going to get any snake or nape dropped on the bad guys, but asked Tom if he could give him some twenty-mike-mike, which he could because strafing a target didn't require as steep a dive angle.

Both F-4s made two passes and the twenty millimeter shells purred like a kitten and a slight vibration tickled my feet as they peppered the landscape. Covey Two Four told us he was sorry, but the weather wasn't going to cooperate.

F-4 revetment

I loved every minute of the hour and fifty minutes I spent as Hiest's back-seater. I even enjoyed sitting in the cockpit waiting, with anxious anticipation, for the alert klaxon to scramble

***

Shortly after Bull Dog returned from LZ English, he had a harrowing experience.

After putting in airstrikes in support of the 26th ROK Infantry Regiment at Miami Beach for more than three-and-a-half hours, his Bird Dog quit on him.

Treebs and Murph were at the club in Phu Cat relaxing after flying two combat missions when word came that Bull Dog was in trouble. They jumped in an O-2 and headed for Miami Beach.

When they arrived they could see Steve and the airplane on Highway 1. The Army had dispatched a helicopter to pick up Bull Dog and the radios from the damaged airplane. When Treebs and Murph arrived in the area, the sun was beginning to dip behind the horizon and the enemy began hosing them with small arms fire. Their tracers were off the mark.

Bull Dog had removed the radios in the damaged plane and helped two Army soldiers who thought they could tie the tail of the Bird Dog to a trailer hitch on a two and a half ton truck and tow it to Tuy Hoa.

The Air Force brass at the TASS and the Army big shots wanted the helicopter out of there before it got shot down, so Bull Dog got in the chopper and away he and the radios went.

Treebs, Murph and the guys towing the helicopter were taking ground fire. With tracers flying, the truck driver panicked and put the pedal to the metal. As the truck's speed increased, the airflow over the wings created lift and the O-1, thinking it's pilot wanted to take off, did exactly that. She became airborne and promptly executed a perfect roll. She crashed inverted and was dragged to death. When the truck driver approached a safe area close to the Air Force Base at Tuy Hoa, he pulled over and cut her mangled carcass loose.

Treebs and Murph landed amid the F-100s at the Tuy Hoa and met up with the two truck drivers and Bull Dog. The five of them were quite shaken and happy to have ended up on the Air Force base. The Army guys left and the three Tums asked the fighter jocks if they could spend the night with them. We worked often with their Hun drivers and they knew us by our Tum call sign. Our guys received a warm welcome and were offered lodging, but only if they could complete a rite of passage. Being strong, healthy Tum FACs, they breezed through the several liters of Purple Passion (the Hun driver's "Tiger Piss") they were forced to drink.

Bull Dog said, "You guys must be tight with your flight surgeons like we are."

The next morning Steve received word that someone from the TASS would soon arrive at Tuy Hoa to assess the battle damage on their aircraft. The guys met Major Dave Fisher. Armed with their AR-15s they drove to the boonies and found the O-1 upside down, surrounded by Vietnamese farmers. Major Fisher didn't even bother to get out of the Jeep. The O-1 was written off as battle damage.

Twenty-Three

March Madness

When I received a letter from the Air Force Personnel Center I knew my tour in Vietnam was coming to a close. I would soon be on my way to train in a jet fighter, or if that wasn't available, an instructor assignment in a Tweet or White Rocket.

WOO HOO! I was going home!

My Walter Mitty moment vanished when I read the words, "First Lieutenant Bernard E. Hale will report to Beale Air Force Base, California, for B-52…" I didn't absorb one word of the remaining text. How could this be happening to me? A FAC has never gotten a B-52 assignment. FACs worked with fighters every day and the transition from FAC to fighter made perfect sense.

I jumped in a Jeep and sped to the 1st Regiment to tell Dave the news, somehow thinking he could undo the disaster. He could make *anything* happen! Dave looked at my orders and said, "Well, Bern, at least you're going to a warm climate. I spent my BUFF (Big Ugly Fat Fucker) time in El Forke Grande (Grand Forks, North Dakota) freezing my ass off."

I was doomed.

I made a trip to base headquarters and asked to talk to someone who knew anything about the assignment process. I was sent to Staff Sergeant Vick who told me I wasn't the first pilot upset about going to SAC. I pleaded with him, "But Sergeant, FACs always get a fighter or instructor slot when they finish a tour in Vietnam."

"Not anymore Lieutenant, it's all about the needs of the Air Force. There's been a recent exodus of SAC guys to the airlines and there's a shortage of bomber and tanker pilots. I'm afraid you've been SACrumcised Lieutenant." With a grin he added, "Good luck, sir."

When I got back to our operations hooch, Snootz was the only guy there and I told him the news.

"You've got to be kidding me, Lizard. I don't think that's ever happened."

"Yep, I'm screwed, Snootzie. A sergeant Vick at headquarters told me SAC is running out of pilots."

Word of the new BUFF driver on the base spread rapidly and the kidding was intense. Chuck Engle wouldn't have handled it well. Ted Barna came up with a steel flywheel the size of a discus that weighed about twenty pounds. He tied a piece of parachute cord to it and dubbed it a "Finger Stretcher." When he presented it to me in front of everyone who wasn't flying, he explained the gift.

"Lizard, a BUFF has eight engines and each one has its own throttle. You're skinny and weak. Those fingers of yours won't wrap around all the throttles you're going to have to manage. You need to start stretching your fingers right away. You have no time to waste."

I was still on the flight schedule, but the O-2 guys were getting the majority of the fragged missions, those prescheduled air strikes on known and suspected enemy locations and LZ prep sorties.

I had three weeks to stretch my fingers.

***

It wasn't because I was leaving soon that the 389th Fighter Squadron decided to have a party, but their timing was good. I was getting short. They mixed a bomb container full of Tiger Piss and the celebration began.

The fighter jocks had nicer quarters than we did. They were single story motel-like rooms with two beds. There was an open area that extended to the flight line that was perfect for tossing a football, baseball or frisbee around. They also had a barbecue pit for moments like this. The hooch was about a mile from the flight line where our Tum operations hooch was located.

Late in the afternoon, Dohrm and I snuck off from the crowd and walked to the flight line to pick up a piece of equipment that Dohrm had made especially for this event. The Tennis Ball Cannon consisted of a launch tube of three tennis ball cans duct-taped together end to end and a firing chamber at the bottom. It held a small amount of lighter fluid which, when ignited, propelled a tennis ball not with the force of a bazooka, but close. The contraption was deadly.

We got it out of our closet and headed back to the party. We came upon one of several crew shuttle vans that were used to move air crews to and from the flight line. They looked like bread trucks. We both had the same thought at the same time. The long walk back to the party was all up hill and we were flight crew members. Sort of. The van was unattended and with the engine idling, seemed to be waiting for us. Dohrm jumped in the van and slid behind the wheel. There was one seat on the driver's side a bench in the back.

I sat on the bench and away we went. Dohrm decided to forgo the road and we headed straight for the party, bumping along the rugged open area. The last words I heard before we were swallowed up in a ditch were, "Hey Lizard, this thing handles pretty good."

Unscathed, we grabbed our cannon and laundry bag full of tennis balls and did the low crawl up the hill, glancing behind for signs of the van's driver or the Air Police. Neither showed up. It was beginning to get dark.

When we were within thirty feet of the rowdy crowd, Dohrm fired the first salvo. It sounded like a Willie Pete going off. We hunkered down, chuckling at the profanity laced tirade coming from the crowd. The guys had no idea where we were, but we knew they would soon form a posse and track us down. These men were trained killers. As fast as Dohrm could load the firing chamber and I could pop a white fuzzy projectile in the cannon, we kept firing and the rowdy pilots kept screaming, threatening to kill us. Their language was atrocious. When we ran out of ammo, we stood and proclaimed a victory.

Dave had his binoculars in our Jeep and we scanned the fading horizon looking for the bread truck. It looked like an Air Force Blue elephant stuck on its side. Somehow we managed to stay out of jail and fly another day.

***

I made nine flights in March and only one was in a Bird Dog. It was a KEL but the bad guys didn't show up. A dry run. One of the O-2 flights was a SEL but like my last O-1 airstrike, this, too, was a bust. No action.

I hung around our operations hooch, helped with the scheduling, hitched a ride to Tiger Town to say good-bye to Bob Smutler and Treebs. There was no going home party, no plaque, Jake's was the last. I didn't care because I had a one-of-a-kind finger stretcher. The day of the raucous farewell parties were over. With Colonel Wis' departure, a malaise seemed to linger over the Tums. Maybe we were just tired, not of each other, but of the seemingly endless war.

Dave received word that his wife had a serious health issue and he left immediately. I didn't get to tell the guy who would forever influence my life, goodbye. His energy, flare for adventure, commitment to the mission and his fellow FACs was contagious. He was our leader. Jake once said of Dave, "Rogers could have won the war singlehandedly if General Westmoreland would have let him." Our Koreans admired him for his courage and the manner in which he supported them. They knew he would always have their back.

Chuck Engle, Snootz and Jim Cross left Vietnam two months after I did. They volunteered to be a part of a clandestine program in Laos. They remained FACs and their new call sign was Raven. Sadly, Jim and Chuck lost their lives in Laos. (For a testimony on Chuck Engle written by Colonel Craig W. Duehring, one of Chuck's fellow Ravens, see appendix A.)

Dohrm was sent to Pleiku but kept his Tum call sign. He received another TDY assignment to Ban Me Thout and had to change his call sign to Walt Zero Three. During that time, Dohrm got wrapped up in the Siege Of Dak Seang. (For a first-person account of Dohrm's participation in this intense battle see appendix B.)

Bull Dog was sent back to LZ English, then to the 5th Special Forces in Pleiku.

Murph, flying Sky Pig, chauffeured me to Cam Ranh Bay where I would hop on the freedom bird the next morning. I checked into the BOQ and walked to the Officer's Club. I sat alone amid rowdy pilots, sipping beer and thinking about the Tums and how I would miss them.

I loved those guys.

Twenty-Four

Home Again, Home Again

The day I dreamed of arrived. It was March 31st, 1970, and I was finally on my way to a reunion with Kay, my family, high school and collegiate friends, and baseball and apple pie.

I woke early and made sure, for the umpteenth time, I had my travel paperwork in order. I stuffed my belongings in the same canvas bag I arrived with, and walked to Base Operations where I checked in for my flight. The waiting area was crowded with officers and enlisted men of all ranks and branches of service. We weren't boarded by rank. This day we were all the same.

Veterans.

One of the first passengers to get onboard, I chose a vacant seat in the first aisle on the left side of the cabin. I remember it vividly, because one of the flight attendants who appeared in the aisle was a classmate of mine at the University of Montana. The last time I was with Dianne Brown, I took her for a flight in a Piper Cherokee. It was May 6th, 1967. My younger brother Pat was in the back seat, and was more enthralled with Dianne than the breathtaking beauty of the Bitterroot Valley as seen from the air.

The chartered plane was full and Dianne busied herself getting everyone settled. As when we began to taxi to the runway, the cabin became deathly very quiet. When we were cleared to takeoff and began to move down the runway, the crowd came alive. When our speed slowly increased, a low murmur began to fill the cabin. As a rowdy football crowd reacts to a kicker approaching the football and the beginning of a homecoming game, the cabin noise rose to a crescendo and exploded in a tremendous roar when we became airborne. Goodbye Vietnam!

The excitement quickly abated and everyone settled down for the long flight ahead. Dianne and I had plenty of time to visit. She wanted an exciting career, one that involved travel. She certainly found it when she went to work for an international charter airline.

Homeward-bound soldiers and airmen who had celebrated the end of their tour of duty all night, fell asleep. The cabin was quiet and I had hours to reflect on what had taken place the past two years.

The year I spent in Lubbock, learning to fly the Air Force way, went by quickly. For the first time in my life I lived side by side with guys from all corners of our country and marveled at how different we were. At twenty-two, I left the only home I'd known and bonded with a group of diverse guys I knew for but a short time, yet would cherish their friendship forever. We had that going-to-war-together thing working.

Then there were the Tums. At Reese, most of us were kids when we met. Our two section leaders, Joe Tarnowski and Dave Sanford, were captains and the rest of us were wet-behind-the-ears lieutenants.

As a second lieutenant Tum, I worked with lieutenants, captains, majors and one lieutenant colonel. They all treated me as a peer. They expected me to be well trained and a player, a pilot prepared for any challenge. Being in the company of Colonel Wis, Dave Rogers, Pat Dowling, Jake Morrison, Rod McClellan and other old heads, I would be crushed if I ever disappointed them. The Bird Dog jocks who followed me: Snootz, Snidley Whiplash, Dohrm, Engle, Larry and Bull Dog had the same attitude, we'd never let one another or our ROKs down..

The O-2 drivers felt the same. We were all alike. Honest, fun loving, ethical and motivated to be the best we could be. We just happened to fly different airplanes.

Volumes have been written about the bond among soldiers who go into combat. As I winged my way home, I thought about the Tums and realized there was no way I could compose a thought that would explain my feelings for those guys and what they meant to me. How much does one love a parent? A sibling? A child? That's all I could come up with.

I recalled my first solo flight in Missoula and how excited I was. The beaming smile on Dick Komberec's face as he cut off the tail of my shirt confirmed my belief that I would obtain my pilot's license.

I thought about the war and how it seemed like a never-ending struggle. To entice peace, we had offered North Vietnam seven bombing halts over the Northern part of their country, beginning in 1965. During each pause, the bad guys were given an opportunity to repair or replace the gun sites and roads we'd damaged or destroyed on the Ho Chi Minh Trail, at a huge cost in lives lost and pilots captured. Despite our peace offerings, our enemy never showed a willingness to negotiate an end to the war. I imagined myself a year or so from now sitting in the cockpit of a B-52 loaded with bombs, winging my way toward Vietnam. Surely the war will be over soon. I had that thought when I was in high school nearly six years ago. *Nah, that'll never happen.*

Our route home took us to Guam where we refueled and were greeted by another flight crew. Our plane was full of drowsy travelers, but when we touched down on American soil, the cabin exploded again with whoops and hollers.

Following a short bus ride to San Francisco and with the help of a very friendly ticket agent, I was able to book a flight to Missoula. The authorities at Travis Air Force Base told us to watch out for violence from antiwar protesters as there had recently been some ugly, violent scenes. We were all in uniform and simply ignored.

Soon I would head north toward the majestic Rocky Mountains.

Twenty-Five

Reunion

My brothers Mike and Pat were seventeen and thirteen years old respectively and neither understood the war or the part I played in the conflict. Pat told me mom spent hours in our basement doing laundry, ironing, smoking cigarettes and crying. In December of 1969, she insisted on having two Christmas trees and one of them would remain untouched until I came home. A few of my high school and college pals, Nels, Bob, Grip, Doug and Truby, Bill, Tod, and Gary often stopped by to tell her they were thinking of her and not to worry, her son would be home soon. Mom loved having them surprise her. No one ever mentioned the Christmas tree.
During my time overseas, Ken Montague, the radio operator who sprinted to the Tiger Town airstrip the day Dohrm and I crashed, hooked me up with two phone calls home. The first was to my mom shortly after Ken and I became friends and I was a regular at Tiger Town. Pat couldn't get her attention before the fragile connection was lost. She was crushed, but knew I was, for the moment, safe. The other time Ken was able to get a long distance connection was after I received my BUFF assignment and was able to tell Kay I would be coming home early.

When the pilot retarded the power on the DC-7 airliner and we began a gentle descent into the Bitterroot Valley, my heart skipped a beat. Flying over the university, my high school, the old neighborhood and the small airport, site of my first flight, took my breath away. Nothing had changed. Time had stood still.

When I deplaned I saw the welcoming committee standing next to the steel fence next to the terminal. They waved and hustled inside to greet me. Mom insisted I embrace Kay first, then she held me tight, tears streaming down her face, breath coming in gasps. It was going to be a very merry Christmas.

Epilogue

Life after the Tums

After spending a month in Montana hanging out with family and friends, Kay and I drove to Castle Air Force Base in Merced, California for my introduction to the B-52. It was a three month training program.

The first day I arrived, my flight instructor, Major Mike Lewis and I walked to the flight line. He said he wanted me to see the inside of the aircraft. We opened the hatch and climbed a ladder to the upper deck where the two pilots and an Electronic Warfare Officer (EWO) were stationed. The EWO was responsible for jamming enemy radar signals. The tail gunner on this model B-52 sat in the tail of the aircraft. In the newer model BUFF the gunner's station was in the upper deck. Two navigator's stations were on the lower level.

I sat in the pilot's seat, leaned forward, looked out the window and said, "Major Lewis, I used to fly lower than this."

In time I learned to enjoy flying the B-52. The pilots and navigators with whom I flew had the same spirit and commitment to the mission we FACs did. We were a fun-loving lot making the best of a wartime situation. They would have been great Tums. I lost friends in Vietnam, Laos and again in the B-52 raids on Hanoi in 1972.

I left the Air Force in 1975. Kay and I had three beautiful girls at the time and they would be joined by a brother two years later. I went to work for a furniture manufacturer in Arkansas, which led to a career in wood products distribution. I moved to Texas in 1982 and Kay and I were divorced three years later.

My wood products career led me to the furniture industry in North Carolina where I live today. I met Janis Harrill and we were married in 1987. We live in Kernersville, North Carolina and are active members of the Main Street United Methodist Church. I am also a member of the Kernersville Lions Club and the Kernersville Chamber of Commerce. We have two poodles, Duke Ellington and Ella Fitzgerald.

My brother, Michael, has four children: Emily Fossum (she married Mitch, an Air Force Academy graduate), Audrey, Andrea and Caleb. Brother Pat has one son, Casey. My daughter, Sheila and her husband Jason Bernstein, have two daughters, Vivian and Lucy.

Over the years, I've kept in touch with many of the Tums, all of whom went on to lead productive lives. They are great Americans.

Ted Barna

Ted followed me to SAC. After our training at Castle Air Force Base in Merced, California, he and his wife, Mary, and their son David, moved to Barksdale Air Force Base in Louisiana. After a twenty-two year career in the Air Force, Ted earned masters and doctoral degrees at the University of South Carolina and subsequently became a university professor of natural sciences at the University of South Carolina.

A career in our nation's capitol followed and Ted currently works as a contractor in the office of the Secretary of Defense. He will retire soon and is putting the finishing touches on a waterfront home in Virginia.

Bob Butler

Bob left Vietnam two months after I did and was assigned to the C-141 aircraft, then flew the Lockheed C-140, a ten-passenger executive jet. Bob transported civilian and military leaders to locations around the globe. He then transitioned back to the C-141 and retired a lieutenant colonel after twenty years in the Air Force. He is now a corporate pilot flying Gulfstream Jet aircraft around the world.

Bob will go kicking and screaming if anyone tries to persuade him to retire.

Dohrm Crawford

Eventually, Dohrm was transferred from Phu Cat to Pleiku then on to Ban Me Thout. Dohrm received a UPT assignment at Webb Air Force Base, Texas and taught in the T-37. When he left the Air Force he went to work for Delta Airlines where he flew for thirty-one years. He also flew for the Louisiana Air Guard and retired the Squadron Commander of the "best fighter squadron in the world."

He and his wife, Sue, have two children, Gray and Sarah, and two "wonderful" granddaughters, Vivika and Zophia.

Pat Dowling

After Vietnam, Pat went to Webb Air Force Base in Texas and instructed in the T-38. His next assignment was at Maxwell Air Force Base where he was an instructor at Squadron Officer School, a military education course for Air Force captains. He was then asked to be an aide to a lieutenant general (three star) and subsequently, a general (four star) of the Air Force requested Pat join his staff. After fulfilling that commitment, Pat got back in the cockpit in Ramstein Air Force Base, Germany, where he was an F-4 instructor pilot.

He resigned from the Air Force in 1980 and worked in the oil and gas business, as well as in real estate.

Steve Drummond

When Steve left Vietnam he was assigned to a C-141 squadron at Travis Air Force Base and was an aircraft commander. He also flew the C-141 for a reserve squadron. Steve flew for four airlines, all of which went bankrupt. He insists it was coincidental. Steve and his wife, Nancy, have one daughter, Casey, who attended college at the University of Montana. Smart woman.

Ted Gamlin

Upon discharge from the Air Force, Ted got a degree in electronics technology from Southern Maine Community College and went into the healthcare industry. He spent thirty years marketing different products to hospitals and universities in the Northeast. Ted enjoyed working for companies like Technicon, Ciba-Corning, Olympus and Sunquest Information Systems.

He got to work with a fellow sales representative out of the Carolinas named John Allen who was an "old F-4 jock." Ted said the fighter pilot reminded him of the young, handsome, fearless, intelligent, professional aviators that comprised the ranks of the Tum FACs. (Sorry, Ted. I couldn't help it.)

He has a son who lives in Kentucky. Ted and his third wife, Beverly, reside in Bow, New Hampshire in their mountaintop retirement home.

Ted has kept active with his ham radio hobby and became a personal trainer. A year and a half ago he was diagnosed with Non-Hodgkins Lymphoma. After chemo treatments and a couple of surgeries, it appears he has it licked.

Ted said the VA provided him with outstanding care.

Tom Hiestand

Hiest left Vietnam in March of 1970 and went to Laughlin Air Force Base, Texas and was a T-37 instructor for two years. He then received an Air Force Institute of Technology assignment and obtained an MBA at the University of Colorado. The AFIT program provided continuing education for selected officers and enlisted military personnel.

He went on to Maxwell Air Force Base and worked in the management analysis area of ROTC. While there, he got to occasionally fly the T-39 Saberliner, a twin engine, executive jet with a crew of two and room for seven passengers. Then it was back to F-4s at Elmendorf Air Force Base, Alaska, his last Air Force assignment. He retired while in Alaska in 1983.

Hiest worked for a neighbor's construction company, did tax work and financial planning. He and his wife Gerri taught school together at a community college. They moved to Oak Harbor, Washington where they live today. Tom and Gerri have five sons.

Larry Howerton

Larry flew the A-1 fighter for seven months before he joined the Tums, and consequently his time as a Tum was short. He returned to the States and was a UPT flight instructor. His subsequent assignment was an F-4, which he flew until he retired.

Gary Lohr

Gary is one of only two radio operators I was able to track down, which is a shame because these guys played a huge role in our ability to accomplish our mission.

When Gary returned from Vietnam in August of 1970, he promptly married his high school sweetheart. When he completed his commitment to the Air Force he took advantage of the GI Bill and earned degrees in accounting and business administration.

He and his wife, Gail, became involved in the real estate industry and purchased a Century 21 franchise. He also moonlighted as a disc jockey.

Bill Lutz

In a career that spanned thirty-eight years, Bill flew nine different aircraft ranging from the O-1 to the Lockheed C-141 transport. Bill received a law degree in 1982 at the Mississippi College School for Law. In 1985, he attended Air Command and Staff College at Maxwell Air Force Base, Alabama. Bill had joined the Mississippi Air National Guard in 1979. He was a captain at the time and flew the C-130. Bill rose to the rank of brigadier general and was Chief of Staff of the Mississippi Air National Guard. He was Assistant to the Commander of Air Force Materiel Command and Commander of Mississippi Air National Guard as a Major General. He retired from the Air Guard in 2006.

Bill's law degree has served him well. He became a Mississippi trial judge and continues to do so part time. He is owner and operator of Lutz Mediation & Arbitration Services. Bill's wife, Catherine, is a two star, Assistant Adjutant General and Commander of the Mississippi Air National Guard, the first woman to achieve that position.

What a couple!

Ken Montague

Ken was assigned to Duluth Air Force Base after he left Vietnam and he and his wife, Judy, moved to Minnesota. He attained the rank of staff sergeant and before he left the Air Force he obtained his private pilot's license. Had I known about his interest in aviation I would have given him some time in the Bird Dog.

After his time in the Air Force, Ken got a degree in chemical engineering from The Ohio State University and went to work for Dow Corning Corporation. Thirty-eight years later he retired from the same company and he and his wife Judy settled on the banks of the Ohio River. Ken obtained a Six Sigma Black Belt, which must have been the Korean influence. His children and grandchildren live close by.

Ken told me, "Life is good."

Jake Morrison

Jake and his wife, Willie, took a break after he left the Air Force. They recharged in a quaint nook in California before he joined Eastern Airlines on the East Coast. Willie taught school in a local village and their son David thrived in the Granite State. Jake joined a hockey club and built a solar house.

I'll bet his bar in Tiger Town is still standing. When I think about it, I bet his bar in Tiger Town is still standing. When Eastern went out of business, they moved to Denver and a job with United Airlines. Jake climbed all the 14,000 foot mountains in the area and David moved his family to Colorado. Life is good for the Morrison family. "We enjoy our best years with our grandchildren," says Jake.

John Murphy

Murph went to SAC after his tour in Vietnam. He was assigned to a KC-135 tanker squadron at Beale Air Force Base, California. Unlike the BUFF and tanker pilots who had to sit alert waiting for the horn to blow, Murph didn't have to do any of that. He refueled the SR-71s.

When he left the Air Force he thought he would be hired by American or World Airways, but he didn't get the call. The call he did receive was from the CIA and he reentered their training program. After training and interim assignments, he entered the clandestine service as an operations case officer.

He's traveled the world over and has homes in Arlington, Virginia and Long Beach, California. Murph plays a lot of golf.

Ted Olson

Ted went to SAC when he left Vietnam and flew the KC-135 tanker. He then transitioned to the B-52, which he flew for five years. He had a TDY assignment to

Guam and flew missions into Vietnam before the end of the war.

He left the Air Force and flew for two charter companies and then went to work for United Airlines. Six years later he landed a job with FedEx and retired after nine years.

Ted is proud of his two "beautiful" children and seven "gorgeous" grandchildren.

Bob Pavelko

After flying the O-2 for the 1st ROK Regiment, Bob became a BUFF driver. He was assigned to Barksdale Air Force Base, Louisiana. He flew missions into Vietnam from Anderson Air Force Base, Guam and also at U-Tapao Royal Thai Air Base, Thailand.

Bob then flew the FB-111A, a two engine tactical jet crewed by a pilot and a WSO. He attained the rank of colonel and retired as the commander of the 42nd Bomb Wing, Loring Air Force Base, Maine. He has two sons, one an Air Force colonel and the other a Marine lieutenant colonel.

Dave Rogers

When he returned home from Vietnam, Dave turned down an offer from the Air Force to become a test pilot and chose to leave the military. He considered medical school, a degree in Aeronautical Engineering, a test pilot's position at Boeing. He chose a mechanical engineering firm and while he was working for the company, went to school at Oregon State University, where he received his engineering degree. Two years later Dave opened a consulting engineering office in Eugene, Oregon. After thirty years he sold the business to his partners.

He accepted an offer to be a part time consultant and he and his wife, Mary, bought a ten acre farm in California. He is an avid mountain biker and is studying jazz piano. He'll never slow down. He has two children and three grandchildren, potential Tum FACs all.

Bill Schoder

After he left Vietnam, Bill was assigned to the Argentine Air Force as an advisor. He then went to Panama as an instructor in the Inter-American Air Forces Academy. He taught use of air power against insurgents. Bill was the only Spanish speaking aircraft commander and instructor pilot in the C-118, the military version of the DC-6 passenger plane.

Bill has a place in the North Georgia mountains and loves to play golf. When he plays, he swears in Spanish.

Bob Snyder

Having WSO experience in the back seat of an F-4, Snidley Whiplash was assigned that aircraft at Bitburg Air Base, Germany. All Snidley wanted to do was fly fighters and that's exactly what he did until he retired from the Air Force. He spent a year in Korea flying the OV-10 and a stint in Hawaii where he was a FAC/ALO inspector. The last fighter he flew was the F-15.

After retirement from the Air Force he went to work for Continental Airlines. His fifteen year career ended in 2003.

Russ Stewart

Russ was one of our first O-2 pilots. He arrived not long after Murphy, Tribo and Butler. He hung out with Dohrm at the Cav. Being an electrical engineer, was able to salvage several defective generators that Dohrm (no surprise) brought home to the Cav hooch.

After Russ left the Air Force, he continued to fly in the capacity of test pilot instructor. He worked for the USAF Test Pilot School as the Chief of Academics and was the Chief of Safety for the Air Force Flight Test Center at Edwards AFB, California.

Ron Tribo

Considering Ron had submitted paperwork to leave the Air Force when he arrived in Vietnam, he had an interesting career. His first assignment was flying the EC-135 and NKC-135 Boeing aircraft in support of Apollo 14, 15 and 16 plus numerous Air Force and Navy missile launches from Cape Kennedy and Vandenberg Air Force Base in California.

His next assignment was an ROTC instructor position at Utah State University. Ron was able to worm his way into a flying slot at Hill Air Force Base in northern Utah. He flew the T-39A corporate jet hauling VIPs around the country. He parlayed that experience into his next job as commander of the Military Airlift Command T-39 detachment.

Next, he studied at the Air War College before moving to Honolulu as an Executive Officer for an admiral. Ron was promoted to colonel in 1981 and returned to the Air Force at Hickham Air Force Base, Hawaii. As the Director of Operations and Vice Commander of the Air Wing he was able to fly T-33s and EC-135s. Ron always worked his way into a cockpit.

Back in the States, he held Vice and Wing Command positions, Director of Training for SAC and an Air Training Command Headquarters position as Assistant Deputy Chief of Staff.

Ron and his wife, Jeri, have two sons, one a Delta pilot and the other a cyber security expert. Six grandchildren "keep them busy."

Frank Wisneski

Colonel Wis, our humble commander, said he, "Couldn't come up with many accomplishments, but has some great memories."

I'm sure being a Tum is on that list. His post-Vietnam assignments include the Pentagon, where he worked in the headquarters of the United States Air Force; he was the vice wing commander at Peterson Air Force Base in Colorado Springs, Colorado; and he was the vice commander of Luke Air Force Base in Arizona.

Colonel Wis is a tutor at the Benet Hill Monastery and president of the Lance Sijan Chapter of the Air Force Association. (Lance Sijan, an Air Force Academy graduate and F-4 pilot, was awarded the Medal of Honor posthumously for his bravery while interred in the Hanoi Hilton prison camp in North Vietnam.)

We were very fortunate to have served under Colonel Wis. He respected us, admired our skill and our spunk. He trusted us to accomplish our mission of supporting our Korean counterparts.

Most of the time I think he really liked us, too.

The Legend of Chuck Engle

Appendix A

By: Craig W. Duehring

Chuck Engle (Raven 26) arrived in Laos during the month of May, 1970, along with another new Raven, Bill Lutz. Both men were assigned to Long Tieng, the headquarters of the legendary Hmong leader, Major General Vang Pao. There were seven or eight pilots assigned there at any given time with only two or three Ravens assigned at the other four locations. At that time, we were experiencing most of the ground fighting that was going on in Laos, although the Ho Chi Minh Trail was a war of its own.

Chuck was an easy guy to like. Strikingly good looking, he was raised on a farm in eastern Indiana and earned a physical education major at Purdue University. His clean, dark features betrayed a touch of his American Indian ancestry. He was dignified in his approach and sincere in his speech, never flippant or verbose. He was possibly the finest natural pilot I have ever known--but a man who was willing to take risks.

On one occasion shortly after his arrival, Chuck and I were searching for enemy soldiers. Finding none, we decided to try a new tactic--high/low. Chuck dropped to a few yards above the ground while I flew in his high six o'clock position, covering his actions. As Chuck jinked his aircraft back and forth, he laughingly called out enemy positions. He could clearly see the startled look on the soldier's faces and I dutifully noted the positions for an airstrike. It wasn't long before a burst of AK-47 fire raked his aircraft, including a bullet that came through his left window, shattering the Plexiglas and passing in front of his eyes. He actually saw the bullet go by. He had been hit in the leg, just above the left ankle with the AK-47 bullet passing completely through his body and rolling loosely on the floor.

We spent the next forty-five minutes in a close formation with me trying to help him overcome the feelings of nausea that threatened to steal his conscious state. An Air America helicopter joined us for the last fifteen minutes of the journey. As we cleared the last ridge line over Long Tieng, I watched my friend circle towards the tiny runway below. As he touched down and dropped the tail wheel to the runway, Chuck saw that he was not aligned with the runway and was heading for a ditch. With tremendous resolve, he picked up his useless leg and smashed it onto the left rudder pedal and simultaneously pulled the mixture to the cut-off position. I saw the aircraft ground loop violently, but it rolled to a stop on the tarmac. Within moments, our resident doctor and the crew chiefs had Chuck out of his plane and onto a waiting Air America Volpar (twin engine turboprop Beechcraft transport) for a fast flight to Udorn, Thailand. Chuck refused to tell his family of his injuries and, likewise, refused to return to the U.S., choosing instead to heal himself among his brethren, first on crutches, then a cane and finally back in the air flying combat missions.

When the dry, winter season arrived, Chuck flew some of his most remarkable missions. On December 30, 1970, Chuck was looking around the northern Plaine des Jarres when he spotted a PT-76 tank parked under a tree. He called for airstrikes, but the A-1s were still a long way out and he was running low on gas. So, he turned the mission over to Park Bunker (Raven 23) and headed home. Tragically, the tank was set out as a trap and Park was shot down by a ZPU-23 (Soviet antiaircraft cannon). Chuck turned back to the scene but was unable to get there before the Raven and his back-seater (Hmong interpreter) were executed by the NVA. It was critical to know if either man was alive and Chuck characteristically volunteered to make a low pass over the one visible body while the A-1s covered his action. All aircraft received extremely heavy ground fire and one of the A-1s was severely damaged but managed to make it home.

Because of Chuck's visual assessment, we knew our friend was dead.

Three days later, an F-4 (call sign Tiger Zero Two) was shot down and again it fell to Chuck, who was closest to the survivors, to begin the task of enemy ground fire suppression and recovery of the crew members. It was a two-day struggle, operating under 1,000 foot overcast, requiring the fighters to strike, as directed by Chuck, within a few yards of the survivors with strafe and napalm. In an incredibly well coordinated effort, the F-4 crew came through the ordeal on the morning of the second day after several extreme close calls. Chuck few to Thailand to celebrate their survival and was treated like the hero he was.

Chuck's greatest challenge took place early in his tour, June 20,1970, the day he earned the Air Force Cross. I saw him do it, from beginning to end. On that day, during the rescue of an OV-10 FAC, Nail 42, I watched Chuck purposefully fly his O-1 Bird Dog between a heavy machine gun and the rescuing Air America helicopter. The bullets riddled his airplane and struck the fuel line that ran down inside the cockpit, spreading aviation fuel down his clothes and onto the floor where the radios were kept. He shut off all but one radio and marked the machine gun for destruction using rockets from his right wing so as not so spark an inferno. I escorted him back to the airfield, and just as we cleared the last mountain ridge, his engine quit from fuel starvation. Chuck easily glided the aircraft the last few miles and gently set it down on the runway while the rest of us mortals watched in awe. Then, without changing his soaked clothes, he jumped into the last O-1 on the ramp and took off again to complete the rescue. For that action, Chuck earned our country's second highest award, the Air Force Cross, a medal he was destined never to receive.

Chuck could make the O-1 Bird Dog fly as no one else possibly could. He often ended his pre-strike fighter briefing by putting the aircraft into a spin, spiraling ever downward until he recovered at the altitude he wanted and then fired a Willie Pete (White Phosphorous rocket) at the target before bringing the nose back to level flight. It was a real crowd-pleaser that suitably impressed the fighter jocks. It was always a great lead into, "Hit my smoke!" He was incredibly brave, more than I could ever be. Whether he was setting an altitude record for the O-1 (19,720 feet) or making a dangerous low pass to help a friend in need, he flew his aircraft to the limits as though it was simply the only way to fly. We held him in the highest esteem.

On the day he crashed, I had driven out to the airport at Vientiane to meet Chuck and go over some awards and decoration write-ups with him. I sat on the ramp in the open Jeep and waited, and waited, and waited. Finally, someone came out from the operations building and told me Chuck had crashed. I asked if Chuck had made it out okay and was told he burned in the wreckage.

I was in total shock. I walked in a daze across the flight line and stumbled against a revetment. Then, in the privacy of my thoughts and the obscurity of the flight line, I fell over and cried, and cried and cried until I had no more tears to shed. As I pulled myself up, I knew I would never feel a loss as great as that again and, so, I promised myself on the spot, that I would never cry again like that for the rest of my life.

I never have.

Colonel Craig W. Duehring retired from the Air Force in 1966 after a twenty-six year career. His final military assignment was U.S. Air Attaché to Indonesia and upon his retirement was Assistant Secretary of the Air Force for Manpower and

Reserve affairs, Washington, DC.

The Siege of Dak Seang

Appendix B

By: Dohrman Crawford

I'm uncomfortable writing about this. For one thing, I don't want anyone to think that I am, to use a fighter pilot term, shining my ass. For another, and most important, all the efforts and courage eventually came to naught, as the unit was overrun a few days later. I was on the scene when that happened and was talking to the American Advisor on the ground as things unfolded. It still bothers me. At least the American Advisor made it out.

I think.

This happened on April 21, 1970. That is a long time in dog years and a long time ago for me, too. However, my memories of that early evening are still pretty good and I'll try my best to tell it straight. I'll try to keep it short and sweet.

During the Siege of Dak Seang, ARVN units were put into the fight around the camp in an attempt to break the siege. There was a lot of action every day. At the time, I was working with the 1st Battalion of the ARVN 42nd Regiment. It was late afternoon, going into sunset when the stuff hit the fan. It had been hitting the fan for a while, but his was a really big deal, a big attack. I had already put in a number of airstrikes that day and only had a few white phosphorous rockets left. I was due to leave the scene in a short while and would have been happier with more gas.

Oh well.

The friendly position looked sort of like a boot sole, seen from above. It was more than a klick (thousand meters) or so from the camp, and just a little distance from the large hill called Nui Eck that loomed over the scene. There were a lot of hills looming, and the clouds were right down to the tops of the hills that surrounded us in all directions, except the river valley that led north to Dak Pek and southernly to Dak To. It was very hazy. The visibility was not so hot and clouds about 2,000 feet. I flew around right under the clouds, as high as I could get because of the danger from small arms and the .51 cal guns the bad guys had all over the place.

As the fight went on, I talked to the good guys who told me they were in danger of being overrun. I believe the guy I talked to is named Frank W. DeLong. They called in artillery from Dak To in an attempt to stop the attack. They were very hard pressed. I asked for, and got a flight of fighters, F-100s, but it took about twenty minutes or so and all the while, the sun kept going down. Around 1830 to 1845, Blade Zero Three and Zero Four, piloted by Captain Stanley J. Smith and Captain Larry D. Crocker showed up. They were mission number 4047. They turned out to be two American heroes.

They flew up from the Dak To area under the clouds, as I gave the briefing and made the rendezvous. I used ground references to describe the friendly position and where the bad guys were, so I could save some rockets for later. By now sunlight was getting dim enough that you could see the flashes of light when the artillery shells hit. In my memory, they looked sort of yellowish and there were a lot of them.

At this point, I asked for a cease fire on the arty (artillery), so we could drop. To my surprise, the friendlies said they would be immediately overrun if they shut off the artillery. No dice, the arty had to keep coming. Hmmm. Arty shells would be falling into the airspace in which I and the fighters would be flying.

I put the situation to the F-100 pilots and they agreed to stay and put in the air strike, despite the artillery fire.

I had the guys drop the five hundred pound bombs in the trees a couple hundred yards away, as the enemy was far too close to the friendlies to use hard bombs. We had napalm and twenty-mike-mike left to work with I orbited right over the friendly position and put in the napalm as close as thirty meters from the good guys, which was their request. They got pretty fired up as the nape did its work and then the F-100s strafed multiple times. They did a fantastic job and the good guys on the ground said they had broken the attack. They also said there was a hail of ground fire directed at us, but I did not hear a single bullet go by my plane. You can hear rounds when they go by a Bird Dog if they are close. An AK-47 sounds like a plastic ruler being snapped and .51 cal sounds like some big fat guy is standing outside the plane and hitting it rapidly with a frying pan.

I can still remember wildly yanking the trusty Bird Dog around like a mad man to keep the fighters in sight, and put in Willie Petes. This may sound phony, but actually, I was too busy to be scared. I was working two radios at once and putting in an airstrike at the same time.

Another day in the life of a FAC. On every fighter pass, the arty was bursting in the area. I can still see those flashes in my mind. Big Sky Theory, I guess. Lots of sky and shells are small.

Long story short, we broke the attack and the fighters headed home. I was getting low on gas but stayed until an Air Force gunship showed up to relieve me. I then set a course for the only lighted runway around, at Pleiku, fifty-five miles away. I landed with almost no gas, but my excuse is that I was a lieutenant and didn't know any better. I should have said, "A lucky lieutenant."

I have never met any of the guys I talked to on the radio. If anyone reading this knows them, please get in touch with me ASAP. I would love to meet them.

For this mission Dohrm was awarded the Silver Star, our Country's third highest award.

One of Dohrm's close friends (and a friend to all Tums), Steve Train, a C-7 Caribou pilot, perished in the siege of Dak Seang. Steve volunteered to lead an emergency resupply mission to the battle site, where ground troops were desperate to receive ammunition. The bad guys had surrounded the embattled special forces camp with .51 calibre gun sights and they shot down Steve and two other courageous C-7 Caribou pilots.

Steve was awarded the Silver Star, posthumously.

Glossary

A-1: WWII vintage single engine fighter-bomber

A-4: Single engine Naval & Marine fighter-bomber

ADF: Automatic direction finder, radio beacon locator

AK-47: Soviet 7.62 mm automatic weapon used by VC & NVA troops

ALO: Air Liaison Officer, Air force Officer advisor to Korean Army Commanders

AO: Area of Operations

ARVN: Army of the Republic of Vietnam

AWOL: Absent Without Leave

BDA: Bomb Damage Assessment

BUFF: Big Ugly Fat Fucker (B-52 Bomber)

BX: Air force Base Exchange

Beaucoup: Much, many (pronounced *boo-coo)*

Bingo Fuel: Enough fuel to return to base

Brown bar: Second Lieutenant

C-7: Twin engine turbo prop, short takeoff and landing cargo and troop transport

C-123: Twin engine military transport that expended Agent Orange

C-141: Lockhead transport aircraft with fifty-seven years longevity

CAR-15: Automatic rifle 5.62mm

CH-47: Twin engine transport helicopter, named Chinook or "Hook"

C-Rations: Canned, precooked meals

CBU: Cluster Bomb Unit small bomb-lets deployed in canisters by fighter aircraft

Charlie: Slang or Viet Cong

CP: Command Post

DASC:	Direct Air Support Center, fighter scheduler and dispatcher
DEROS:	Date of Estimated Return From Overseas
DMZ:	Demilitarized Zone
Daisy Cutter:	Fuse extender that detonates ordnance above ground level
Dust Off:	Helicopter medical evaluation
ETA:	Estimated Time of Arrival
F-4:	Two-place interceptor/fighter bomber used by Air Force and Marines
F-100:	Single engine jet fighter bomber, known as the "Hun"
FAC:	Forward Air Controller
FNG:	Fucking New Guy
Frag:	Daily pre-planned air strike
Flight Surgeon:	Medical Doctor on flying status
G.I.:	Government Issue
G-Suit:	Anti-gravity suit
GIB:	Guy in Back, Weapon System Operator
Good Stick:	Excellent Pilot
HE:	High Explosive
Hun:	F-100 Super Saber, single engine jet fighter
High Drags:	Bomb fitted with steel fins that deploy upon release, creating drag which slows the weapon's descent, which allows the fighter pilot to safely exit the impact area.
Hooch:	Any structure where one slept, worked, or hung out
Huey:	UH-1 helicopter, Vietnam workhorse
IFR:	Instrument Flight Rules, poor weather, instruments required
Jink:	Abrupt back and forth movement of the control stick.
KEL :	Known enemy Location

KBA:	Killed by Air
Klick:	1,000 meters, slightly longer than a half mile
LZ:	Landing Zone
M-79:	49mm single shot grenade launcher carried by some TUMs
MIL:	Military power
MIA:	Missing in Action
MP:	Army Military Policeman
MPC:	Military Pay Currency, substitute for greenbacks
Mama-San:	Domestic maid
Milk Run:	Easy mission
Nape:	Napalm, a petroleum based incendiary weapon
NCO:	Non Commissioned Officer
NVA:	North Vietnamese Army
PSP:	Pierced Steel Planking, runway material
PX:	Post Exchange
REMF:	Rear Echelon Motherfucker
R&R:	Rest and Relaxation
ROE:	Rules of Engagement
RON:	Remain Over Night
ROTC:	Reserve Officer Training Corps
RTB:	Return to Base
ROMAD:	Radio Operator, Maintenance, and Driver
SAC:	Strategic Air Command
SEL:	Suspected Enemy Location
Shack:	Direct hit on a target

Shit Hot:	Person, place or thing considered to be outstanding
Short-Timer:	GI with but a few days until DEROS
Smoke Grenade:	Smoke Bomb
Snake eyes:	General purpose high drag bombs: Mark 82 - 500lb. bomb
Sortie:	Operational Military Flight
STOL:	Short Takeoff and Landing aircraft
TASS:	Tactical Air Support Squadron, headquarters for ROMADs and FACs
TDY:	Temporary Duty
Twenty-Mike-Mike:	Twenty millimeter cannon
UHF:	Ultra high frequency radio
UPT:	Undergraduate Pilot Training
USO:	United Service Organizations
VC:	Viet Cong
VFR:	Visual Flight Rules
VR:	Visual Reconnaissance
Winchester:	Out of Ammunition
WIA:	Wounded in Action
WSO:	Weapons Systems Officer (GIB)
Zoomie:	Air Force Academy Graduate

THE END